ST/ESA/328

Department of Economic and Social Affairs
Division for Social Policy and Development
Secretariat of the Permanent Forum on Indigenous Issues

STATE OF
THE WORLD'S
INDIGENOUS
PEOPLES

United Nations
New York, 2009

DESA

The Department of Economic and Social Affairs of the United Nations Secretariat is a vital interface between global policies in the economic, social and environmental spheres and national action. The Department works in three main interlinked areas: (i) it compiles, generates and analyses a wide range of economic, social and environmental data and information on which States Members of the United Nations draw to review common problems and to take stock of policy options; (ii) it facilitates the negotiations of Member States in many intergovernmental bodies on joint course of action to address ongoing or emerging global challenges; and (iii) it advises interested Governments on the ways and means of translating policy frameworks developed in United Nations conferences and summits into programmes at the country level and, through technical assistance, helps build national capacities.

Note

The views expressed in this publication do not necessarily reflect those of the United Nations. The designations employed and the presentation of the material in this publication do not imply the expression of any opinion whatsoever on the part of the Secretariat of the United Nations concerning the legal status of any country or territory or of its authorities, or concerning the delimitations of its frontiers.

The term "country" as used in the text of the present report also refers, as appropriate, to territories or areas.

The designations of country groups in the text and the tables are intended solely for statistical or analytical convenience and do not necessarily express a judgement about the stage reached by a particular country or area in the development process.

Mention of the names of firms and commercial products does not imply the endorsement of the United Nations.

Symbols of United Nations documents are composed of capital letters combined with figures.

ST/ESA/328
United Nations publication
Sales No. 09.VI.13
ISBN 92-1-130283-7
Copyright © United Nations, 2009
All rights reserved
Printed by the United Nations, New York

Acknowledgements

The State of the World's Indigenous Peoples has been a collaborative effort in which a number of experts and organizations have participated.

The thematic chapters were written by Joji Carino, Duane Champagne, Neva Collings, Myrna Cunningham, Dalee Sambo Dorough, Naomi Kipuri and Mililani Trask. The introduction was written by the Secretariat of the Permanent Forum on Indigenous Issues.

The Secretariat of the Permanent Forum on Indigenous Issues oversaw the preparation of the publication. Elsa Stamatopoulou, Chief of the Secretariat provided overall leadership throughout the entire process of preparing this publication. Broddi Sigurdarson was managing editor for the production of the publication from its inception.

Important contributions were made by Sonia Smallacombe, Carol Pollack, Juan Fernando Nuñez, Maria Luz Aragon, Ekaterina Gorbunova and Anna Satarova. Contributions were also made by Oksana Burnabaeva, Olga Khovenmei, Bonney Hartley, Tobias Langenbach and Elizabeth Martinez.

Special gratitude goes to the Russian Association of the Indigenous Peoples of the North (RAIPON) and the Yamal Nenets Autonomous Okrug for organizing an expert Group Meeting in Salekhard, Russian Federation which brought together the authors and other experts for a three day meeting in preparation for this publication. The efforts of Pavel Sulyandziga were particularly valuable in organizing this meeting. Other individuals also contributed to this meeting. They include: Rodion Sulyandziga, Yana Dordina, William Langeveldt and Oksana Ilyina.

Special acknowledgements go to the editor, Diana Vinding and also to Ziad Al-Kadri and Marko Srdanovic of the UN Graphic Design Unit, Department of Public Information.

Jomo Kwame Sundaram, Assistant-Secretary-General for Economic Development, and Anisuzzaman Chowdhury of the Department of Economic and Social Affairs provided invaluable comments.

Foreword to the State of the World's Indigenous Peoples

By Mr. Sha Zukang, Under-Secretary-General for Economic and Social Affairs

Indigenous peoples are custodians of some of the most biologically diverse territories in the world. They are also responsible for a great deal of the world's linguistic and cultural diversity, and their traditional knowledge has been and continues to be an invaluable resource that benefits all of mankind.

Yet, indigenous peoples continue to suffer discrimination, marginalization, extreme poverty and conflict. Some are being dispossessed of their traditional lands as their livelihoods are being undermined. Meanwhile, their belief systems, cultures, languages and ways of life continue to be threatened, sometimes even by extinction.

Increasingly, governments are recognizing these threats, and matching such recognition with action. From land claims settlements and constitutional amendments to important symbolic actions such as apologies for past treatment of indigenous peoples, governments around the world are making important steps towards addressing indigenous peoples' concerns.

In responding to the challenges they continue to face, indigenous peoples have engaged the international community, calling for a Declaration on the Rights of Indigenous Peoples and a permanent forum at the United Nations that meets regularly to discuss indigenous peoples' issues and make recommendations to the UN system and beyond.

The United Nations has committed its unwavering support to a future where all indigenous peoples will enjoy peace, human rights and well-being, and has responded to indigenous peoples' demands, welcoming them as partners. The United Nations Declaration on the Rights of Indigenous Peoples was adopted in September 2007, and the Permanent Forum on Indigenous Issues meets annually at UN Headquarters, bringing together indigenous peoples, Member States, NGOs, UN agencies and other intergovernmental organizations.

Much work remains to be done in advancing the implementation of the United Nations Declaration on the Rights of Indigenous Peoples. One condition for facilitating the implementation of the Declaration is information about the state of the world's indigenous peoples. The Permanent Forum recognized this in its first session when it recommended that the United Nations system produce a publication "on the state of the world's indigenous peoples, containing data on indigenous peoples and discussing issues relating to indigenous peoples in the thematic areas within the Forum's mandate."[1]

Responding to this request, the Department of Economic and Social Affairs reached out to experts on indigenous issues who have contributed the material for this publication. The chapters are based on the thematic areas within the Permanent Forum's mandate, and highlight some major issues indigenous peoples face.

In a world confronted by multiple crises, indigenous peoples remain committed to their struggles, and their cultures continue to be vibrant while their traditional knowledge is an invaluable source of ingenuity. This publication will be a useful tool for strengthening partnerships and cooperation with indigenous peoples.

---

[1] Permanent Forum on Indigenous Issues, Report on the first session (12-24 May 2002) E/2002/43/Rev.1 Para 8.

Table of Contents

Introduction

By the Secretariat of the United Nations Permanent Forum on Indigenous Issues

The United Nations is commonly seen as one of humankind's most ambitious projects, striving to attain human rights, development and peace and security for all. In many ways, the ambitious, lofty nature of its goals is both the United Nations' greatest strength and its greatest challenge. Despite unprecedented progress made during the United Nations' first sixty years, there remains a lingering frustration that the poorest of the poor, the most marginalized and discriminated against, still do not enjoy their basic human rights, development or security.

Indigenous peoples' concerns have not always been represented at the United Nations and, for the first decades of existence of the Organization, their voices were not heard there. This has slowly changed and the United Nations system has, in recent years, taken a number of steps to atone for past oversights, increasingly building partnerships with indigenous peoples.

There has been a vigorous and dynamic interface between indigenous peoples—numbering more than 370 million in some 90 countries—and the United Nations, an interface which, difficult as it is, has produced at least three results: a) a new awareness of indigenous peoples' concerns and human rights; b) recognition of indigenous peoples' invaluable contribution to humanity's cultural diversity and heritage, not least through their traditional knowledge; and c) an awareness of the need to address the issues of indigenous peoples through policies, legislation and budgets. Along with the movements for decolonization and human rights, as well as the women's and environmental movements, the indigenous movement has been one of the most active civil society interlocutors of the United Nations since 1945.

The situation of indigenous peoples in many parts of the world continues to be critical: indigenous peoples face systemic discrimination and exclusion from political and economic power; they continue to be over-represented among the poorest, the illiterate, the destitute; they are displaced by wars and environmental disasters; the weapon of rape and sexual humiliation is also turned against indigenous women for the ethnic cleansing and demoralization of indigenous communities; indigenous peoples are dispossessed of their ancestral lands and deprived of their resources for survival, both physical and cultural; they are even robbed of their very right to life. In more modern versions of market exploitation, indigenous peoples see their traditional knowledge and cultural expressions marketed and patented without their consent or participation. Of the some 7,000 languages today, it is estimated that more than 4,000 are spoken by indigenous peoples. Language specialists predict that up to 90 per cent of the world's languages are likely to become extinct or threatened with extinction by the end of the century.[1] This statistic illustrates the grave danger faced by indigenous peoples.

A brief history of indigenous issues at the international level

For centuries, since the time of their colonization, conquest or occupation, indigenous peoples have documented histories of resistance, interface or cooperation with states, thus demonstrating their conviction and determination to survive with their distinct sovereign identities. Indeed, indigenous peoples were often recognized as sovereign peoples by states, as witnessed by the hundreds of treaties concluded between indigenous peoples and the governments of the United States, Canada, New Zealand and others. And yet as indigenous populations dwindled,

---

[1] Language Vitality and Endangerment. UNESCO

and the settler populations grew ever more dominant, states became less and less inclined to recognize the sovereignty of indigenous peoples. Indigenous peoples themselves, at the same time, continued to adapt to changing circumstances while maintaining their distinct identity as sovereign peoples.

In 1923, Cayuga Chief Deskaheh, the representative of the Six Nations of the Iroquois travelled to Geneva, to the League of Nations, to plead for the cause of his people. He waited a whole year to obtain recognition from the League but was not received and returned home to North America. Although he was not granted an audience by the League, he did sustain a remarkably successful PR campaign in Europe, where he found a much more receptive audience in the media and general public than he did amongst the delegations in the League.

A similar journey was made the following year by Maori religious leader W.T. Ratana to protest at the breakdown of the Treaty of Waitangi, concluded in 1840 between representatives of the British Crown and Maori chiefs in New Zealand, a treaty that gave Maori ownership of their lands. Ratana first travelled to London with a large delegation to petition King George V, but he was denied access. He then sent part of his delegation to Geneva to the League of Nations and arrived there later himself, in 1925, but was also denied access.

Indigenous issues received scant attention from the international community until the last three decades of the twentieth century. One exception was in the 1950s, when concerns about situations of forced labour among "native populations" prompted the International Labour Organization to work on what became, in 1957, Convention No. 107, entitled "Convention Concerning the Protection and Integration of Indigenous and Other Tribal and Semi-Tribal Populations in Independent Countries". This Treaty was later criticized as assimilationist by the indigenous movement, which had become more visible at the international level in the 1970s. This would eventually lead to the adoption of ILO Convention No. 169 in 1989.

A great number of indigenous peoples' organizations, were established at national and international level in the 1960s and 1970s, spurred on by the decolonization era and a more general growth in non-governmental organizations. The issues that fuelled the movement ranged from broken treaties and loss of land to discrimination, marginalization, conflict and gross violations of human rights, including massacres. Although most of the activities of the nascent international indigenous movement took place outside the environs of the United Nations, indigenous peoples' voices were at last being heard, and the UN was finally willing to listen to these voices.

In 1972, the United Nations Sub-Commission on Prevention of Discrimination and Protection of Minorities launched a Study on the problem of discrimination against indigenous populations, later known as "the Martínez Cobo study", the name of the Special Rapporteur appointed to prepare the report.[2] The study began at a time when the international indigenous movement was growing rapidly throughout the Americas, the Caribbean, the Arctic, Australia, New Zealand, the Philippines, Bangladesh and elsewhere. This framed the nascent international indigenous movement in human rights terms—a landmark that has characterized the movement since.

The Study created a momentum that, together with the advocacy work of the indigenous movement, led, in 1982, to the establishment of the first United Nations mechanism on indigenous peoples' issues, namely the Working Group on Indigenous Populations of the Sub-Commission. In 1983, in an unprecedented breakthrough, the Working Group decided to allow the participation of representatives of indigenous peoples and their organizations.

Between 1984 and 1993, indigenous issues gained increased momentum, as witnessed by the establishment of the UN Voluntary Fund for Indigenous Populations (1985), the adoption of ILO Convention No. 169 on Indigenous

---

[2] Martínez Cobo (1986/7).

and Tribal Peoples in Independent Countries (1989), the proclamation of the International Year of the World's Indigenous People (1993) and, subsequently, the proclamation of two separate International Decades of the World's Indigenous People (1995-2004 and 2005-2014).[3]

The First Decade, launched in 1994 and completed in 2004, adopted the special theme of "partnership in action" and its programme of action was meant to raise awareness about, and integrate, indigenous issues into the intergovernmental and, by extension, the governmental agendas. The First Decade helped to promote awareness and solidified indigenous issues on the agenda of the United Nations and some of its agencies. Indigenous peoples themselves also took advantage of the Decade, documenting and providing information about human rights violations and carving themselves a niche within various international fora. During the course of the First Decade a number of other achievements were made:

◈ August 9 was declared as the annual International Day of the World's Indigenous People

◈ The Special Rapporteur on the situation of human rights and fundamental freedoms of indigenous people was appointed by the Commission on Human Rights

◈ A fellowship programme for indigenous people was established within the Office of the High Commissioner on Human Rights (OHCHR).

The other major goal of the first Decade was the establishment of the United Nations Permanent Forum on Indigenous Issues, by the Economic and Social Council in 2000. Despite these important steps forward, a number of challenges remained, most importantly the lack of implementation by states of programmes that promote the development and rights of indigenous peoples and the United Nations' role in assisting them. The other unfinished matter was the Draft Declaration on the Rights of Indigenous Peoples, which had not been adopted during the first Decade, despite great efforts by all sides.

In 1993, the Working Group completed a Draft Declaration on the Rights of Indigenous Peoples, a document held in high esteem by indigenous peoples, created with their participation and expressing indigenous peoples' aspirations.

In 1994, the Draft Declaration was approved by the Sub-Commission and, in 1995, the Commission on Human Rights established a Working Group to examine and fine-tune the Draft Declaration. The negotiations were difficult and indigenous representatives again participated actively in the process, which eventually culminated, in June 2006, in the historic decision taken during its first session by the Human Rights Council—the body that succeeded the Commission on Human Rights—to adopt the Declaration. Just over a year later, on 13 September 2007, the General Assembly adopted the United Nations Declaration on the Rights of Indigenous Peoples, which marked a major milestone in the work of the United Nations and indigenous peoples´ struggle for the protection and promotion of their rights.[4]

The Working Group on indigenous populations was abolished in 2007 and replaced with the Expert Mechanism on the Rights of Indigenous Peoples.[5] The Expert Mechanism is a subsidiary body of the Human Rights Council, composed of five experts, which provides thematic expertise on the rights of indigenous peoples to the Council, focusing mainly on studies and research-based advice. The Mechanism may also suggest proposals to the Council for consideration and approval, although the mechanism does not adopt resolutions or decisions.

---

[3] United Nations Organization (2004).
[4] United Nations General Assembly Resolution (2007).
[5] The Expert Mechanism on the rights of indigenous peoples.

In 2001, the Commission on Human Rights decided to establish a Special Rapporteur on the human rights and fundamental freedoms of indigenous people to examine the situation of indigenous peoples worldwide on the basis of communications received and country-specific visits. The first Special Rapporteur, Rodolfo Stavenhagen, a well-known Mexican anthropologist, presented annual reports to the Commission on Human Rights—and, since 2006—to the Human Rights Council[6] and the General Assembly. Mr. Stavenhagen was succeeded by the Native American law professor, Mr. S. James Anaya on 1 May 2008.

The establishment of the Permanent Forum on Indigenous Issues (UNPFII) in 2000 came after a ten-year process of international consultation following the Vienna Conference of 1993. The Forum has a broad mandate, namely to discuss economic and social development, culture, the environment, education, health and human rights and to advise the Economic and Social Council and the United Nations system on all matters pertaining to its mandate, promote the coordination and integration of indigenous issues in the United Nations system, raise awareness about indigenous issues and produce information materials on indigenous issues. This high-level body in the United Nations' hierarchy demonstrates the increasing political engagement of states in terms of cooperating with indigenous peoples to address a multiplicity of issues. More than 1,500 indigenous participants from all parts of the world attend the annual sessions of the UNPFII in New York, in addition to representatives from some 70 countries and around 35 UN agencies and inter-governmental entities.

The concept of indigenous peoples

In the forty-year history of indigenous issues at the United Nations, and its even longer history at the ILO, considerable thinking and debate have been devoted to the question of the definition or understanding of "indigenous peoples". But no such definition has ever been adopted by any United Nations-system body.

One of the most cited descriptions of the concept of "indigenous" was outlined in the José R. Martínez Cobo's Study on the Problem of Discrimination against Indigenous Populations. After long consideration of the issues involved, Martínez Cobo offered a working definition of "indigenous communities, peoples and nations". In doing so, he expressed a number of basic ideas forming the intellectual framework for this effort, including the right of indigenous peoples themselves to define what and who indigenous peoples are. The working definition reads as follows:

> *Indigenous communities, peoples and nations are those which, having a historical continuity with pre-invasion and pre-colonial societies that developed on their territories, consider themselves distinct from other sectors of the societies now prevailing on those territories, or parts of them. They form at present non-dominant sectors of society and are determined to preserve, develop and transmit to future generations their ancestral territories, and their ethnic identity, as the basis of their continued existence as peoples, in accordance with their own cultural patterns, social institutions and legal system.*
>
> *This historical continuity may consist of the continuation, for an extended period reaching into the present of one or more of the following factors:*
>
> > *a. Occupation of ancestral lands, or at least of part of them*
> >
> > *b. Common ancestry with the original occupants of these lands*

---

[6] The Special Rapporteur's reports may be accessed on the website of the Office of the High Commissioner for Human Rights, www.ohchr.org

c. Culture in general, or in specific manifestations (such as religion, living under a tribal system, membership of an indigenous community, dress, means of livelihood, lifestyle, etc.)

d. Language (whether used as the only language, as mother-tongue, as the habitual means of communication at home or in the family, or as the main, preferred, habitual, general or normal language)

e. Residence in certain parts of the country, or in certain regions of the world

f. Other relevant factors.

On an individual basis, an indigenous person is one who belongs to these indigenous populations through self-identification as indigenous (group consciousness) and is recognized and accepted by these populations as one of its members (acceptance by the group).

This preserves for these communities the sovereign right and power to decide who belongs to them, without external interference.[7]

During the many years of debate at the meetings of the Working Group on Indigenous Populations, observers from indigenous organizations developed a common position that rejected the idea of a formal definition of indigenous peoples at the international level to be adopted by states. Similarly, government delegations expressed the view that it was neither desirable nor necessary to elaborate a universal definition of indigenous peoples. Finally, at its fifteenth session, in 1997, the Working Group concluded that a definition of indigenous peoples at the global level was not possible at that time, and this did not prove necessary for the adoption of the Declaration on the Rights of Indigenous Peoples.[8] Instead of offering a definition, Article 33 of the United Nations Declaration on the Rights of Indigenous Peoples underlines the importance of self-identification, that indigenous peoples themselves define their own identity as indigenous.

Article 33

1. Indigenous peoples have the right to determine their own identity or membership in accordance with their customs and traditions. This does not impair the right of indigenous individuals to obtain citizenship of the States in which they live.

2. Indigenous peoples have the right to determine the structures and to select the membership of their institutions in accordance with their own procedures.

ILO Convention No. 169 also enshrines the importance of self-identification. Article 1 indicates that self-identification as indigenous or tribal shall be regarded as a fundamental criterion for determining the groups to which the provisions of this Convention apply.

Furthermore, this same Article 1 contains a statement of coverage rather than a definition, indicating that the Convention applies to:

a) tribal peoples in independent countries whose social, cultural and economic conditions distinguish them from other sections of the national community and whose status is regulated wholly or partially by their own customs or traditions or by special laws or regulations;

---

[7] Martínez Cobo (1986/7), paras. 379-382.
[8] Working Group on Indigenous Populations (2006a) and (2006b), paras. 153-154.

b) peoples in independent countries who are regarded as indigenous on account of their descent from the populations which inhabited the country, or a geographical region to which the country belongs, at the time of conquest or colonization or the establishment of present state boundaries and who irrespective of their legal status, retain some or all of their own social, economic, cultural and political institutions.

The concept of indigenous peoples emerged from the colonial experience, whereby the aboriginal peoples of a given land were marginalized after being invaded by colonial powers, whose peoples are now dominant over the earlier occupants. These earlier definitions of indigenousness make sense when looking at the Americas, Russia, the Arctic and many parts of the Pacific. However, this definition makes less sense in most parts of Asia and Africa, where the colonial powers did not displace whole populations of peoples and replace them with settlers of European descent. Domination and displacement of peoples have, of course, not been exclusively practised by white settlers and colonialists; in many parts of Africa and Asia, dominant groups have suppressed marginalized groups and it is in response to this experience that the indigenous movement in these regions has reacted.

It is sometimes argued that all Africans are indigenous to Africa and that by separating Africans into indigenous and non-indigenous groups, separate classes of citizens are being created with different rights. The same argument is made in many parts of Asia or, alternatively, that there can be no indigenous peoples within a given country since there has been no large-scale Western settler colonialism and therefore there can be no distinction between the original inhabitants and newcomers. It is certainly true that Africans are indigenous to Africa and Asians are indigenous to Asia, in the context of European colonization. Nevertheless, indigenous identity is not exclusively determined by European colonization.

The Report of the Working Group of Experts on Indigenous Populations/Communities of the African Commission on Human and Peoples' Rights therefore emphasizes that the concept of indigenous must be understood in a wider context than only the colonial experience.

> *The focus should be on more recent approaches focusing on self-definition as indigenous and distinctly different from other groups within a state; on a special attachment to and use of their traditional land whereby ancestral land and territory has a fundamental importance for their collective physical and cultural survival as peoples; on an experience of subjugation, marginalization, dispossession, exclusion or discrimination because these peoples have different cultures, ways of life or modes of production than the national hegemonic and dominant model.*[9]

In the sixty-year historical development of international law within the United Nations system, it is not uncommon that various terms have not been formally defined, the most vivid examples being the notions of "peoples" and "minorities". Yet the United Nations has recognized the right of peoples to self-determination and has adopted the Declaration on the Rights of Persons Belonging to National or Ethnic, Religious and Linguistic Minorities. The lack of formal definition of "peoples" or "minorities" has not been crucial to the Organization's successes or failures in those domains nor to the promotion, protection or monitoring of the rights accorded to these groups. Nor have other terms, such as "the family" or "terrorism" been defined, and yet the United Nations and Member States devote considerable action and efforts to these areas.

In conclusion, in the case of the concept of "indigenous peoples", the prevailing view today is that no formal universal definition of the term is necessary, given that a single definition will inevitably be either over- or under-

---

[9] Report of the African Commission's Working Group of Experts on Indigenous Populations/communities.

inclusive, making sense in some societies but not in others. For practical purposes, the commonly accepted understanding of the term is that provided in the Martínez Cobo study mentioned above.

Looking forward

After decades of little or no attention from the international community, indigenous peoples are increasingly making their voices heard and building partnerships with the United Nations system and beyond. This is equally true for the national and local levels and there are countless examples of good practices whereby indigenous peoples work in cooperation with governments and local authorities in countries across the globe.

But there are still also countless examples of bad practices and, as mentioned above, the situation of indigenous peoples in many parts of the world remains extremely precarious. Some examples of this situation will be given in this volume, but it is beyond its scope to address all issues that concern indigenous peoples. It is not an attempt to provide an exhaustive or definitive analysis of indigenous issues. It is, however, an attempt to raise awareness of the most important issues and challenges that indigenous peoples face, as well as to highlight some of the possible steps that can be taken to address these challenges.

With the adoption of the United Nations Declaration on the Rights of Indigenous Peoples in September 2007, an important step has been taken and it is safe to say that indigenous issues have never been more prominent within the United Nations system. The Declaration has the potential to become extremely influential. This potential, however, can only be realised if indigenous peoples, states, civil society and the UN system make use of the Declaration and make it a living document that has real relevance for indigenous peoples across the world. Already, there is evidence that this will be the case. The Declaration has been adopted as national law in Bolivia and is already being referred to and used in courts of law in other countries.

About this publication

This publication will discuss many of the issues addressed by the Declaration on the Rights of Indigenous Peoples. It is divided into seven chapters, based on the six mandated areas of the Permanent Forum on Indigenous Issues, in addition to a chapter on emerging issues;

The first chapter, written by Joji Carino, emphasizes both self determination and the principle of free, prior and informed consent, which in practice, means that indigenous peoples themselves must be free to determine their own development. This entails that indigenous peoples' rights to their own lands and territories must be respected and that indigenous peoples need to develop their own definitions and indicators of poverty and well-being. Although global statistics on the situation of indigenous peoples are not readily available, it is clear that indigenous peoples suffer disproportionately from poverty, marginalization, lack of adequate housing and income inequality. Traditional modes of livelihood, such as fishing, hunting and gathering, livestock cultivation or small scale agriculture are under a great amount of stress from phenomena such as neo-liberalism and commodification, privatization, climate change and conflict. Many of these challenges are faced not only by indigenous peoples, but by all of humanity, and as the chapter concludes: "Indigenous peoples have vital contributions to make in addressing the contemporary challenges to renew ecological and social ethics and relationships, and in the fulfilment of peace, human rights and sustainable development."

In the second chapter, Naomi Kipuri discusses various definitions of culture, emphasising the remarkable contribution that indigenous peoples make to cultural diversity across the globe. Although it is estimated that indigenous peoples are some 370 million, or less than 6 per cent of the global population, they speak an overwhelming majority of the world's estimated 7,000 languages, and are the stewards of some of the most biologically diverse areas accumulating an immeasurable amount of traditional knowledge about their ecosystems. Indigenous cultures face the dual and somewhat contradictory threats of discrimination and commodification. On the one hand, indigenous peoples continue to face racism and discrimination that sees them as inferior to non-indigenous communities and their culture as a hindrance to their development. On the other hand, indigenous peoples are increasingly recognized for their unique relationship with their environment, their traditional knowledge and their spirituality, leading to a commodification of their culture which is frequently out of their control, providing them no benefits, and often a great deal of harm.

The chapter on Environment, written by Neva Collings, begins by looking at the major environmental issues that indigenous peoples are facing today. The chapter emphasizes indigenous peoples' spiritual, cultural, social and economic connection with their traditional lands and their tradition of collective rights to land in contrast with dominant models of individual land ownership, privatization and development which frequently lead to dispossession of indigenous peoples' land. In addition to these threats, indigenous peoples face the consequences of rapid climate change, especially in the Arctic and the Pacific islands, while mitigation efforts have exacerbated the situation, putting increased pressure on their lands, such as deforestation for biofuel plantations. The chapter reviews some of the international legal frameworks and mechanisms for environmental protection, from the Rio Summit in 1992 to the Declaration on the Rights of Indigenous Peoples, adopted in 2007, and how indigenous peoples have used these mechanisms. A final section of the chapter looks at how international environmental law is being implemented, and which are the major gaps and challenges indigenous peoples have to confront at the local and national levels.

The Education chapter by Duane Champagne illustrates the stark contrast in access to education between indigenous and non-indigenous students. At all levels, and in all regions of the world, indigenous peoples tend to have lower levels of literacy, enjoy fewer years at school and are more likely to drop out of school. Education is seldom provided to indigenous children in their native languages and it is frequently offered in a context that is culturally inappropriate and has few and inadequate facilities. Far too often, those who do get an education are forced to assimilate within the dominant culture, unable to find jobs in their communities. Despite discouraging overall trends, there are a great number of initiatives that point the way forward for indigenous education, where the community as a whole is involved, where teachers speak both the dominant language and the relevant indigenous language, where ultimately indigenous peoples have the freedom to choose whether they pursue their careers in their own communities or elsewhere.

The Health chapter, written by Myrna Cunningham[10] emphasizes the interdependence between health and other factors, such as poverty, illiteracy, marginalization, environmental degradation and (the lack of) self determination. These forces, inherited from colonization, make indigenous peoples in general, and indigenous women and children in particular, vulnerable to poor health. The result is that indigenous peoples experience disproportionately high levels of maternal and infant mortality, malnutrition, cardiovascular illnesses, HIV/AIDS, malaria, tuberculosis, diabetes, and in virtually all other indicators of poor health, including mental health. Indigenous peoples have poor access to state health systems while there is a palpable lack of recognition and support for indigenous peoples' own health systems. Any successful plan to provide health care for indigenous peoples must involve intercultural health system where Western and indigenous health systems are practiced with equal human, technological and financial resources and where indigenous peoples are involved in all decision making processes involving their health and health care provisions.

---

[10] Written in collaboration with the Center for Indigenous Peoples' Autonomy and Development (CADPI) in Nicaragua.

In the Human Rights chapter, Dalee Sambo Dorough stresses the indivisibility and interrelatedness of indigenous peoples' rights and how their human rights are intrinsically related to their right to self-determination, self-determination being indeed a pre-condition to the exercise of all other rights. From the Universal Declaration on Human Rights to the Declaration on the Rights of Indigenous Peoples, there are a significant number of international instruments that protect the human rights of indigenous peoples, and there have been marked improvements in recent years. However, indigenous peoples continue to face grave human rights abuses on a daily basis, from dispossession of land to violence and murder. Often the most serious of these abuses are committed against indigenous persons who are defending their rights and their lands and territories. There is therefore a serious gap between indigenous peoples' internationally recognized human rights and their enjoyment of those rights in reality which needs to be addressed through human rights education, more effective oversight and greater commitments from states.

The last chapter of this publication, written by Mililani Trask, looks at some of the emerging issues affecting indigenous peoples, including violence and militarism, effects of conservation, globalization, migration and urbanization, and indigenous peoples living in voluntary isolation. These issues are in many ways interrelated and a common theme is indigenous peoples' vulnerability in the face of outside pressures and the need to develop specific policies that address this vulnerability, while simultaneously ensuring that the principle of free, prior and informed consent is respected and that indigenous peoples participate in decision making processes that affect their well-being. This is indeed the underlying theme of this publication.

Overview of main international responses

1957 - ILO Convention 107 on Indigenous and Tribal Populations is adopted
(http://www.ilo.org/ilolex/english/convdisp1.htm)

1972 - The Study of the Problem of Discrimination against Indigenous Populations (also known as the Martínez Cobo study) – is launched

1982 - The Working Group on Indigenous Populations is established by the UN
(http://www.ohchr.org/english/issues/indigenous/groups/groups-01.htm)

1984 - The Martínez Cobo Study is submitted to the UN 1985 - The Voluntary Fund for Indigenous Populations is created

1989 - ILO Convention No. 169 concerning Indigenous and Tribal Peoples in Independent States
(http://www.ilo.org/ilolex/english/convdisp1.htm) is adopted

1992 - The Rio Earth Summit adopts the Convention on Biological Diversity (http://www.biodiv.org/convention/default.shtml)

1993 - The World Conference on Human Rights recommends the establishment of a Permanent Forum on Indigenous Issues

1993 - International Year of the World's Indigenous People

1994 - The first International Decade for Indigenous People is launched (1994-2004)

1994 - The Voluntary Fund to support small-scale projects during the Decade is created

1998 - First Roundtable on Intellectual Property and Indigenous Peoples organized by the World Intellectual Property Organization - WIPO (http://www.wipo.int)

2000 - Establishment of the United Nations Permanent Forum on Indigenous Issues (UNPFII)
(http://www.un.org/esa/socdev/unpfii/index)

2001 - The mechanism of a Special Rapporteur on the Human Rights and Fundamental Freedoms of Indigenous People is established by the Commission on Human Rights
(http://www.ohchr.org/english/issues/indigenous/rapporteur/)

2002 - A Voluntary Fund for Indigenous and Local Communities is established by the CBD (http://www.cbd.int)

2003 - A Voluntary Fund is established by the UN to support the Permanent Forum

2005 - The Second International Decade for Indigenous People is launched (2005-2015), including a fund to support small-scale projects

2005 - A Voluntary Fund for Indigenous and Local Communities is created by WIPO

2007 - The UN Declaration on the Rights of Indigenous Peoples is adopted by the UN General Assembly
(http://www.un.org/esa/socdev/unpfii/en/declaration.html)

2007 - The new Expert Mechanism on the Rights of Indigenous Peoples is established by the Human Rights Council

List of References

African Commission on Human and Peoples' Rights (ACHPR). 2005. Report of the African Commission's Working Group of Experts on Indigenous Populations/communities. Banjul and Copenhagen: ACHPR and IWGIA.

The Expert Mechanism on the rights of indigenous peoples was established by Human Rights Council Resolution 6/36, which was adopted without a vote on 14 December 2007.

Martínez Cobo, José. 1986/7. "Study of the Problem of Discrimination against Indigenous Populations". UN Doc. E/CN.4/Sub.2/1986/7 and Add. 1-4. Available online at http://www.un.org/esa/socdev/unpfii/en/second.html.

UNESCO. 2003. "Language Vitality and Endangerment." Document submitted by Ad Hoc Expert Group on Endangered Languages to the International Expert Meeting on UNESCO Programme Safeguarding of Endangered Languages, UNESCO Paris, 10–12 March 2003.

United Nations Organization. 2004. Draft Programme of Action for the Second Decade. UN Doc. A/60/270. Available at UNPFII website http://www.un.org/esa/socdev/unpfii.

United Nations Organization. 2007. Declaration on the Rights of Indigenous Peoples. Resolution A/61/L.67 September 2007. Available online at UNPFII Web site http://www.un.org/esa/socdev/unpfii/en/declaration.html

Working Group on Indigenous Populations (WGIP). 1996a. Working Paper by the Chairperson-Rapporteur, Mrs. Erica-Irene A. Daes, on the concept of "indigenous people". UN Doc. E/CN.4/Sub.2/AC.4/1996/2, 10 June 1996.

Working Group on Indigenous Populations (WGIP). 1996b. Report of the WGIP on its fourteenth session. UN Doc. E/CN.4/Sub.2/1996/21, 16 August 1996.

CHAPTER I

POVERTY AND WELL-BEING

- By Joji Carino

As long as we have waters where the fish can swim
As long as we have land where the reindeer can graze
As long as we have woods where wild animals can hide
we are safe on this earth

When our homes are gone and our land destroyed
— then where are we to be?

Our own land, our lives' bread, has shrunk
the mountain lakes have risen
rivers have become dry
the streams sing in sorrowful voices
the land grows dark, the grass is dying
the birds grow silent and leave

The good gifts we have received
no longer move our hearts
Things meant to make life easier
have made life less

Painful is the walk
on rough roads of stone
Silent cry the people of the mountains

While time rushes on
our blood becomes thin
our language no longer resounds
the water no longer speaks

(Paulus Utsi, "As long as…")

Introduction

Paulus Utsi, the Saami poet,[1] echoes the lament of many indigenous peoples about the ravages caused by industrial development upon nature and traditional cultural values. He describes a longing to maintain traditional lifestyles close to nature and the ensuing loss of meaning when engulfed by modern economic development. Captured in the poem are underlying cultural values and definitions of what constitutes indigenous peoples' well-being and sustainable development and, in its absence, indigenous peoples' despair.

---

[1] Paulus Utsi was born in 1918 and died in 1975. His poem "As long as…" is translated by Roland Thorstensson and reprinted in In the Shadow of the Midnight Sun: Contemporary Sami Prose and Poetry (1998), Harald Gaski (ed.).

From the Asian region, John Bamba, an indigenous Dayak from Kalimantan, similarly summarizes the underlying principles for living a good life, based on the Dayak's traditional cultural values. They are the values of sustainability, collectivity, naturality, spirituality, process-orientation, domesticity and locality. These are contrasted with prevailing modern values — productivity, individualism, technology, rationality, efficiency, commercialism, and globalization — that have become predominant principles in present-day social and economic development that can undermine a balanced human-nature relationship. The ensuing chaos is seen as cultural poverty, defined from a Dayak perspective as arising from the inability to practice customary principles and values, and to live a good life.

Cultural poverty: A Dayak perspective

The following seven principles summarize the way in which the Dayak achieve their ideal of life, based on their cultural values and how they compare with modern values:

◈ Sustainability (biodiversity) versus productivity (monoculture)

◈ Collectivity (cooperation) versus individuality (competition)

◈ Naturality (organic) versus engineered (inorganic)

◈ Spirituality (rituality) versus rationality (scientific)

◈ Process (effectiveness) versus result (efficiency)

◈ Subsistence (domesticity) versus commerciality (market)

◈ Customary law (locality) versus state law (global)

Failure to achieve these ideals is believed to result in *barau* (Jalai Dayak): a situation when nature fails to function normally, and thus results in chaos. *Barau* is a result of *Adat** transgression—a broken relationship with nature. "Poverty" for the Dayak is linked directly with failure to exercise the *Adat* that governs the way in which the people should live.

* Adat: set of local and traditional laws.

Source: Bamba (2003).

These insights from two indigenous intellectuals underline the central importance of cultural values in defining the social and economic well-being of indigenous peoples. Any measures of indigenous peoples' social and economic development must necessarily start from indigenous peoples' own definitions and indicators of poverty and well-being.

Indigenous leaders addressing the UN General Assembly's Special Session, five years after the Rio Conference on Environment and Development, stated, "Sustainable development and self-determination are two sides of the same coin."[2] This echoes a statement on poverty adopted in May 2001 by the Committee on Economic, Social and Cultural Rights, which recognizes that poverty constitutes a denial of human rights and defines poverty as a human condition characterized by the deprivation of the resources, capabilities, choices, security and power necessary for the enjoyment of an adequate standard of living and other civil, cultural, economic, political and social rights.[3]

> [sustainable development and self-determination are two sides of the same coin]

This chapter presents an overview of issues linked to modern economic development and the impoverishment of indigenous peoples, the status and trends in the practice of traditional occupations, indicators relevant to indigenous peoples' well-being and sustainable development, and corporate globalization and sustainability of indigenous communities. It also contains some core findings of selected thematic or country case studies relevant to the subject of indigenous peoples and development.

> "If a villager had cut trees in this place, the elders would have fined them so much. But because it is the Government, they will not dare say anything". — a villager, Cambodia[4]

New threats of globalization

The global ascendancy of neo-liberal economics and the entrenchment of corporate power in international and national affairs have deepened inequalities between and within nations and largely undermined efforts toward sustainable development. Based on a belief that the market should be the organizing principle for social, political and economic decisions, policy makers promoted privatization of state activities and an increased role for the free market, flexibility in labour markets, and trade liberalization. The benefits of these policies frequently fail to reach the indigenous peoples of the world, who acutely feel their costs, such as environmental degradation and loss of traditional lands and territories.

> "At present, villages do not have serious problems of land use. But the next generation of indigenous peoples will not have enough land for their field and paddy rice agriculture". — a farmer, Cambodia[5]

Since the 1980s there has been a global trend to liberalize Mining Codes. This is aimed at increasing foreign investment into the extractives sector and providing increased assurance of profit on investment for mainly British, Canadian, US

---

[2] Statement made at the 19th Special Session of the United Nations General Assembly 1997 on Earth Summit + 5. Reproduced in Posey (2000).

[3] Committee on Economic, Social and Cultural Rights (2001). Statement on Substantive Issues Arising in the Implementation of the International Covenant on Economic, Social and Cultural Rights: Poverty and the International Covenant on Economic, Social and Cultural Rights. Adopted on 4 May 2001.

[4] Asian Development Bank (2002)

[5] Asian Development Bank (2002).

and Australian financed mining companies. Investors were given commitments against nationalization and the previous trend, especially in the global South to regard resource industries as strategic national interests in need of protection. Many nationalized mineral extraction enterprises were sold to transnational corporations. According to Professor James Otto then of the Colorado School of mines by 2003 more than 105 countries had liberalized their Mining Codes along these lines. Countries such as the Philippines and Colombia revised their mining codes, facilitating large-scale mining by foreign companies, which intensified the pressure on indigenous lands and weakened or overrode the legal protections previously enjoyed by indigenous peoples.[6]

According to the recently concluded meeting of the African Initiative on Mining, Environment and Society: "In recent times, international investment agreements and contracts with African governments in the extractive sector in particular have significantly increased. By the middle of 2008, more than 2600 bilateral investment treaties have been signed between individual African governments and private corporations and northern governments. Despite their intent to clarify and codify rules around expropriation, these treaties tended to reinforce structures of exploitation and Africa's peripheral status in global political economic order. They have been effective in protecting the interest of foreign direct investment (FDI), constraining public policy space, limiting environmental protection, undermining human rights including labour and community livelihood, and ultimately legalizing capital flight out of the continent." [7]

In Australia the Native Title legislation has provided some increased negotiating powers to indigenous peoples, obliging mining companies to consult with communities and to recognize some wider social responsibilities. This has resulted in some improvements in the proportion of Indigenous Peoples employed in mining within indigenous areas. However disputes over and resistance to mining projects remain common. In Panama, the San Blas Kuna territory is constitutionally protected, as is the Yanomami territory in Northern Brazil. Nevertheless, mining companies and other extractive corporations tend to have few requirements to consider the environmental or social impact of their activities on indigenous peoples. This is especially the case in southeast Asia and many African countries due to the non-recognition of customary land rights. Even where some legislation protecting indigenous peoples' land rights exists, it is frequently not implemented or is overpowered by conflicting legislation that is designed to attract foreign investment. Whether it is gold mining in Guatemala, nickel extraction in Indonesia, the Chad-Cameroon oil pipeline, or the gas pipeline in Camisea in the Peruvian Amazon, the effects have been devastating on the indigenous peoples whose territories are destroyed by highly polluting technologies and disregard of local communities' right to the environment. "The widespread practice of dumping toxic waste in indigenous territories has been the cause of many abortions and cases of cancer and other diseases among indigenous women".[8] Such practices are found on indigenous territories both in the global North and South including for example

[indigenous peoples bear disproportionate costs from resource-intensive and resource-extractive industries]

---

[6] Tebtebba (2005).
[7] African Initiative on Mining, Environment and Society (2009)
[8] Stavenhagen (2007), para. 52.

the Navajo territories in the south-western United States which is both a location for uranium mining and nuclear waste disposal.

As the pressures on the Earth's resources intensify, indigenous peoples bear disproportionate costs from resource-intensive and resource-extractive industries and activities such as mining, oil and gas development, large dams and other infrastructure projects, logging and plantations, bio-prospecting, industrial fishing and farming, and also eco-tourism and imposed conservation projects. These pressures also accelerate some unsustainable economic activities undertaken by indigenous peoples themselves, notably where indigenous rights have not been respected, thus leaving communities with insufficient land and resources. According to one observer, "In particular, many indigenous peoples have been gravely affected as environmental and social crises—such as the displacement of communities, the deterioration of health and severe environmental degradation—have increasingly disrupted and brought chaos to their lives".[9]

[the implementation of privatization policies has had a profound effect on the economic practices of many communities]

The effects of privatization on Russian reindeer herders

Since the break up of the Soviet Union in 1991, Northern Russia has undergone considerable changes. One of these changes has been the privatization of the economy, leading to significant economic decline in northern regions. The implementation of privatization policies has had a profound effect on the economic practices of many communities, in particular in the north-eastern regions, including Yakutia, Chukotka, Magadan, and Kamchatka. These communities specialize in breeding reindeer. As a result of the central government's disinvestment, the domestic reindeer population fell by more than one-third between 1991 and 1999, from 2.2 million head to 1.4 million. One result of the reduction of this economic activity has been a more settled way of life, instead of following the reindeer.

However, in certain areas, where the supply networks that supported production and distribution were cut off or became intermittent, people have actually had to make greater investment in hunting, fishing and trapping activities in order to support themselves. Among the Dolgan and the Nganasan, more isolated now than in the past 30 years, the main source of protein comes from subsistence hunting, fishing and harvesting.

Although privatization has destabilized many communities in Northern Russia, it has also created more variation among areas, with some seeing a resurgence of traditional subsistence means of economic support and so reaffirming the continuing need for understanding and treatment of indigenous conceptions of economy and relations to the land.

Source: Arctic Human Development Report (2004), 80.

---

[9] Sawyer and Terence Gomez (2008), 16.

Agriculture and food security

The WTO Agreement on Agriculture, which promotes export competition and import liberalization, has allowed the entry of cheap agricultural products into indigenous peoples' communities, thereby compromising their sustainable agricultural practices, food security, health and cultures. The view has been put forward that small-scale subsistence production, which characterizes many indigenous economies, does not contribute to economic growth. That "... economic growth will only come about if subsistence lands are rapidly converted into large-scale, capital intensive, export-oriented commercial production. This takes the form of huge agricultural monocrop plantations, commercial mines and/or plantation forest projects, all of which drive people from their lands".[10]

> *"Once you sell land, it means hunger for your family. There is nowhere to go to clear land anymore".* — former indigenous landowner, Vietnam[11]

Thus, small-scale farm production is giving way to commercial cash-crop plantations, further concentrating ancestral lands in the hands of a few agri-corporations and landlords. The conversion of small-scale farming to cash-crop plantations has further caused the uprooting of many community members from rural to urban areas.

National legislation that is compliant with WTO agreements, combined with the liberalization of trade and investment regimes promoted by the donor community since the early 1980s, are undermining national legislation and regulations protecting indigenous rights and the environment. Indigenous Peoples have put forward these examples of the adverse impacts of WTO agreements.[12]

The WTO Agreement on Agriculture (AOA) requirements for the liberalization of agricultural trade and the deregulation of laws which protect domestic producers and crops has resulted in the loss of livelihoods of indigenous corn producers in Mexico because of the dumping of artificially cheap, highly subsidized corn from the USA. The contamination of traditional corn varieties in Mexico by genetically modified corn is also a very serious problem. Indigenous vegetable production in the Cordillera region of the Philippines has been similarly devastated by the dumping of cheap vegetables. The drop in commodity prices of coffee has impoverished indigenous and hill tribe farmers engaged in coffee production in Guatemala, Mexico, Colombia, and Vietnam. All these are made possible due to high export subsidies and domestic support provided to agribusiness corporations and rich farmers in the United States and the European Union.

There has been an upsurge in infrastructure development, particularly of large hydroelectric dams, oil and gas pipelines, and roads in indigenous peoples territories to support operations of extractive industries, logging corporations, and export processing zones. For example, infrastructure development under Plan Puebla Panama has destroyed ceremonial and sacred sites of indigenous peoples in the six states of southern Mexico and in Guatemala.

The General Agreement on Services (GATS) allows privatization of basic public services such as water and energy, and coverage is being expanded to include environmental services (sanitation, nature and landscape protection), financial services, and tourism, among others. This has spurred massive general strikes and protests such as those led by indigenous peoples in Bolivia.

---

[10] Tauli-Corpuz (2006), 39.
[11] Asian Development Bank (2002).
[12] The International Cancun Declaration of Indigenous Peoples, 5th WTO Ministerial Conference - Cancun, Quintana Roo, Mexico, 12 September 2003.

The patenting of medicinal plants and seeds nurtured and used by indigenous peoples, like the *quinoa, ayahuasca*, Mexican yellow bean, *maca, sangre de drago, hoodia*, etc. is facilitated by the World Trade Organization (WTO) Agreement on Trade-Related Aspects of Intellectual Property Rights (TRIPS). This contains requirements for national legislation to protect copyrights, patents, trademarks and other forms of intellectual property, allowing the patenting of life forms for micro-organisms and non-biological and microbiological processes of production of plants and animals. This constitutes a threat to the protection and promotion of indigenous knowledge. Furthermore, these policies have subjected indigenous peoples to the uncertainties of the marketplace, thus decreasing their food security and threatening their traditional livelihoods as illustrated by the discussion on Greenland and Northern Russian communities.

> *"They now even charge for domestic animals such as cats or dogs, which they used to give away for good luck".* — a woman interviewed, Viet Nam[13]

[large dams have dispro-
portionately impacted
indigenous peoples]

The above discussion points to the fact that neo-liberalism has frequently been imposed on indigenous peoples, and that under structural adjustment programmes, multinational corporations have extracted resources from indigenous territories without the free, prior and informed consent of the indigenous peoples involved, providing little or no compensation for the communities with adverse impacts on their livelihood and cultural/spiritual life. As a result, the indigenous peoples are made worse-off beyond what is evident in the quantitative (monetary) indicators of poverty and well-being.

Large dams and indigenous peoples

Large dams became symbols of modern development in the twentieth century, and recently have also epitomized the unequal economic, social and environmental impacts of "unsustainable development". The World Commission on Dams (WCD) knowledge base revealed that large dams have disproportionately impacted indigenous peoples and that future dam building also targets their lands disproportionately. They have suffered from loss of lands and livelihood, cultural losses, fragmentation of political institutions, breakdown of identity and human rights abuses.

Dam planning and projects are characterized by serious procedural failures that relate directly to indigenous communities. The distinctive characteristics of affected peoples are often ignored in project planning, as are customary rights. Environmental and social assessments are either absent or inadequate. Resettlements are frequently ill-planned.

---

[13] Asian Development Bank (2002).

> Compensation and reparations are tardy and inadequate. Participatory mechanisms are typically weak, with no negotiations or prior informed consent. Within national societies, indigenous peoples are often subject to social exclusion and prevalent discrimination, exacerbating these failures.
>
> WCD's detailed study of the water and energy sectors exemplifies the underlying problems with externally-imposed development projects that fail to respect the rights of indigenous peoples. Such top-down decision-making processes have impoverished indigenous peoples wherever they live, in developed and developing countries throughout the world, paving the way for demands to gain the free, prior and informed consent of indigenous peoples to any programmes and projects affecting them.
>
> *Source: WCD (2000), 97-130.*

Impoverishment of indigenous peoples

Indigenous peoples suffer from the consequences of historic injustice, including colonization, dispossession of their lands, territories and resources, oppression and discrimination as well as lack of control over their own ways of life. Their right to development has been largely denied by colonial and modern states in the pursuit of economic growth. As a consequence, indigenous peoples often lose out to more powerful actors, becoming among the most impoverished groups in their respective countries.

> *"Before the plantation came in, our lifestyle was prosperous. If we needed fruits, we just went to the forest. It was the same if we needed medicines, we just went to the forest. But since this company came in and burned our forest, everything has gone. Our life became difficult. The forest fire has been a disaster for us".* — a member of the Adat community, Indonesia[14]

Indigenous peoples continue to be over-represented among the poor, the illiterate, and the unemployed. Indigenous peoples number about 370 million. While they constitute approximately 5 per cent of the world's population, indigenous peoples make up 15 per cent of the world's poor.[15] They also make up about one-third of the world's 900 million extremely poor rural people.[16]

> *"If you go to visit a household and cannot meet them for two weeks or a month, you can be sure that they are poor people.*

while they constitute approximately 5 per cent of the world's population, indigenous peoples make up 15 per cent of the world's poor

[14] Asian Development Bank (2002).
[15] IFAD (2007).
[16] IFAD (2007).

Only poor people cannot afford to work near the village, as there is often no fertile land left. They often stay in the forest for weeks with their children". — a district indigenous officer, Viet Nam[17]

Indigenous peoples also face huge disparities in terms of access to and quality of education and health. In Guatemala, for example, 53.5 per cent of indigenous young people aged 15-19 have not completed primary education, as compared to 32.2 per cent of non-indigenous youth.[18] Although infant and child mortality has been steadily decreasing throughout Latin America over the last four decades, child mortality is still 70 per cent higher among indigenous children. Furthermore, malnutrition is twice as frequent among indigenous children in the region.[19] In Nepal, while some indigenous peoples, such as the Thakali, Byasi and Hyolmo, have literacy rates that surpass the national average, 30 of the country's indigenous peoples still fall far below it.[20]

Indigenous peoples also suffer from discrimination in terms of employment and income. According to the ILO, indigenous workers in Latin America make on average about half of what non-indigenous workers earn. Approximately 25-50 per cent of this income gap is "due to discrimination and non-observable characteristics, such as quality of schooling".[21]

In different parts of the world, differential progress is being made by indigenous peoples in their social and economic development, reflecting specific national legal and policy frameworks with regard to recognizing, respecting and promoting their rights. Historical and ongoing colonialism has trapped many of them in conditions of deepening impoverishment, even as others have made important advances in asserting recognition of their distinct identities as indigenous peoples and promoting models of development with cultural identity and integrity, applying a human rights-based approach. It is clear that the advancement of indigenous peoples' social and economic development is predicated on international and national recognition of their human rights and on pursuing development strategies based on their own definitions and indicators of poverty and well-being.

Statistics on the situation of indigenous peoples are not readily available because few countries collect data disaggregated by ethnicity. Nonetheless, it is possible to build a picture of indigenous peoples' social and economic development through the use of selected national and regional information, and through analysis of information gleaned from the Human Development Index and the Human Poverty Index.

The following information from countries where national statistics are available is indicative of the poverty situation of indigenous peoples in different countries and regions.

Living conditions of indigenous peoples in Australia, Canada New Zealand and the United States

Poverty and well-being of indigenous peoples is an issue not only in developing countries, as it is often thought. Even in developed countries, indigenous peoples consistently lag behind the non-indigenous population in terms of most indicators of well-being. They live shorter lives, have poorer health care and education and endure higher unemployment rates. Those indigenous persons who do enjoy full employment earn significantly less than their non-indigenous counterparts. A native Aboriginal child born in Australia today can expect to die up to 20 years earlier

[17] Asian Development Bank (2002).
[18] ECLAC (2005), 101.
[19] ECLAC (2007), 191.
[20] UNDP (2004), 63.
[21] ILO (2007), 27.

than his non-indigenous compatriot.[22] Obesity, type 2 diabetes and tuberculosis are now major health concerns amongst indigenous peoples in developed countries. Smoking and substance abuse are more common amongst indigenous peoples, while suicide rates, and incarceration rates are significantly higher. These problems are more pronounced in urban areas, where indigenous peoples are detached from their communities and cultures, yet never fully embraced as equal members of the dominant society. Indigenous peoples are also more likely to suffer from violent crime.

A recent study, applying UNDP's Human Development Index[23] to indigenous peoples in Australia, Canada, New Zealand and the United States, showed clearly that indigenous people lag significantly behind the general populations in these countries. This discrepancy is particularly pronounced in Australia, where Australian non-indigenous HDI scores rose steadily in the 1990s but remained stagnant amongst Aboriginal and Torres Strait Islanders. According to the study, the HDI of Australia's indigenous peoples is similar to that of Cape Verde and El Salvador. Although the gap has narrowed in Canada, New Zealand and the United States, there is still a significant HDI gap in all three countries between the indigenous and non-indigenous population.[24] In 2001, Australia ranked third; the United States, seventh; Canada, eighth; and New Zealand, twentieth in the HDI rankings, while U.S. American Indian and Alaska Natives ranked thirtieth; Canadian Aboriginals, thirty-second; New Zealand Maori, seventy-third, and Australian Aboriginal and Torres Strait Islanders, one hundred third.[25] In all four countries, predominantly English-speaking settler cultures have supplanted indigenous peoples to a large extent, leading to enormous indigenous resource losses, "the eventual destruction of indigenous economies and a good deal of social organization, precipitous population declines and subjection to tutelary and assimilationist policies antagonistic to indigenous cultures".[26]

Australia. These HDI scores are mirrored by other indicators. In Australia, the indigenous unemployment rate was 15.6 per cent in 2006, or just over three times higher than the non-indigenous rate, while the median indigenous income was just over half of the non-indigenous income.[27] Although some progress has been made in Australia in recent years, particularly in education, the gap between indigenous and non-indigenous peoples' quality of life by virtually all standards is still very significant. Indigenous households are half as likely to own their own

> even in developed countries, indigenous peoples consistently lag behind the non-indigenous population

---

[22] Cooke, Mitrou, Lawrence, Guimod & Dan Beavon (2007).

[23] The Human Development Index (HDI) is a summary composite index that measures a country's average achievements in three basic aspects of human development: health, education, and a decent standard of living. Health is measured by life expectancy at birth; education is measured by a combination of the adult literacy rate and the combined primary, secondary, and tertiary gross enrolment ratio; and standard of living is measured by GDP per capita (PPP USD).

[24] Cooke, Mitrou, Lawrence, Guimod & Beavon (2007).

[25] Cooke, Mitrou, Lawrence, Guimod & Beavon (2007).

[26] Cornell, Stephen (2006).

[27] Altman, Biddle & Hunter (2008).

homes, (34 per cent of indigenous households owned their homes, compared to 69 per cent of the non-indigenous population), and they are more likely to live in overcrowded conditions (in 2006, a quarter of the indigenous population of Australia was reported to be living in overcrowded conditions). The situation is particularly serious in rural and remote communities where people frequently do not have access to affordable adequate food, water and housing and have poor access to basic services and infrastructure. In 2001, for example, nearly half of all aboriginal communities (46 per cent) with a population of 50 or more had no connection to a town water supply.[28] Indigenous adults in Australia are twice as likely as non-indigenous adults to report their health as fair or poor, are twice as likely to report high levels of psychological stress, and are twice as likely to be hospitalized. Ultimately, indigenous Australians' life expectancy is around 20 years lower than non-indigenous life expectancy.

Canada. Canada recognizes that key socio-economic indicators for Aboriginal people are unacceptably lower than for non-Aboriginal Canadians. Aboriginal peoples' living standards have improved in the past 50 years, but they do not come close to those of non-Aboriginal people. The Royal Commission on Aboriginal Peoples (RCAP) reports that following:

◆ Life expectancy is lower and illness is more common. In 2000, "life expectancy at birth for the registered Indian population was estimated at 68.9 years for males and 76.6 years for females. This reflects differences of 8.1 years and 5.5 years respectively, from the 2001 Canadian population's life expectancies". Moreover, the rate of premature mortality (when a person dies before the age of 75 due to suicide or unintentional injury) is almost four-and-a-half times higher.[29]

◆ Fewer children graduate from high school, and far fewer go on to colleges and universities. Many indigenous communities have poor access to schools. About 70 per cent of First Nations students on-reserve will never complete high school. Graduation rates for the on-reserve population range from 28.9 per cent to 32.1 per cent annually. Just about 27 per cent of the First Nations population between 15 and 44 years of age hold a post-secondary certificate, diploma or degree, compared with 46 per cent of the Canadian population within the same age group.[30]

◆ Aboriginal people have poorer access to jobs. In 2005, for example, the unemployment rate of Canada's western provinces of Manitoba, British Columbia, Alberta and Saskatchewan was as high as 13.6 per cent among indigenous people, but only 5.3 per cent among the non-indigenous population.[31]

◆ Many more spend time in jails and prisons. Aboriginals make up about 19 per cent of federal prisoners, whilst they are 4.4 per cent of the total population. Between 1997 and 2000, they were 10 times more likely to be accused of homicide than non-aboriginal people. The rate of indigenous in Canadian prisons climbed 22 per cent between 1996 and 2004, while the general prison population dropped 12 per cent.[32]

The restrictions put on Aboriginal peoples' ability to protect, meaningfully benefit from and freely dispose of their land and resources constitute the main obstacle to real economic development among First Nations, Métis and Inuit. As a result of land loss and severe limitations set by the various levels of government on the free use of and continuing benefit from their natural resources, Aboriginal people have become increasingly dependent on

---

[28] Bolstridge, Jill A. (2008).
[29] Health Canada (2007)
[30] Assembly of First Nations (2009).
[31] Statistics Canada (2005)
[32] Gorelick (2007)

welfare measures undertaken by the federal or provincial governments. This accounts for the large disparities between Aboriginal people and other Canadians.[33]

The Canadian Council on Social Development identified poverty as one of the most pressing problems facing Aboriginal peoples, particularly in cities, where 60 per cent of Aboriginal children live below the poverty line. In Winnipeg, 80 per cent of inner-city Aboriginal households reported incomes below the poverty line, a much higher percentage than for poor non-Aboriginal families.

Housing is a major problem confronting Aboriginal people, with the RCAP reporting that houses occupied by Aboriginal people are twice as likely to be in need of major repairs as compared to houses of other Canadians. Aboriginal homes are generally overcrowded, and are 90 times more likely to be without piped water. On reserves, more than 10,000 homes have no indoor plumbing, and one reserve in four has a substandard water or sewage system. Approximately 55 per cent live in communities where half of the houses are inadequate or sub-standard, manifested in deteriorated units, toxic mould, lack of heating and insulation, and leaking pipes. On the other hand, some negotiated agreements between the Government and First Nations have provided resources for repairs and the building of adequate new homes, as in the case of Mistissini, a Cree community in Québec.

United States. In the United States of America, an evaluation of the 2000 census and a study in January 2005 by Harvard University[34] showed that socio-economic conditions for Native Americans had improved between 1990 and 2000. The authors of the study stressed that the most important reason for the improvements was self-determination, allowing tribes to break away from the overall pattern of intractable poverty. It allows Native American tribes to have decision-making power in their own lands and to be able to exercise this decision-making power efficiently.[35]

Despite these trends, the average income of Native Americans is still less than half the average for the United States overall.[36] Almost a quarter of Native Americans and Alaska Natives live under the poverty line in the United States, compared to about 12.5 percent of the total population.[37]

Native American life expectancy is on average 2.4 years lower than that of the general population. Moreover, Native Americans and Alaska Natives have higher death rates than other Americans from tuberculosis (600 per cent higher), alcoholism (510 per cent higher), motor vehicle crashes (229 per cent higher), diabetes (189 per cent higher), unintentional injuries (152 per cent higher), homicide (61 per cent higher) and suicide (62 per cent higher).[38]

Dropout rates from primary schools are significantly higher among Native American Students compared to their non-indigenous counterparts and the performance of those who stay in school, lags behind others. This pattern is also visible in higher education, where only 7.6 per cent of Native Americans have a bachelor's degree, compared

---

[33] RCAP estimated that, since Confederation (1867), two-thirds of the lands in the possession of indigenous peoples—lands essential to indigenous peoples' enjoyment of their basic human rights— have been "whittled away" through appropriation, theft, encroachment and the environmental consequences of policies and activities imposed on indigenous peoples without their consent. According to RCAP, this has been a central factor behind pervasive problems of impoverishment, ill health and social stress afflicting indigenous communities across Canada.
[34] Taylor and Kalt (2005).
[35] Cornell, Stephen (2006).
[36] Taylor and Kalt (2005).
[37] United States Census Bureau (2005)
[38] Indian Health Service (2006).

with 15.5 per cent of the total population.[39] This education deficit clearly has an impact on economic outcomes. While the total unemployment rate in the United States declined from 6.5 to 5.9 per cent between 1994 and 2003, during the same period, it increased from 11.7 to 15.1 per cent among American Indians and Alaska Natives.[40]

The 2000 census estimated 18 per cent of all Native American households on Native American land being crowded (more than one person per room), compared to 6 per cent nationwide. 13 per cent of Native American and Alaska Native homes lack safe and adequate water supply and/or waste disposal facilities, compared to 1% of homes for the United States general population.[41]

A 1999 study of the Bureau of Justice Statistics found that rates of violence in every age group among Native Americans are higher than those of other ethnicities in the United States and that nearly a third of all Native American victims of violence are aged between 18 and 24.[42] Indigenous women are also particularly vulnerable to sexual violence. Native American women, for example, are 2.5 times more likely to be raped or sexually violated than women in the United States in general.[43]

New Zealand. New Zealand is another country ranking high in global comparisons of human development, but where there exist persistent disparities between Maori and non-Maori in areas such as paid work, economic standard of living, housing, health and justice.

A recent survey by the Ministry of Social Development showed that in all but four basic socio-economic indicators, Maori were worse off than European New Zealanders. Comprising just under 15 per cent of the New Zealand population, Maori account for 40 per cent of all convictions in the courts and 50 per cent of the prison population. The unemployment rate for the Maori is over twice as high as the national average (7.7 per cent vs. 3.8 per cent).[44] Household income is 70 per cent of the national average. Maori life expectancy is nearly 10 years lower than non-Maori; they are four times more likely to live in an overcrowded house (since 1991, the proportion of Maori who own their own home has fallen from 61.4 per cent to 45.2 per cent).[45]

Educational improvements have been made as recently as the 1986-1996 period, as New Zealand's official Statistic Agency states: "The proportion of Maori with a post-school (tertiary) qualification increased from 16.1 per cent in 1986 to 22.6 per cent in 1996. The comparable increase for non-Maori was from 33.3 per cent to 35.5 per cent". However, in "1996, a higher proportion of non-Maori had a post-school qualification than a school qualification or no qualification, whereas Maori were more likely to have no qualification".[46]

As stated by the UN Special Rapporteur on the situation of human rights and fundamental freedoms of indigenous people, Rodolfo Stavenhagen, at the end of his visit to New Zealand in 2005: "All these issues are considered by Maori the result of a trans-generational backlog of broken promises, economic marginalization, social exclusion and cultural discrimination".[47]

---

[39] Tsai & Alanis (2004).
[40] Freeman, C., and Fox, M. (2005), 122.
[41] Indian Health Service (2009).
[42] Bureau of Justice Statistics (1999).
[43] Amnesty International (2007), 2.
[44] New Zealand Department of Labour (2008).
[45] Housing New Zealand Corporation (2008).
[46] Statistics New Zealand (1998) p. 51.
[47] Stavenhagen (2005).

Poverty and land rights in Latin America

A World Bank study on indigenous peoples and poverty in Latin America concluded that "poverty among Latin America's indigenous population is pervasive and severe".[48] This study, which documented the socio-economic situation of around 34 million indigenous people in the region, representing 8 per cent of the region's total population, showed that the poverty map in almost all the countries coincides with indigenous peoples' territories. A similar study in the region by the Inter-American Development Bank observed that being poor and being indigenous were synonymous. Its report on Mexico concluded that indigenous peoples live in "alarming conditions of extreme poverty and marginality…Virtually all of the indigenous people living in municipalities with 90 per cent or more indigenous people are catalogued as extremely poor".[49] The difference between the indigenous and non-indigenous is often striking, where, for example in Paraguay, poverty is 7.9 times higher among indigenous peoples, compared to the rest of the population. In Panama, poverty rates are 5.9 times higher, in Mexico 3.3 times higher, and in Guatemala, indigenous peoples' poverty rates are 2.8 times higher than the rest of the population.[50] As can be seen from Figure I.1, despite significant changes in poverty rates overall, the proportion of indigenous peoples in the region living in poverty did not change much in most countries from the early 1990s to the early 2000s.

Poverty for indigenous and non-indigenous peoples in Latin America, 1980s to 2000s

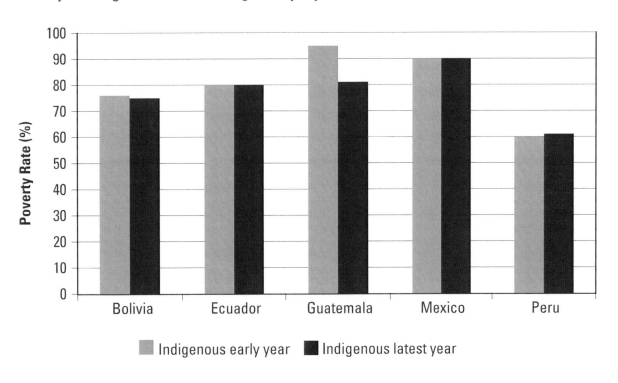

Source: World Bank (2007).

Studies of socio-economic conditions of indigenous peoples in Latin America show that being indigenous is associated with being poor and that over time, that condition has stayed constant. Studies also show that

---

[48] Hall and Patrinos (2005).
[49] Plant (1998).
[50] ECLAC (2007), 152.

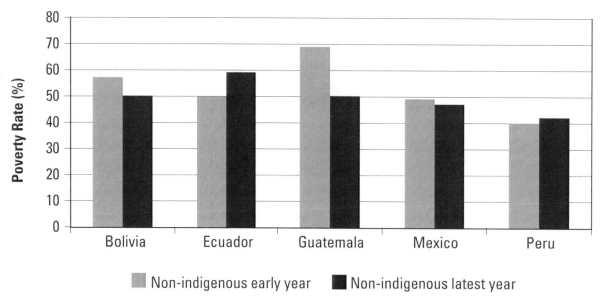

Non-indigenous early year ■ **Non-indigenous latest year**

Source: World Bank (2007).

indigenous peoples' poverty has not diminished over time, including over the period of the first International Decade of the World's Indigenous People, 1994-2004.[51] Indigenous peoples also suffer from many other disadvantages. Even when they have access to secondary or higher education, they are frequently unable to convert that to significantly greater earnings or to reduce the poverty gap with the nonindigenous population. This finding holds for countries where indigenous peoples are a small fraction of the overall population, such as Mexico[52] and Chile,[53] as well as in countries where a large portion of the population is indigenous, such as in Bolivia.[54]

> studies also show that indigenous peoples' poverty has not diminished over time

Over the past 20 years or more, indigenous organizations in Latin America have put great efforts into safeguarding their land rights through mapping, demarcation and titling of their territories. This process, which began in the 1980s and reached its peak in the 1990s, has led to an increased, albeit varying, degree of recognition of indigenous lands in national laws. In Colombia, indigenous peoples comprising 2 per cent of the population have gained the legalization of indigenous territories corresponding to one-third of the national territory. In 2004, Brazilian State had recognized over 15 million hectares as indigenous reserves, while in Peru the indigenous peoples of the Amazon had achieved the titling of 7 million hectares of land, or approximately 10 per cent of the Peruvian Amazon. A total of 18 million hectares are under claim by the indigenous peoples of Peru. In the south of the continent, the recovery of indigenous territories has been more difficult and the colonial structures more ingrained.

Although land titling has been a fundamental step and a great achievement for the indigenous communities in Latin America, they are still far from having real

[51] Hall and Patrinos (2006)
[52] Ramirez (2006)
[53] Hopenhayn (2003).
[54] Feiring (2003).

control over their territories. Land titles and deeds do not always correspond to the communities' full areas of use and subsistence. In many countries, indigenous lands and territories face serious threats from the activities of oil and lumber companies. In Colombia, the armed conflict has driven thousands of indigenous peoples from their lands.[55]

India: Poverty among the Scheduled Tribes

Research by the Institute of Human Development, India, has shown how official statistics could shed light on the discrimination experienced by indigenous peoples.[56] Analysis of official data on Scheduled Tribes and Scheduled Castes[57] from the UNDP Human Development Index (HDI) and the Planning Commission of the Government of India showed that while the caste system discriminates against the poorest caste – the *Dalits* – the level of poverty among Scheduled Tribes is deeper, despite the constitutional rights that apply uniquely to them. It was also found that while poverty among the general population had declined between 1993-1994 and 1999-2000, there had been little change in poverty levels among indigenous peoples. The Scheduled Castes have fared better than Scheduled Tribes in terms of poverty reduction. The poverty gap between Scheduled Castes and other groups in India has decreased while that between the Scheduled Tribes and other groups has widened.

Similar results were found using the Human Poverty Index (HPI). Whilst India is considered a middle-ranked country in the UNDP HPI ranking of countries, the indigenous communities as a group are comparable to Sub-Saharan countries, which are ranked in the bottom 25. By taking into account the poverty of indigenous peoples, the MDG goal of halving poverty by 2015 may not be achieved in India.

Scheduled Tribes also score lower in education, health and other social and economic aspects measured by the HDI. Indigenous communities in India are typically rural, and poverty among rural communities is higher than that in urban areas. There are few people without land among the Scheduled Tribes, but their lands have low productivity. The more productive lands, especially in low-lying areas, have been taken over by other communities. There is also less job diversification among Scheduled Tribes. Deprived of formal education and with little access to capital, they fail to find work, either self-employed or within regular jobs, ending up in casual employment or in agriculture.

On the status of and trends in the practice of traditional occupations

A narrow focus on income levels, while providing useful information on disparities within countries between indigenous peoples and the rest of the population, cannot capture the entire picture of indigenous peoples' poverty and marginalization, nor measure their well-being. A major criticism of mainstream poverty and human development indicators is their standard application for culturally diverse groups and their non-inclusion of domains or themes which are considered significant or important for indigenous peoples. The emphasis on quantitative measurements and the considerably less attention given to subjective judgments and cultural perceptions make these measurements less insightful and relevant.

One interesting indicator proposed for traditional knowledge, innovations and practices is the *status of and trends in the practice of traditional occupations*. This indicator tries to capture the continuity and change in

---

[55] Wiben Jensen (2004).

[56] Sarkar, Mishra, Dayal and Nathan (2006).

[57] Scheduled Castes (SCs) and Scheduled Tribes (STs) are Indian communities that are explicitly recognized by the Constitution of India as requiring special support to overcome centuries of discrimination by mainstream Hindu society. SCs are also known as Dalits, and STs as Adivasi.⊠Ed.

indigenous peoples' relationships and access to ecosystem resources and services over time. When combined with information about changes in land-use patterns, including percentage of lands and resources under local control as well as demographic changes, this indicator can begin to measure changes in the livelihoods of indigenous peoples. Degradation of ecosystems, landscapes and resources in indigenous peoples' territories will clearly affect their exercise of traditional occupations and, hence, their economic and social well-being. The contribution of subsistence activities to individual and household consumption and to income is another indicator of social and economic change.

Because indigenous peoples define happiness as closely linked with the state of nature and their environment, indigenous peoples' well-being necessarily encompasses their access, management and control over lands, territories and resources under customary use and management, all of which are critical for their own sustainable development. The following examples highlight indigenous peoples' vulnerabilities while also demonstrating their vitality and the benefits of their traditional occupations and livelihood.

Pastoralists

Pastoralism is a livelihood strategy and management system based on raising and herding of livestock. It has been estimated that pastoralism is practised on 25 per cent of the global land area, providing 10 per cent of the world's meat production[58]. Pastoralism is common in areas where rainfall and climatic patterns are erratic and generally dry, necessitating mobility in search of fresh pasture and water. Pastoralists who specialize in livestock breeding include the Quechua and Aymara llama and alpaca breeders in the Andes, Mongol horse breeders in central Asia, Saami reindeer herders in northern Europe and Siberia, and the Bedouin in Arabia. Today, most pastoralists are in Africa, including the Tuareg camel breeders in the Sahara, the Maasai cattle breeders of Eastern Africa or the Fulani cattle breeders of the West African savannah. Pastoralism is particularly important in sub-Saharan Africa, accounting for about 20 per cent of national GDPs.[59] Pastoralism accounts for 80 per cent of the agricultural GDP of Sudan, 84 per cent in Niger, and 50 per cent in Kenya. Ethiopia's pastoralist-dominated leather industry is second only to the country's coffee industry in terms of foreign trade. In the former Soviet Union, pastoralist products of Kazakhstan supplied 25 per cent of Soviet lamb and 20 per cent of Soviet wool. China-sourced cashmere (65-75 per cent of the world's cashmere fibre) comes from the western and northern pastoral zones of Inner Mongolia, Xinjiang and the Tibetan plateau.[60]

Pastoralism is a sophisticated system of production and land management, proven to be an economically viable, environmentally sustainable and remarkably effective livelihood in the world's drylands. Pastoralists are also custodians of rich biological diversity, both in terms of their livestock and managed ecosystems. The grazing, browsing and fertilization associated with livestock production, supports and maintains, significant floral diversity. Where pastoralism has been abandoned, it has resulted in the disappearance of grasslands and their associated diversity, replaced with desertification. Moreover, pastoralism is the source of identity, culture, heritage and traditions for some 200 million people.

Nevertheless, pastoralists are often minority groups in their countries far removed from the political elites, and whose occupations are undervalued in the modern economy. Their territories often lie

[58] Nori, Taylor & Sensi (2008), 5
[59] Ibid.
[60] Hatfield & Davies (2006), 10

across national borders, giving rise to significant jurisdictional and political problems, such as restrictions on trans-border movement, and militarization. Pastoralists and their livelihoods are under constant and persistent threat from economic modernization.

Colonial governments considered pastoralist lands as unoccupied ownerless lands, while post-colonial governments have seen these as under-utilized and poorly managed. Such discriminatory public policies have justified State expropriation of pastoralist lands for sedentary agriculture, resource extraction or infrastructure development, national parks or nature reserves, with devastating effects on both the environment and on the pastoralist peoples themselves. These negative approaches are beginning to provide some lessons:

> Indeed, both government and privatization of lands have demonstrated poor effectiveness in pastoral areas. In his satellite imagery assessments of grassland degradation under different property regimes in parts of central Asia crossed by international boundaries, including northern China, Mongolia and southern Siberia, Sneath (1998) revealed large differences in degradation processes under different resource access rights patterns. Grazing resources in Mongolia— which have allowed pastoralists to continue their traditional group-property institutions involving large-scale movements between seasonal pastures— were much less degraded than those administered through Russian and Chinese policies involving state-owned agricultural collectives and permanent settlements.[61]

Studies from Africa have in fact shown that pastoral systems are two to 10 times more productive than ranching alternatives in the drylands. "Despite gross underinvestment and neglect, both in the production system and in the producers themselves, pastoralism continues to contribute healthily to national economies and export earnings".[62]

Pastoral ways of life are threatened not only by the direct actions of states, development practitioners and environmentalists, but also by climate change. It is notoriously difficult to predict the effects of increasing greenhouse gas emissions, but rising global temperatures will certainly bring about severe changes to pastoralists' territories in the medium and long term. It is nevertheless very likely that a great number of pastoralists will have to deal with increasingly dry and less fertile lands. In addition to changing rainfall patterns, other major effects include biodiversity shifts, changing wind patterns, more frequent floods and droughts, heat waves

[pastoralism is practised on 25 per cent of the global land area]

---

[61] Nori, Taylor and Sensi (2008)
[62] Hatfield and Davies (2006), 5

and tropical cyclones. Therefore, it is essential that their primary coping tool—mobility—be respected rather than restricted.

In recent years, pastoralists have been making their voices heard at the international level, such as the United Nations Permanent Forum on Indigenous Issues and meetings related to the Convention on Biological Diversity. United Nations agencies such as IFAD, FAO and UNDP have also, in recent years, improved their understanding of pastoralism and developed working relationships with pastoralists. At the world gathering of nomadic and transhumant pastoralists in Segovia in 2007, the participants adopted the Segovia Declaration of Nomadic and Transhumant Pastoralists, which welcomed the Declaration on the Rights of Indigenous Peoples. Furthermore, the Declaration contains 16 policy recommendations aimed at respecting and promoting pastoralists' rights. These recommendations include the need to respect pastoralists' customary laws and leadership, assuring their access to healthcare, education and markets and their right to cross-border mobility. The Segovia Declaration also highlighted some of the major concerns of pastoralists.

> *Despite the crucial contribution of nomadic and transhumant pastoralism to livelihoods and to national economies and its role in preserving the fragile ecosystems of the planet, in many countries we are not receiving the necessary attention and support. We are subject to discrimination and social exclusion. In some countries, we are subject to dispossession of natural resources, forced or induced sedentarization and displacement, ethnic cleansing and ethnocide, in direct violation of human rights, and as a consequence of conflicts and adverse and ill-designed policies, legislation and development programmes. Both privatization and government confiscation ("nationalization") of common resources usually lead to land use change having dramatic effects on the overall viability of pastoral systems and on the environment—both in terms of land degradation and pollution. These policies and changes exacerbate poverty of people and erosion of biological diversity, force people into migration, and deprive our peoples of their subsistence base, cultural values, spirituality and dignity.[63]*

Arctic region, including Russia and Northern Europe

In Greenland, the political and economic changes of the post-war period led to crucial changes in traditional Greenlandic fishing/hunting culture, as well as in traditional social structures. Industrialization, the transition to a cash economy, educational mobility and increased urbanization have transformed Greenlandic society away from the subsistence production of extended families in small, closed communities and toward wage earning in a more globalized and open society. Today, most people in Greenland, and in the Arctic in general, have adapted their lifestyles, mixing traditional activities with paid jobs. These changed relationships with the living and the non-living resources affect family structures, diets, consumption patterns, occupations and sources of income, housing, health, education, attitudes, values and aspirations. In 1945, it was estimated that 66 per cent of the Greenlandic labour force, out of a population of 21,412 individuals, was involved in hunting and fishing. In 1996, this proportion had decreased to approximately 25 per cent, including people working in the modern fishing industry.[64]

---

[63] Segovia Declaration of Nomadic and Transhumant Pastoralists (2007)
[64] Andersen and Poppel (2002), 191–216.

Despite this, traditional methods for producing food have proved to be resilient. The symbolic value of hunting, fishing and herding has been maintained or has even increased,[65] as these are a key part of identity.[66] Furthermore, it is known that customary harvesting practices still form a significant part of the dietary intake of households and communities in many parts of the Arctic. In Alaska, recent studies indicate that rural villages have an annual production that generally varies between 69.5 and 301.8 kg per capita. For the Canadian Arctic, the annual harvest in edible weight varies between 84 and 284 kg per capita. The latter value would be equivalent to production before other sources of food were available. In Greenland, a majority of the households eat traditionally-produced food five times or more per week.[67]

Food from land and sea is one of the few substitutes for imports in the Arctic and, in several regions, its contribution to food intake is central, especially when international commodity prices fluctuate and the price of imported food increases. It is also important for its contribution to the meaning of life because customary activities create links both between past and present and between people living in the same community.

Arctic economies of all sorts have a narrow economic base predicated on the raw natural resources available. Economies are not diversified, and there is only a narrow range of viable means of economic support in a particular location. As such, many Arctic communities are subject to boom-and-bust cycles, due to either the volatility of the world markets for raw materials (for instance, oil and gas in Arctic Canada and Arctic Russia) or to specific actions or consumer trends (for instance, bans on the import or sale of seal products and sudden change in the rules governing the use of whales and other marine mammals). This same characteristic of narrow dependence on nature also demands a sharper focus on the impacts of climate change, which are already observable in the Arctic, a place where the continuing effects of climate change are likely to be especially severe.

[traditional methods for producing food have proved to be resilient]

Following years of negative lobbying campaigns by conservation organizations in Europe, the sealskin industry has collapsed, with devastating impacts on the Inuit. The sale of sealskins was once the main source of cash income for many Inuit families, and seal hunting was central to traditional culture and values. The loss of this revenue has been catastrophic beyond its economic impacts, including negative social, cultural, nutritional and psychological effects.[68]

[65] Condon, Collings, and Wenzel (1995).
[66] Ingold (1995), 41-68.
[67] Arctic Human Development Report (2004), 74.
[68] Kuptana (1996).

Forest Peoples of Africa

There are between 250,000 and 300,000 Forest Peoples, or "Pygmies",[69] in the Central African rainforests whose ways of life as hunters and gatherers are in rapid and critical decline.[70] These are the Mbuti (or Bambuti) and Efe of the Ituri Forest in the Democratic Republic of Congo (DRC); the Baka of South-eastern Cameroon and Northwestern Congo Brazzaville; the Aka (or Ba-Aka) of Northern Congo Brazzaville and the Central African Republic; the Batwa in Rwanda, Burundi, Eastern DRC, and South-western Uganda; the Bakola of Southwestern Cameroon and the Basua (numbering only perhaps 65 to 70 people) in Western Uganda. The ongoing marginalization of these groups has particularly been accelerated by the political upheavals and civil war in the region.

Traditionally, "Pygmy" peoples lived in small nomadic bands in the forest, hunting and gathering forest products and exchanging them with settled farming communities for salt, metal tools and other items. Their forest territories extended over thousands of hectares, but have never been formally recognized, either in state law or the customary laws of farming communities. "Pygmy" peoples are now facing unprecedented pressures on their lands, forest resources and societies, as forests are logged, cleared for agriculture or turned into exclusive wildlife conservation areas. They are becoming outcasts on the edge of dominant society as they become settled in villages, increasingly dependent on the cash economy but unable to enjoy the rights accorded to other citizens, and marginalized from policies and decision-making. As these pressures intensify, "Pygmy" peoples are suffering increasing poverty, racial discrimination, violence and cultural collapse. Throughout Central Africa, their traditional way of life is disappearing, and their incomparable knowledge of the forest is being lost.

> Their forest territories extended over thousands of hectares, but have never been formally recognized

The Batwa peoples are among those who have been completely dispossessed of their forest lands through clearance of forests for development projects and conservation areas, and they can no longer practice forest-based livelihoods. Of the estimated 70-87,000 Batwa in the Great Lakes region, probably less than 7,000 have direct and regular access to forest today. There is a second, smaller group of Batwa in the region: fisher folk who live mostly on the shores of Lake Kivu; they are unlikely to number more than 3,000 and are today prevented from openly fishing because they do not have fishing licences.

The remaining group of 60,000 to 76,000 Batwa in Rwanda, Burundi, Uganda and Eastern Democratic Republic of Congo no longer have access to forests, have little or no land, and are desperately poor. A great many are now dependent

---

[69] The term "Pygmy" is a generic term used to describe all the distinct hunter-gatherer indigenous peoples living in, or originating from, the forests of Central Africa. All of them, however, designate themselves by their own specific names (for instance, Mbuti, Efe, Twa, etc.). As some people consider "Pygmy" to be a derogatory term, it is used in this publication in quotation marks.—Ed.

[70] This section is based on Kenrick (2000). See also the Web site of the Forest Peoples Programme at http://www.forestpeoples.org

upon their neighbours for their livelihoods, which leads to situations where Batwa must work on villagers' fields at just the times of year when they should be planting or harvesting their own small farm plots. They may have to borrow food to survive, creating a culture of debt whereby they form a ready source of cheap labour. The Batwa in Rwanda, whose forests have been destroyed, are referred to as "potters", as that occupation has become the main source of income and even identity for the Batwa as a people. This source of income is now increasingly threatened by industrialized pottery. Between 1978 and 1991, there was a 40-per cent fall in the Batwa population of Rwanda, compared to a 50-per cent rise in the population of other Rwandans. Although research is very limited, it is likely that this population decline is due to extreme poverty, poor access to health care and the loss of land and traditional livelihoods. It is estimated that under 2 per cent of the Batwa population have sufficient land to cultivate, very few own livestock, and most are either squatters or tenants on other peoples' land.[71] Rwandan authorities refuse to recognize the Batwa as indigenous or even as a separate ethnic group, claiming to do so would undermine the country's reconciliation process.

Batwa living in the Democratic Republic of Congo have also lost their territories and thus their traditional livelihoods. A majority of the Batwa in the DRC are not documented as citizens, like other Congolese, preventing them from legally owning land, as land entitlements are tied to Congolese nationality.[72] The livelihoods and well-being of the few Batwa who still live in the forests have further been threatened by conflict and the militarization of their territories and by natural resource extraction, such as logging and mining, not only in Rwanda and the DRC, but throughout Central Africa.

As a result, what used to be mainly a nomadic group that moved across long distances in the forest in pursuit of game and plants is gradually settling down. Most members of pygmy communities now work as day labourers and servants on farms that do not belong to them, or practice small-scale, informal mining activities. Some resort to begging.[73]

In recent years, Batwa organizations and communities working with non-governmental organizations like the Forest Peoples Programme have been organizing and struggling to secure land and regain access to forest resources, engaging with government and donors to improve policies and laws and uphold their rights as citizens. This is taking place alongside work to improve livelihoods through pottery enterprises and new ways of earning money to pay for health care, schooling and housing, and to build up reserves of money and livestock.

In other parts of the region, "Pygmies" still have access to forests, although this is decreasing every year. These peoples include the Mbuti and Efe (of which there are 35,000 - 40,000); the Aka or Ba-Aka (25,000 - 30,000); the Baka (35,000 - 50,000), and the Bakola or Bagyeli (3,000 - 4,000). All of these groups continue, to varying degrees, as hunter-gatherers; however, significant sedentarization is taking place, and many "Pygmies" work for long or short periods for outsiders such as logging companies, meat traders and conservationists.

In these countries, indigenous communities and organizations are working to secure their lands and increase their access to forest through dialogue with neighbouring Bantu farming communities and with conservation agencies, governments and regional forest planners. Support NGOs are helping indigenous peoples to document and formally map their customary land use in order to support their land claims and are providing legal advice on how to secure their land rights. By providing information and facilitating community meetings, isolated "Pygmy" groups are able to meet and develop new forms of representation in order to engage more effectively with outside agencies and defend their rights.[74]

---

[71] Mugarura and& Ndemeye (2003).
[72] IRIN (2006), 9-10.
[73] IRIN (2006), p. 8.
[74] See Forest Peoples Programme at http://www.forestpeoples.org

East and South East Asia: Rice culture in Ifugao, Philippines

Indigenous peoples' traditional livelihoods are threatened not only by extractive industries or huge development projects, but also by efforts that are aimed at preserving and celebrating indigenous peoples' cultures and the environment. In some cases, indigenous peoples have been forced off their lands for the establishment of natural parks, whilst even the World Heritage designation can have unintended consequences.[75]

> in some cases, indigenous peoples have been forced off their lands for the establishment of natural parks

The Ifugao rice terraces in the Central Cordillera, Philippines, have been widely recognized as an outstanding cultural heritage. They became a "national landmark" in 1973, were declared "living cultural landscapes" and put on the UNESCO list of World Heritage in danger in 1995, and were listed as one of the world's best examples of soil and water conservation technology by the American Society of Civil Engineers in 1996.

However, the protection of the terraces for their aesthetic and ethnological importance fails to support their function as an ongoing sustainable economy. Indeed, the attention attracted by the labelling of the terraces as "heritage" can compromise the continued sustainability of management by introducing requirements, seen by many in the community as static and confining. At the same time, the heightened attention has stimulated tourism and associated risks to traditional management.

The growing market for wooden handicrafts and cash crops leads to intensified forest harvesting, and there has also been an increase in the construction of buildings to accommodate the needs of the tourists. These buildings exemplify the clash between the land management values under traditional practices as compared with the "heritage sites" of the UNESCO list. Whilst land management of the past placed most importance and protection on the forested areas above the terraces in their roles as water sources and soil stabilizers, the "heritage" view delineates the terraces from the rest of the landscape as the places of greatest importance and protection, hence more recent houses are built for the most part in the "*muyong*"[76] zone of the mountain, above the terraces. [77]

Pacific: Traditional fishing in Vanuatu

One of the fundamental aspects of the traditional indigenous fishing practices in Vanuatu is the way in which the traditional resource management practices are intimately interspersed with area-specific cosmologies.[78] Marine resource management was never formally compartmentalized outside the context of culture and religion.

---

[75] Guimbatan and Buguilat Jr. (2006), 59-67.
[76] Muyong is the local name for a traditional system of forest use and management.
[77] Guimbatan and Buguilat Jr. (2006), 59-67.
[78] This section is based on Hickey (2007), 147-169.

This is expressed in a system of taboos placed on areas to be fished prior to harvesting, preventing people from disturbing the water in order to encourage fish to enter the area. The system of taboos is multifaceted and parallels many of the strategies in resource management based on Western scientific principles, including privileged-user rights; species-specific prohibitions; seasonal closures, protected areas and behavioural prohibitions. The enforcement of these taboos, now called "*bans*" so as to differentiate them from the older spiritual practices, is largely managed by indigenous law systems, such as the village leaders and the village court.

The traditional practice of protected areas offers "a mosaic of refugia or sanctuaries for mobile marine life" which has, led to economic opportunities for the communities. In some areas, abundant marine life has been used to attract tourists wishing to see sea turtles or dugongs that have become unwary and even tame after having been protected for several years by the closure system.

Many taboos now used are contemporary expressions of earlier traditional practices, adapted flexibly to maintain a sustainable economy. However, it is has to be noted that contemporary taboos tend to be less firmly rooted in tradition and are less ritualized, and there is decreased reliance upon supernatural sanctioning. Consequently, they command less respect than traditional ones, which is a matter of concern. This is a situation made more acute by the influence of the Church, particularly in its characterization of traditional beliefs as "heathen and uncivilized".

[a growing number of indigenous peoples are today living in urban areas]

Indigenous Peoples living in urban areas

A growing number of indigenous peoples are today living in urban areas. This is the result of, among other things, the deterioration in and dispossession of lands, the forced evictions, and the lack of local employment opportunities that many indigenous people experience. ECLAC has estimated that in one in three indigenous individuals in Guatemala and México live in urban areas.[79] In Bolivia, Brazil and Chile, more than half of the indigenous population lives in urban areas. Cases studies from a UN-Habitat-OHCHR[80] report reveal that indigenous peoples in urban settings live in dismal conditions, frequently experiencing extreme poverty. Many of these people live in informal settlements and slums that often occupy territories susceptible to inundations, erosion, land- and mudslides, or are located in the vicinity of garbage dumps and polluting factories. Most slums and informal settlements are severely overcrowded, insecure and unsanitary, and without any urban infrastructure such as potable water, electricity, proper sanitation or garbage collection. It is common in many

[79] ECLAC (2007), 168.
[80] UN-Habitat and OHCHR (2005).

cities of the world to see increasing numbers of indigenous workers and beggars. Indigenous women in particular are affected by these conditions, as they are also often the victims of discrimination and physical abuse.[81]

Indigenous peoples in urban areas often become an almost invisible population because of the abstract and non-geographically clustered nature of the community, and because of the continued existence of stereotypes regarding indigenous peoples. There are several push- and pull-factors that prompt indigenous peoples to migrate to the cities, including poverty, environmental factors, the privatization of lands and territories, employment opportunities and access to health care and education.[82]

Often, when delivering services for indigenous peoples, all indigenous peoples are classified under one label as 'special needs', and there is no undertaking to understand the complexities of difference and the need to provide services in a different way, based on the experiences of the various indigenous groups residing in the cities. Involving indigenous peoples in decision-making affecting their communities in the urban situation is extremely important as it places indigenous peoples on an equal platform in seeking solutions.

Indigenous youth and children residing in urban areas are often portrayed in a way that sensationalizes problems such as destructive behaviour or risk-prone lifestyles. Meaningful activities that achieve positive outcomes for youth are empowering and need to provide opportunities for the development and affirmation of cultural identity and cultural knowledge and skills. Cultural activities in the form of drama, music and art, for example, are being used increasingly to raise awareness about relevant social concerns and to help youth speak out on issues that affect them.

Despite a few benefits of living in urban areas, such as proximity to social facilities, in most cases indigenous peoples have substantial difficulties. The underlying racism and discrimination toward indigenous peoples is felt every day, despite the increasing multicultural nature of cities. The lack of employment and income-generating activities, limited access to services and inadequate housing continue to be the main challenges that indigenous peoples living in urban areas face. In general, disrespect for a wide range of human rights and fundamental freedoms of indigenous peoples is often a main underlying cause for persisting poverty among urban indigenous communities. In many cases, indigenous peoples are trying to deal with their economic and social conditions in what is often a very hostile environment.

[the underlying racism and discrimination toward indigenous peoples is felt every day]

---

[81] UN-Habitat and OHCHR (2005), 178.
[82] See UNHABITAT, OHCHR, SPFII, ECLAC & IOM (2007) for a detailed discussion on some of the primary issues related to urban indigenous peoples.

Many indigenous city dwellers maintain reciprocal relationships with family and their homelands and build associations and relations as a form of finding their own space and socio-cultural continuum outside of their traditional homes – a coping mechanism that helps minimize conflicts brought about by the drastic change and demands of urbanization. The livelihood and employment strategies pursued by indigenous urban dwellers build on traditional skills; but many end up in low-paying work. Some examples are marketing of handicrafts; trading of traditional herbs and remedies; as construction workers by Igorot men skilled in building rice terraces and Maasai males serving as security guards reflecting their traditional role as warriors in East Africa. Others are also exploited as tourist attractions. Many have livelihoods as petty traders, menial and domestic workers and low-paid service workers, as well as being a source of cheap labour in the city. On the other hand, indigenous urban dwellers have raised the visibility of indigenous issues through advocacy and public actions in the cities.[83]

The Millennium Development Goals and Indigenous Peoples

The Millennium Declaration, signed by 147 Heads of State and Government in September 2000, and the Millennium Development Goals (MDGs) have provided an opportunity for a renewed focus on indigenous peoples in the international development debate. As the United Nations Permanent Forum on Indigenous Issues stated during is fourth session, "Indigenous peoples have the right to benefit from the Millennium Development Goals and from other goals and aspirations contained in the Millennium Declaration to the same extent as all others".[84]

The adoption of the United Nations Declaration on the Rights of Indigenous Peoples by the General Assembly in September 2007, in particular Articles 41 and 42,[85] provides a crucial opportunity and call to action for states and the UN system to integrate indigenous visions of development into their work toward the achievement of the MDGs.

> if the Millennium Development Goals are to be reached by 2015, they must be underpinned by a human rights-based approach to development that emphasizes universality, equality, participation and accountability

---

[83] UNCSD12 (2004) Indigenous People's Discussion Paper on Water, Sanitation and Human Settlements*

[84] UNPFII (2005).

[85] Article 41 reads as follows: The organs and specialized agencies of the United Nations system and other intergovernmental organizations shall contribute to the full realization of the provisions of this Declaration through the mobilization, inter alia, of financial cooperation and technical assistance. Ways and means of ensuring participation of indigenous peoples on issues affecting them shall be established.
Article 42 reads as follows: The United Nations, its bodies, including the Permanent Forum on Indigenous Issues, and specialized agencies, including at the country level, and States shall promote respect for and full application of the provisions of this Declaration and follow up the effectiveness of this Declaration.

During the fourth and fifth sessions of the United Nations Permanent Forum on Indigenous Issues, many indigenous peoples, through their organizations, made statements about the urgent need to redefine the MDGs and approaches to their implementation so as to include the perspectives, concerns, experiences and world views of indigenous peoples. There is also a need for full and effective participation of indigenous peoples in the implementation of the Goals.[86]

If the Millennium Development Goals are to be reached by 2015, they must be underpinned by a human rights-based approach to development that emphasizes universality, equality, participation and accountability. Working with indigenous peoples on the MDGs also requires a culturally sensitive approach based on respect for and inclusion of indigenous peoples' world-views, perspectives, experiences, and concepts of development.

Reviews of MDG reports from approximately 40 countries in Africa, Latin America and Asia and the Pacific have found that, with very few exceptions, indigenous peoples' input has not been included in national MDG monitoring and reporting.[87] The reviews also highlight clear gaps in data on indigenous peoples and the MDGs. Although many of the reports discuss the disparities affecting indigenous peoples, very few of them actually provide disaggregated data. Another gap identified in the reviews is the lack of mechanisms through which to ensure the input and participation of indigenous peoples themselves in the design, implementation and monitoring of policies designed to achieve the MDGs.

The following are a few key recommendations to better integrate indigenous peoples' issues into MDG programmes and policies:[88]

◈ The human rights-based approach to development should be operationalized by states, the UN system and other intergovernmental organizations. The recognition of indigenous peoples as distinct peoples and the respect for their individual and collective human rights is crucial for achieving a just and sustainable solution to the widespread poverty that affects them.

◈ Policies must be put in place to ensure that indigenous peoples have universal access to quality, culturally-sensitive social services. Some areas of particular concern are inter-cultural/bilingual education and culturally sensitive maternal and child healthcare.

◈ MDG-related programmes and policies should be culturally sensitive and include the active participation and free, prior and informed consent of indigenous peoples so as to avoid loss of land and natural resources for indigenous peoples and the accelerated assimilation and erosion of their cultures. United Nations Country Teams in Bolivia and Kenya, for example, have established indigenous peoples' advisory committees to guide programming on indigenous peoples' issues.

◈ States and the UN System must make greater efforts to include indigenous peoples in MDG monitoring and reporting, including the production of national MDG reports, as well as in the implementation, monitoring and evaluation of MDG-related programmes and policies that will directly or indirectly affect them. Improved disaggregation of data is indispensable to properly monitor progress toward MDG achievement in countries with indigenous populations and should be a key priority for Governments and the UN System. Several initiatives are currently underway to improve data disaggregation at both

---

[86] UNPFII (2006).

[87] These desk reviews are available online at http://www.un.org/indigenous

[88] These recommendations are drawn from the UNPFII's fourth and fifth sessions, as well as from the Desk Reviews of national MDG Reports carried out annually by the Secretariat of the UNPFII.

national and regional levels. ECLAC, for example, has played a key role in improving data on indigenous peoples in Latin America, and UNPFII has organized a series of regional meetings on indicators of well-being for indigenous peoples.

Indicators relevant to indigenous peoples' well-being and sustainable development

In recent years, there has been a concerted process to define global indicators for indigenous peoples' well-being and sustainable development. The global campaign to eradicate extreme poverty embodied in the Millennium Development Goals (MDGs) has also given impetus to identifying the poorest populations in each country, including indigenous peoples, for targeted interventions. The Convention on Biological Diversity (CBD) has adopted the 2010 Biodiversity Target to significantly reduce the rate of biodiversity loss, and one of its focal areas is the protection of traditional knowledge, innovations and practices.[89]

In 2006 and 2007, various regional and thematic workshops were organized on the topic of indicators relevant to indigenous peoples. This was part of a broader effort in recent years by United Nations bodies, governments, research agencies and indigenous bodies to measure status and trends in the social and economic development of indigenous peoples using indigenous- defined and culturally appropriate indicators. The following core issues and thematic areas have been identified[90] in terms of framing meaningful indicators to measure status of and trends in indigenous peoples' well-being at global, regional, national and local levels:

◈ Security of rights to territories, lands and natural resources

◈ Integrity of indigenous cultural heritage

◈ Gender

◈ Respect for identity and non-discrimination

◈ Fate control and self-determination

◈ Full, informed and effective participation

◈ Culturally-appropriate education

◈ Health

◈ Access to infrastructure and basic services

◈ Extent of external threats

◈ Material well-being

◈ Demographic patterns of indigenous peoples

---

[89] CBD 2010 Biodiversity Target at http://cbd.int/2010-target
[90] A global synthesis report on Indicators of Indigenous Peoples' Well-being, Poverty and Sustainability was submitted to the UN Permanent Forum on Indigenous Issues in 2008, see UNPFII (2008). The report was the culmination of more than two years of effort to capture indicators, in various workshops with indigenous peoples' participation. See UNPFII (2006), (2007a) and (2008).

The Millennium Ecosystem Assessment which, in 2001-2005, carried out an in-depth study into the present state of ecosystems and human well-being, highlights in its report messages which are highly relevant when assessing indigenous peoples' well-being.

From the Millennium Ecosystem Assessment

The pattern of "winners" and "losers" associated with ecosystem changes, and in particular the impact of ecosystem changes on poor people, women and indigenous peoples, has not been adequately taken into account in management decisions. Changes in ecosystems typically yield benefits for some people and exact costs on others, who may either lose access to resources or livelihoods, or be affected by externalities associated with the change. For several reasons, groups such as the poor, women, and indigenous communities have tended to be harmed by these changes.

Many changes in ecosystem management have involved the privatization of what were formerly common pool resources. Individuals who depended on those resources (such as indigenous peoples, forest-dependent communities, and other groups relatively marginalized from political and economic sources of power) have often lost rights to the resources.

Poor people have historically lost access to ecosystem services disproportionately as demand for those services has grown. Coastal habitats are often converted to other uses, frequently for aquaculture ponds or cage-culturing of highly valued species such as shrimp and salmon. Despite the fact that the area is still used for food production, local residents are often displaced, and the food produced is usually not for local consumption but for export. Many areas where overfishing is a concern are also low-income, food-deficit countries. Significant quantities of fish are caught by large distant water fleets in the exclusive economic zones of Mauritania, Senegal, Gambia, Guinea Bissau, and Sierra Leone, for example. Much of the catch is exported or shipped directly to Europe, while compensation for access is often low compared with the value of the product landed overseas. These countries do not necessarily benefit through increased fish supplies or higher government revenues when foreign distant water fleets ply their waters.

Source: Millennium Ecosystem Assessment (2005), 13 and 62.

Concluding Remarks

The biggest challenge faced by indigenous peoples and communities in relation to sustainable development is to ensure territorial security, legal recognition of ownership and control over customary land and resources, and the sustainable utilization of lands and other renewable resources for the cultural, economic and physical health and well-being of indigenous peoples.

Indigenous peoples' economies now represent the greatest continuity with pre-industrial modes of production and traditional livelihoods in the contemporary world. These economies, representing sustained interaction and adaptation with particular locations and ecosystems, are among the longest-standing and most proven examples of "sustainable development" in the twenty-first century.

Indigenous peoples carry millennial knowledge founded in generations of hunting and agricultural practices, land management and sustainable water use, and agriculture-related engineering and architecture. The maintenance of these cultural and spiritual relationships with the natural world is key to their survival as peoples or civilizations. The Mayans are the "Corn People", for example, while the Gwich'in Athabascans are "Caribou People". Traditional clan systems among Seminole people include the Bear, Eagle and even Sweet Potato clans.

The maintenance of these cultural and spiritual relationships is also vital to the conservation of biodiversity. This historical interdependence and relationship with specific ecosystems underpins the technical and scientific contributions of indigenous knowledge to critical research related to sustainable development based on an ecosystem approach. Many traditional practitioners are experts at reading indicator species that provide very early warning signals of impending environmental or food catastrophes and changes such as global warming.

Historical developments have all wrought significant changes on the social and economic position of indigenous peoples, progressively incorporating them into centralized states and privatized lands and resources. Indigenous peoples have cited the 500-year-old colonial encounter, the establishment of post-independence states, modernization and economic globalization as key milestones affecting their status and well-being.

> the biggest challenge faced by indigenous peoples and communities in relation to sustainable development is to ensure territorial security, legal recognition of ownership and control over customary land and resources

The present crises of biodiversity loss and climate change, resulting from the fossil fuel-based industrialized economy, are wreaking serious havoc on indigenous peoples' economies and environments, making the start of the twenty-first century a time of rapid change and adaptation for indigenous peoples.

An historical perspective and understanding of indigenous peoples' vital contribution to sustainable development is very important so that policies and actions can be taken at the international, regional, national and local levels in order to ensure the continued well-being of indigenous peoples. The future of indigenous peoples is closely linked with solutions to the crises in biodiversity and climate change, which must incorporate respect, protection and promotion of indigenous peoples' rights as an essential component of a global strategy. "Sustainable Development" has become the mainstream challenge of the twenty-first century— combining economic development, environmental sustainability and social equity between and within societies.

The advance of globalization has had profound impacts on indigenous peoples' traditional resource-based subsistence economies and livelihoods. Globalization has created a bridge between the centre and the periphery and intensified the inter-linkages and interdependencies between modern and traditional societies. This deepening incorporation of indigenous peoples into global economic systems, moving toward their full integration, has serious ramifications for the diversity of economies and livelihoods.

Indigenous peoples are at the cutting edge of the crisis in sustainable development. Their communities are concrete examples of sustainable societies, historically evolved in diverse ecosystems. Today, they face the challenge of extinction or survival and renewal in a globalized world. One clear criterion for sustainable development and the implementation of Agenda 21 must be actions taken to ensure indigenous peoples' rights and welfare.

The past 10 years have also seen an intensification of conflicting trends in addressing the imbalances in social and ecological relationships that underpin the global crisis in sustainable development:

> ◈ the rise of economic neo-liberalism and corporate globalization and the attendant commoditization and "privatization" of social and ecological values; and

> ◈ the resurgence of indigenous peoples' movements, local community and citizen's movements and transnational partnerships asserting the primacy of sustainable local communities and cultures and ecological integrity.

[
the future of indigenous peoples is closely linked with solutions to the crises in biodiversity and climate change
]

This conflict is evident in the disjuncture between global economic, financial and trade decisions, which are constricting national and local options and efforts to define flexible sustainable development paths, as encouraged by the global policy dialogue on environment and sustainable development. This lack of coherence in global policy processes is frustrating the implementation of positive measures supportive of indigenous peoples' self-determination and sustainable development.

Traditional wisdom and modern scientific knowledge confirm the un-sustainability of contemporary economic relations. The economic and social systems perpetrated by colonialism, modern development and contemporary economic globalization have progressively deepened fundamental imbalances in human relationships with nature and within society. Today, we are facing unprecedented changes in natural systems caused by global warming, as well as violent social conflicts underpinned by social exclusion and inequality.

The solutions to these challenges require the utmost contribution from the entire world's peoples and members of society through open and democratic governance structures at all levels.

List of references

Aboriginal Healing Foundation. 2003. "Aboriginal Domestic Violence in Canada". In The Aboriginal Healing Foundation Research Series. Ottawa: The Aboriginal Healing Foundation. Available on line at http://www.ahf.ca/pages/download/28_38

African Initiative on Mining, Environment and Society (AIMES) (2009). Statement Eleventh Annual Strategy Meeting of the African Initiative on Mining, Environment and Society the June 24-26th, Nairobi, Kenya

Amnesty International. 2007. The Maze of Injustice: The failure to protect Indigenous women from sexual violence in the USA. London: Amnesty International.

Andersen, Thomas and Poppel, Birger. 2002. "Living conditions in the Arctic". Social Indicators Research 58. Netherlands: Kluwer Academic Publishers.

Arctic Human Development Report. 2004. Societies and Cultures: Change and Persistence. Lead authors Yvon Csonka, University of Greenland, Nuuk, Greenland, and Peter Schweitzer, University of Alaska Fairbanks, U.S.A. Available at http://hdr.undp.org/en/reports/regionalreports/other/arctic_2004_en.pdf

Asian Development Bank. 2002. Indigenous peoples/Ethnic minorities and poverty reduction. Regional Report. Manila: Asian Development Bank.

Assembly of First Nations Canada, 2009. "Fact Sheet: The Reality for First Nations in Canada" . Available online at http://www.afn.ca/article.asp?id=764 (status: 03/10/2009)

Bamba, John. 2003. "Seven fortunes and seven calamities – Cultural poverty from an indigenous perspective" in Indigenous Affairs, Indigenous Poverty: An issue of Rights and Needs, No.1/2003: 26-35. Copenhagen: IWGIA. Available online at http://www.iwgia.org

Bentzon, A. W. and Agersnap, T. 1971. Urbanization, Industrialization and Changes in the Family in Greenland during the Reform Period since 1950. Copenhagen.

Bolstridge, Jill A. 2008. Invisible people. In The New Black Magazine. Online magazine. Birmingham, U.K.. Available at http://www.thenewblackmagazine.com/xtact.aspx? (status: 03/10/2009)

Bureau of Justice Statistics. 1999. American Indians and Crime. U.S.Department of Justice. Washington D.C. Available online at: http://www.ojp.usdoj.gov/bjs/pub/pdf/aic.pdf

Caruso, Emily, Cholchester, Marcus, MacKay, Fergus, Hildyard, Nick and Nettleton, Geoff. 2005. "Synthesis Report: Indigenous Peoples, Extractive Industries and the World Bank", in Extracting Promises: Indigenous Peoples, Extractive Industries and the World Bank, Second Edition. Baguio City: Tebtebba Foundation.

Condon, R., Collings, P. and Wenzel, G.. 1995. "The best part of life: Subsistence hunting, ethnicity, and economic adaptation among young adult Inuit males". Arctic 48(1), 31.

Convention on Biological Diversity (CBD). n.d. 2010 Biodiversity Target. Availableon line at http://cbd.int/2010-target

Cooke, Martin, Mitrou, Francis, Lawrence, David, Guimod, Eric and Beavon, Dan. 2007. Indigenous well-being in four countries: An application of the UNDP's Human Development Index to Indigenous Peoples in Australia, Canada, New Zealand and the United States. BMC International Health and Human Rights. Availabble online at http://www.biomedcentral.com/1472-698X/7/9

Cornell, Stephen. 2006. "Indigenous Peoples, Poverty and Self-Determination in Australia, New Zealand, Canada and the United States". In Joint Occasional Papers on Native Affairs (No. 2). Harvard Project on American Indian Economic Development. Cambridge: Harvard University, U.S.A.

Economic Commission for Latin America and the Caribbean (ECLAC). 2005. Objetivos de desarrollo del milenio: Una mirada desde América Latina y el Caribe. Santiago: United Nations.

Economic Commission for Latin America and the Caribbean (ECLAC). 2007. Panorama social de América Latina 2006. Santiago: United Nations.

Feiring, B. with MRG Partners. 2003. Indigenous Peoples and Poverty: The Cases of Bolivia, Guatemala, Honduras and Nicaragua. London: Minority Rights Group International.

Freeman, C., and Fox, M., 2005. Status and Trends in the Education of American Indians and Alaska Natives (NCES 2005-108). U.S. Department of Education, National Center for Education Statistics. Washington, D.C.: U.S. Government Printing Office. Available online at http://nces.ed.gov/pubs2005/2005108.pdf

Gaski, Harald, ed. 1998. In the Shadow of the Midnight Sun: Contemporary Sami Prose and Poetry. Seattle: University of Washington Press.

Gorelick, Melissa. 2007. "Discrimination of aboriginals on native lands in Canada: A comprehensive crisis". In UN Chronicle Vol. 3, 2007 Available online at: http://www.un.org/Pubs/chronicle/2007/issue3/0307cont.htm

Greenland Statistics/Grønlands Statistik. 2003. Statistisk årbog (Statistical Yearbook). Nuuk: Grønlands Statistik /Atuagkat.

Guimbatan, Rachel and Buguilat, Teddy Jr. 2006. "Misunderstanding the notion of conservation in the Philippine rice terraces – cultural landscapes". International Social Science Journal LVIII(58),1/187.

Hall, Gillian and Patrinos, Harry Anthony. 2006. Indigenous Peoples, Poverty and Human Development in Latin America: 1994-2004. New York, N.Y.: Palgrave McMillan.

Hatfield, Richard and Davies, Jonathan. 2006. Global Review of the Economics of Pastoralism. Nairobi: World Initiative for Sustainable Pastoralism, International Union for the Conservation of Nature. Available online at http://www.landcoalition.org/pdf/07_rev_econom_pastor.pdf

Hazlehurst, Kayleen, and Dunn, Albert (1988). "Aboriginal criminal justice". In Australian Institute of Criminology. Trends and issues in crime and criminal justice (No. 13). On line article. Available at http://74.125.47.132/search?q=cache:SPLhpqMSlIUJ:www.aic.gov.au/publications/tandi/ti13.pdf+Hazlehurst,+Ka yleen,+Dunn,+Albert+(1988).&hl=en&ct=clnk&cd=2&gl=us (status: 03/10/2009)

Health Canada. 2007. "First Nations Comparable Health Indicators" Available online at: http://www.hc-sc.gc.ca/ fniah-spnia/diseases-maladies/2005-01_health-sante_indicat-eng.php

Hickey, Francis R. 2007. "Traditional Marine Resource Management in Vanuatu: Worldviews in Transformation". In Fishers' Knowledge in Fisheries Science and Management, Part II, Chapter 1. Paris: UNESCO.

Housing Assisting Council Website. Available at http://www.ruralhome.org/manager/uploads/NativeAmerInfoSheet.pdf (status: 03/10/2009)

Housing New Zealand Corporation. 2008. "Maori Housing Trend Report 2008." Available at http://www.hnzc. co.nz/utils/downloads/0781374DF912C27AC059E7956A48B05E.doc

Indian Health Service. 2006. "Facts on Indian Health Disparities" Available at: http://info.ihs.gov/Files/DisparitiesFacts-Jan2006.pdf

Indian Health Service, 2009. "IHS Fact Sheets: Safe Water and Waste Disposal Facilities" Available online at: http://info.ihs.gov/SafeWater.asp

Ingold, T. 1995. "Work, identity and environment: Finns and Saami in Lapland." In Arctic Ecology and Identity, ed. S. Mousalimas. Budapest: Akadémiai Kiadó.

Integrated Regional Information Networks (IRIN) 2006. Minorities under siege: Pygmies today in Africa. IRIN Humanitarian News and Analysis. UN Office for the Coordination of Humanitarian Affairs. Available online at http://www.irinnews.org/pdf/in-depth/Pygmies-today-in-Africa-IRIN-In-Depth.pdf

International Fund for Agricultural Development (IFAD) 2007. Statistics and key facts about indigenous peoples. Rome: IFAD. Available online at http://www.ruralpovertyportal.org/web/guest/topic/statistics/tags/indigenous%20peoples

International Labour Organization (ILO) 2007. Equality at work: Tackling the challenges. Global Report under the follow-up to the ILO Declaration on Fundamental Principles and Rights at Work. Report of the Director General. International Labour Conference 96th Session 2007. Geneva: ILO

Kenrick, Justin. 2000. "The Forest Peoples of Africa in the 21st Century". Indigenous Affairs, Hunters and Gatherers, 2/2000:10-25. Copenhagen: IWGIA. Available online at http://www.iwgia.org

Kuptana, Rosemary. 1996. "ICC and Indigenous Economic Development". Paper presented at the seminar "Indigenous Peoples Production and Trade", 15-17 January 1996, Copenhagen, organd by Nordic Council of Ministers.

Millennium Ecosystem Assessment. 2005. Ecosystems and Human Well-being: Synthesis. Washington, D.C.: Island Press. Available online at http://millenniumassessment.org/documents/document 356 aspx.pdf

Mugarura, Benon with Ndemeye, Aniced. 2003. Batwa Land Rights in Rwanda. Micro Study. London: Minority Rights International. Available online at http://www.minorityrights.org/download.php?id=93

New Zealand Department of Labour. 2008. Maori Labour Market Factsheet, September 2008. Available online at http://www.dol.govt.nz/publications/lmr/lmr-quick-facts-maori.asp

Nori, Michele, Taylor, Michael, Sensi, Alessandra. 2008. Browsing on fences: Pastoral land rights, livelihoods and adaptation to climate change. Nottingham: International Institute for Environment and Development.

Phillips, Janet. 2007 and Carrington, Kerry. 2003. Domestic Violence in Australia—An overview of the issues. E-Brief online only. Available at http://www.aph.gov.au/library/INTGUIDE/sp/Dom_violence.htm (status: 03/10/2009)

Plant, Roger. 1998. Issues in Indigenous Poverty and Development. Washington D.C.: Inter-American Development Bank.

Posey, Darrell A., ed. 2000. Cultural and Spiritual Values of Biodiversity. New York, NY: United Nations Environment Program/London: Intermediate Technology Publications.

Ramírez, A. 2006. "Mexico", in G. Hall and H.A. Patrinos, (eds.), Indigenous Peoples, Poverty and Human Development in Latin America. London: Palgrave McMillan.

Royal Commission on Aboriginal Affairs. 1996. Report on Aboriginal Peoples. Available online at http://www. ainc-inac.gc.ca

Sarkar, Sandip, Mishra, Sunil, Dayal Harishwar and Nathan, Dev. 2006. Development and Deprivation of Scheduled Tribes in India: What the Figures Tell. Delhi: Institute of Human Development.

Sawyer, Suzana and Gomez, Edmund Terence. 2008. Transnational Governmentality and Resource Extraction: Indigenous Peoples, Multinational Corporations, Multilateral Institutions and the State. Identities, Conflict and Cohesion Programme Paper No. 13. Geneva: United Nations Research Institute for Social Development.

Segovia Declaration of Nomadic and Transhumant Pastoralists. 2007. La Granja, Segovia, Spain, 13 September 2007. Available online at http://www.nomadassegovia2007.org/declaration.html

Statistics New Zealand. 1998. New Zealand Now – Maori (Census 96). Wellington. Statistics New Zealand.

Statistics Canada. 2005. "Labour Force Survey: Western Canada's off-reserve Aboriginal population" Available online at: http://www.statcan.gc.ca/daily-quotidien/050613/dq050613a-eng.htm

Stavenhagen, Rodolfo. 2005. Statement issued in Press Release "UN Expert on Human rights of Indigenous People Concludes Visit to New Zealand 25 November 2005". Available online at http://www.unhchr.ch/huricane/huricane.nsf/view01/593D9C547C710084C12570C400369649?opendocument

Stavenhagen, Rodolfo. 2006. "Mission to New Zealand." Report of the Special Rapporteur on the situation of human rights and fundamental freedoms of indigenous people to the UN Economic and Social Council, Addendum 3. UN DOC E/CN.4/2006/78/Add.3 13 March 2006.

Stavenhagen, Rodolfo. 2007. Report of the Special Rapporteur on the situation of human rights and fundamental freedoms of indigenous people, Rodolfo Stavenhagen to the United Nations General Assembly (A/HRC/4/32).

Tauli-Corpuz, Victoria. 1999. TRIPS and its potential impacts on indigenous peoples. Echoes 15/1999, World Council of Churches, Geneva, Switzerland, pp.17-19. Available online at http://www.wcc-coe.org/wcc/what/jpc/trips2.html

Tauli-Corpuz, Victoria. 2006. "World bank and IMF Impacts on Indigenous Economies", in Paradigm Wars: Indigenous Peoples' Resistance to Economic Globalization, eds. Jerry Mander and Victoria Tauli-Corpuz

Taylor, Jonathan B. and Kalt, Joseph B. 2005. American Indians on Reservations: A Data-book of Socioeconomic Change Between the 1990 and 2000 censuses. Harvard Project on American Indian Economic Development, Malcolm Wiener Center for Social Policy, John F. Kennedy School of Government, Harvard University. Available at http://www.ksg.harvard.edu/hpaied/pubs/documents/AmericanIndiansonReservationsADatabookofSoicioeconomicChange.pdf

Tsai, Grace & Alanis, Luisa. 2004. The Native American Culture: A Historical and Reflective Perspective. In National Association of School Psychologists Communiqué, Vol. 32 No. 8. Available online at: http://www.nasponline.org/publications/cq/cq328native.aspx

United Nations Development Programme (UNDP) 2004. Nepal Human Development Report 2004: Empowerment and Poverty Reduction. Kathmandu: UNDP. Available online at http://hdr.undp.org/en/reports/nationalreports/asiathepacific/nepal/nepal_2004_en.pdf

UN-HABITAT, OHCHR, SPFII, ECLAC & IOM. 2007. Report of the International Expert Group Meeting on Urban Indigenous Peoples and Migration, Santiago de Chile, 27-29 March 2007. Available online at http://www.un.org/esa/socdev/unpfii/documents/6session_crp8_en.doc

United Nations Permanent Forum on Indigenous Issues (UNPFII). 2005. Report on the Fourth Session. UN Doc. E/2005/43 Available online at http://www.un.org/indigenous

United Nations Permanent Forum on Indigenous Issues (UNPFII). 2006. Report on the Fourth Session. UN Doc. E/2006/43 Available online at http://www.un.org/indigenous

United Nations Permanent Forum on Indigenous Issues (UNPFII). 2006. Report of the Meeting on Indigenous Peoples and Indicators of Well-being. UN Doc. E/C.19/2006/CRP, 3. April 2006. Available online at http://www.un.org/esa/socdev/unpfii

United Nations Permanent Forum on Indigenous Issues (UNPFII). 2007a. African Regional Expert Working Group on Indicators of Well-being and Indigenous Peoples. UN Doc. E/C.19/2007/CRP. 3 November 2006. Available online at http://www.un.org/esa/socdev/unpfii

United Nations Permanent Forum on Indigenous Issues (UNPFII). 2007b. Asia regional workshop: Indicators Relevant for Indigenous Peoples, the Convention on Biological Diversity and the Millennium Development Goals. UN Doc. E/C.19/2007/CRP. 10 November 2006. Available online at http://www.un.org/esa/socdev/unpfii

United Nations Permanent Forum on Indigenous Issues (UNPFII). 2008. Indicators of well-being, poverty and sustainability relevant to indigenous peoples. UN Doc. E/C.19/2008/9, 20 February 2008. Available online at http://www.un.org/esa/socdev/unpfii

United States Bureau of Justice 1999 Statistics. Online Web Site. Available at http://www.ojp.usdoj.gov/bjs/pub/pdf/aic.pdf (status: 03/10/2009)

United States Census Bureau. 2005. Census Bureau, March Current Population Survey (CPS), 1994 to 2003. Available online at http://nces.ed.gov/pubs2005/nativetrends/ind_8_2.asp

United States Census Bureau. 2005. Press Release: Income Stable, Poverty Rate Increases, Percentage of Americans Without Health Insurance Unchanged. Available online at: http://www.census.gov/Press-Release/www/releases/archives/income_wealth/005647.html

United States Census Bureau. 2008a. News Release, 26 August 2008. Available online at http://www.census.gov/Press-Release/www/releases/archives/income_wealth/012528.html

United States Census Bureau. 2008b. News Release: Facts for Features, 16 October 2008. Available online at http://www.census.gov/PressRelease/www/releases/archives/facts_for_features_special_editions/012782.html

Wessendorf, Katrin (ed.) a. o. 2008. "The Indigenous World 2008". Copenhagen: International Work Group for Indigenous Affairs.

Wiben Jensen, Marianne. 2004. "Editorial" Indigenous Affairs, Land Rights: A Key Issue, No. 04/2004:4. Copenhagen: IWGIA. Available online at http://www.iwgia.org

World Bank. 2007. Economic Opportunities for Indigenous Peoples in Latin America, Washington D.C.: The World Bank.

World Commission on Dams (WCD). 2000. "Dams and Development, A New Framework for Decision-making." Report of the World Commission on Dams. U.K.: Earthscan Publications.

CHAPTER II

CHAPTER II

CULTURE

By Naomi Kipuri

Culture has been defined as "that complex whole which includes knowledge, belief, art, morals, law, custom, and any other capacities and habits acquired by man as a member of society".[1] In other words, culture is a patterned way of life shared by a group of people. Culture encompasses all that human beings have and do to produce, relate to each other and adapt to the physical environment. It includes agreed-upon principles of human existence (values, norms and sanctions) as well as techniques of survival (technology).[2] Culture is also that aspect of our existence which makes us similar to some people, yet different from the majority of the people in the world... it is the way of life common to a group of people, a collection of beliefs and attitudes, shared understandings and patterns of behaviour that allow those people to live together in relative harmony, but set them apart from other peoples.[3]

> culture is also that aspect of our existence which makes us similar to some people, yet different from the majority of the people in the world...

Indigenous peoples have rich and diverse cultures based on a profound spiritual relationship with their land and natural resources. Dichotomies such as nature vs. culture do not exist in indigenous societies. Indigenous peoples do not see themselves as outside the realm of nature, but as part of nature, and they have their own specific attachment to their land and territory and their own specific modes of production based on a unique knowledge of their environment. Nor do indigenous peoples emphasize a radical duality between the sacred and the mundane as happens in Western culture. In many indigenous cultures, social and political institutions are part of the cosmic order,[4] and it is on the basis of their worldview, beliefs, values and customs that indigenous peoples define their own forms of governance, as well as their customary laws and norms. Another salient characteristic of indigenous cultures is that they are based on a collective perspective. In the same way that indigenous peoples consider their lands and resources to be collective assets, they see their cultural values and activities—their identity—as a function of the group, not individuals.[5] This also applies to the ownership and custody of their cultural heritage, which is collective.[6]

Indigenous communities have kept their cultures alive by passing on their worldview, their knowledge and know-how, their arts, rituals and performances from one generation to the next. Preserving their cultural heritage has also included speaking and teaching their own languages, protecting their sacred and significant sites and objects. It has also included defending and holding onto their lands and territories, since these are fundamental for sustaining them as peoples and cultures.

---

[1] Tylor (1871), 1.
[2] Rossi (1980).
[3] Friedl and Pfeiffer (1977), 283-284.
[4] Champagne (2007), 79.
[5] Gomez (2007).
[6] Daes (1995), para. 5.

It is this all-encompassing nature of indigenous cultures that makes them unique and so different from the cultures of those groups that hold the political, economic and social power in the nation-states in which they live. But because indigenous peoples have been excluded from the decision-making and policy frameworks of the nation-states in which they live, and because they have been subjected to processes of domination and discrimination, their cultures have been viewed as being inferior, primitive, irrelevant, something to be eradicated or transformed. In addition, they have continued to experience the loss of access to lands, territories and natural resources. The result has been that indigenous cultures today are threatened with extinction in many parts of the world.

In order to assess the current situation of indigenous cultures, this chapter presents a brief overview of some of the fundamental elements of indigenous cultures—such as lands and languages, spirituality, social institutions and traditional knowledge. However, it is important to bear in mind that indigenous cultures can be understood only in a holistic and comprehensive way, and that their various "elements" should be seen as essentially interconnected with and dependent on each other.

This chapter also looks at some of the threats and challenges indigenous cultures are facing today—in the form of misappropriation by outsiders, globalization, commodification and tourism—as well as some of the new openings and opportunities brought about by the broad international recognition of indigenous cultural rights as well as by a growing appreciation of indigenous peoples' invaluable contribution to humanity's cultural diversity and heritage.

Land, language and identity

Among the many markers of indigenous cultural identity, the attachment to land and the use of an indigenous language are two of the most significant.

Land

The importance of land and territories to indigenous cultural identity cannot be stressed enough. The survival and development of indigenous peoples' particular ways of life, their traditional knowledge, their handicrafts and other cultural expressions have, since time immemorial, depended on their access and rights to their traditional lands, territories and natural resources. But land is not only the basis of the indigenous economy. Indigenous peoples also have a deep spiritual relationship with the land; they feel at one with their ancestral territory and feel responsible for the healthy maintenance of the land—its waters and soils, its plants and animals—for both themselves and future generations.[7] Land is where their ancestors are buried and where sacred places are visited and revered.

Very often, people identify themselves by taking the name of the place to which they belong. In Maasailand, for example, sub-groups are named after their particular area of origin. Thus the IlKaputiei are from Kaputiei, Ilpurko are from Purko, IlMatapato are from Matapato, etc. Hence, the place is also the people. In this way, the notion of "pertaining to the land" is embedded in indigenous peoples' cultural identities. This is also reflected in the common understanding of indigeneity as expressed in various international documents, including ILO Convention No. 169, which all reflect the special and intimate attachment of indigenous peoples to their lands and territories and its fundamental importance for their collective physical and cultural survival as peoples.[8]

---

[7] Young (2000), 57.
[8] These international documents include—besides ILO Convention No. 169 (1989)—the Study on the Discrimination against Indigenous Peoples (Martínez Cobo Study) from 1986/7 and the Working Group on Indigenous Populations' Working Paper on the concept of "indigenous peoples" from 1996.

Indigenous peoples are often defined as the original peoples of the land who lost their land and were displaced and marginalized by colonizers or by a group of people who arrived at some later date. Although this pattern of displacement and marginalization of indigenous peoples is found throughout the world, given the extensive and complicated history of human migration in many part of Africa, being the "first peoples in a land" is not a necessary pre-condition for acceptance as an indigenous people. Rather, indigenous identity relates more to a set of characteristics and practices than priority of arrival. For example, several populations of nomadic peoples, such as the Tuareg of the Sahara and Sahel regions, now inhabit areas in which they arrived comparatively recently; their claim to indigenous identity status (endorsed by the African Commission on Human and Peoples' Rights) is based on their marginalization as nomadic peoples in states and territories dominated by sedentary agricultural peoples. This does not, however, prevent them from identifying themselves through and with the land that may have sustained them for several generations, shaped their culture, and to which they have become spiritually attached, since this is where their ancestors are buried.

The centrality of land in the lives of indigenous peoples has been recognized by the Permanent Forum in the following words:

> Land is the foundation of the lives and cultures of indigenous peoples all over the world. This is why the protection of their right to lands, territories and natural resources is a key demand of the international indigenous peoples' movement and of indigenous peoples and organizations everywhere. It is also clear that most local and national indigenous peoples' movements have emerged from struggles against policies and actions that have undermined and discriminated against their customary land tenure and resource management systems, expropriated their lands, extracted their resources without their consent and led to their displacement and dispossession from their territories. Without access to and respect for their rights over their lands, territories and natural resources, the survival of indigenous peoples' particular distinct cultures is threatened.

> Land rights, access to land and control over it and its resources are central to indigenous peoples throughout the world, and they depend on such rights and access for their material and cultural survival. In order to survive as distinct peoples, indigenous peoples and their communities need to be able to own, conserve and manage their territories, lands and resources.[9]

Land is the basis for the lives, cultures and identities of indigenous peoples. Rights over lands, territories and natural resources are among the most important and also the most contentious issues that indigenous peoples, at both the national and international level, have debated with governments. Since the colonial period, indigenous peoples have been dispossessed of their lands or faced the threat of dispossession and forced removal, leading to increased poverty, erosion of cultures and even outright extinction or complete assimilation. Although indigenous peoples today continue to face the threat of dispossession of lands, a great deal of progress has been made in recent years in terms of legislative reforms and policy making. Nevertheless, there is a persistent implementation gap between the laws passed and daily reality for indigenous peoples. This implementation gap is observed both between national legislation and international standards on the one hand, and the day-to-day reality on the other. Indigenous peoples-related legislation is sometimes inconsistent with other laws, and there is generally a lack of proper mechanisms for monitoring the effectiveness of such legislation and its application. State bureaucracies are often slow and poorly equipped to react to new legislation favouring indigenous peoples. Thus, indigenous

---

[9] UNPFII (2007c), paras 5-6.

peoples have frequently looked to international instruments and international and national judicial systems to fill in the implementation gap, with some successes.

The United Nations Declaration on the Rights of Indigenous Peoples addresses lands, territories and natural resources thoroughly, including the right to maintain spiritual relationships with the land, the right not to be forcibly removed or dispossessed, the right for indigenous peoples to have their own land tenure systems, the right to redress for land that has been taken or damaged and the right to conservation and protection of the environment. Article 26 contains some of the most important language on land:

> *Article 26*
> 1. *Indigenous peoples have the right to the lands, territories and resources which they have traditionally owned, occupied or otherwise used or acquired.*
> 2. *Indigenous peoples have the right to own, use, develop and control the lands, territories and resources that they possess by reason of traditional ownership or other traditional occupation or use, as well as those which they have otherwise acquired.*
> 3. *States shall give legal recognition and protection to these lands, territories and resources. Such recognition shall be conducted with due respect to the customs, traditions and land tenure systems of the indigenous peoples concerned.*

In addition to the Declaration, some significant progress has been made at the national level. This holds particularly true regarding legislative reforms, respecting indigenous peoples' collective rights to land. In Northern Canada, for example the Nunavut land claim agreement grants approximately 25,000 Inuit title to around 350,000 square kilometres of lands and resources. In South America, some of the most advanced legal frameworks for indigenous land tenure are in Bolivia, Brazil, Colombia, Costa Rica, Ecuador, Nicaragua, Panama, Paraguay and Peru, enshrined in legislation and often in constitutions as well. Indigenous peoples' collective rights to land are also recognized in Australia, New Zealand, Northern Europe and the Russian Federation. The situation in Asia varies greatly. Cambodia and the Philippines have enacted legislation that recognizes communal land rights, while in India, there is constitutional protection of indigenous lands in areas of Northeast India. In Africa, very few countries recognize indigenous peoples' rights to land, although in South Africa and Botswana, some peoples have had success in having their land claims recognized.[10]

In many cases, these legislative reforms are a direct consequence of court decisions in favour of indigenous peoples and their demand for the recognition of their ancestral lands, while in other cases, these reforms correspond with changing international standards. In all cases, these reforms are a direct consequence of indigenous peoples' resistance and demands that their rights be respected, protected and fulfilled.

Landmark cases

Calder v. British Columbia (1973) Canada
The Calder case reviewed the existence of "aboriginal title" claimed by the Nisga'a people of British Columbia, Canada. The Nisga'a argued that they possessed land rights over their traditional territories and had never surrendered or lost their rights to the land. Chief Frank Arthur Calder lost the case, based on a procedural point, but the lasting result of the Supreme Court decision was that the Court recognized that Aboriginal title to land existed prior to the colonization of the continent and was not

---

[10] IWGIA (2004), 4-7.

merely derived from statutory law. This resulted in the Government of Canada's overhauling its land claim negotiation processes.

Source: University of Saskatchewan online library (2008)

Mabo v. Queensland (1992) Australia

In 1992, the High Court of Australia held that the common law of Australia recognizes native title to land, rejecting the doctrine that Australia was terra nullius (land belonging to no-one) at the time of European settlement. The decision stated that native title can continue to exist where Aboriginal and Torres Strait Islander people have maintained their connection with the land through the years of European settlement and that the content of native title is to be determined according to the traditional laws and customs of the Aboriginal and Torres Strait Islander people involved. The case had been led by Eddie Mabo of the Meriam people from the Mer (Murray) Islands of the Torres Strait. Mr. Mabo died before the decision was rendered by the High Court.

Source: Aboriginal Law Bulletin (1993)

Mayagna Awas Tingni v. Nicaragua (2001) Nicaragua

When a private company was granted logging concessions over their traditional lands, the Sumu people of the village of Awas Tingni brought their case to the Inter-American Court of Human Rights. The Court concluded that Nicaragua had violated the right to judicial protection and to property and that the American Convention of Human Rights protected indigenous peoples' collective rights to their traditional territories. This was the first time that the Inter-American Court had issued a judgment in favour of the rights of indigenous peoples to their ancestral land, and as such, is a key precedent for defending indigenous rights in the Americas.

Source: Anaya & Grossman (2002)

Alexkor Limited v. The Richtersveld Community (2003) South Africa

On 14 October 2003, the Constitutional Court of South Africa decided that the Nama people who had been dispossessed of their diamond-rich land in the 1920s had exclusive rights to their traditional territories and its resources. The Court found that a change in sovereignty does not destroy pre-existing property rights and that the Nama people had unlawfully been dispossessed of their lands based on racial discrimination.

Source: Agreements, treaties and negotiated settlements project (2007)

Sagong Bin Tasi v. Keajaan Negeri Selangor (2005) Malaysia

The plaintiffs, seven indigenous Temuans of the Bukit Tampoi village, charged that their eviction and dispossession of land for the construction of a highway was illegal and that they deserved compensation for the loss of 38 acres of land that had been taken from them. The High Court of Malaysia ruled that the Temuans had native title under common law over their lands and that the defendants must pay the Temuans substantial compensation. This ruling affirmed that Malaysian law does indeed recognize customary proprietary rights of indigenous peoples over their lands and territories.

Source: Current Law Journal (2005)

> **Sesana v. Botswana (2006) Botswana**
> In December 2006, the Botswana High Court ruled that the 2002 eviction and displacement of indigenous San peoples from their ancestral lands in the Central Kalahari Game Reserve (CKGR) was unlawful and unconstitutional, as was the government's decision to terminate the provision of basic services to the San peoples within the CKGR. The court recognized that the San, as indigenous peoples, have the right to live, hunt and gather on their ancestral land inside the CKGR and that they should not have to apply for permits to enter it.
>
> *Source: South African Legal Information Institute (2006)*

Land thus plays a crucial role in the culture of indigenous peoples. Even indigenous city dwellers—whether they are indigenous Australians or Mapuche in Chile—remain determined to retain their links to the land.[11] Losing access to their lands and territories, on the other hand, makes indigenous peoples feel deprived of their material and spiritual sustenance. Traditional livelihoods are discontinued, traditional knowledge lost, rituals linked to the land or ancestral spirits can no longer take place,[12] and social disintegration is often a result.[13]

Indigenous languages

Maintaining distinct languages, at least in part, has also been seen as an essential part of being indigenous.[14] Language is a system of symbols, or words arranged to convey meaning, and enables people to communicate either verbally or in writing. Language is an important component of one's identity. It is fundamental to understanding values, beliefs, ideology and other intangible aspects of culture. It enables people to communicate as specific peoples and determines participation, access to knowledge, leadership and depth of understanding.[15]

It is usually estimated that there are between 6,000 and 7,000 oral languages in the world today. Most of these languages are spoken by very few people, while a handful of them are spoken by an overwhelming majority of the world. About 97 per cent of the world's population speaks 4 per cent of its languages, while only 3 per cent speaks 96 per cent of them.[16] A great majority of these languages are spoken by indigenous peoples, and many (if not most) of them are in danger of becoming extinct. These are languages that are spoken by only a handful of elders and are not being acquired by children and, as the remaining native

[it has been estimated that roughly 90 per cent of all existing languages may become extinct within the next 100 years]

---

[11] Young (2000), 58; Bello (2007), 14.
[12] Kenrick (2000), 10.
[13] Wesley-Esquimaux (2007), 7.
[14] See, among other documents, ILO Convention No.169 and WGIP (1996).
[15] See UNESCO (2008), 2. UNESCO also underlines the key role languages play in the various pillars of sustainable development and in achieving the Millennium Goals.
[16] See, for example, Skutnabb Kangas (2000) and UNESCO (2003).

speakers die, one by one, the languages are dying with them. In fact, it has been estimated that roughly 90 per cent of all existing languages may become extinct within the next 100 years.[17]

The extinction of a language is a great loss for humanity; it constitutes the invaluable loss of traditional knowledge and cultural diversity. But for the indigenous peoples themselves, the loss is even greater, especially since many of the indigenous languages exist only orally and cannot, therefore, be retrieved once they are no longer spoken. The loss of a language is thus "a cause of intense grief and disorientation to hundreds of thousands of indigenous men and women who struggle to be themselves without the words to say what that means."[18] Language, furthermore, is not only a communication tool, it is often linked to the land or region traditionally occupied by indigenous peoples; it is an essential component of one's collective and individual identity and therefore provides a sense of belonging and community. When the language dies, that sense of community is damaged.

Indigenous languages have been dying, not only as a result of unintended consequences of colonization and globalization, but also because of deliberate assimilation policies that sought to deny indigenous peoples their own identities and cultures. Indigenous languages were dismissed as the "gibbering of monkeys" or "barbaric tongues" that were to be eradicated to make way for an English (or French or Spanish, etc.) that "all who are civilized can understand".[19] These assimilation policies lead to the destruction of languages and can thus be considered a form of ethnocide or linguistic genocide.[20]

Recovering their land and their lost language

Elsie Vaalboi was born in the early 1900s in the Southern Kalahari, South Africa. Her people, the ǂKhomani, are the last San society of South Africa. In the 1970s, both the apartheid government and experts on Bushman* cultures decreed that the ǂKhomani had ceased to exist. Linguists announced that the language had died out.

Elsie Vaalboi knew the ǂKhomani language. But her children did not, nor did her neighbours. She believed she was the last ǂKhomani speaker on earth.

In the late 1990s, one of Elsie Vaalboi's sons, Petrus, began to work with the South African San Institute (SASI). They met with ǂKhomani families who were squatters at Welkom, a community at the edge of the Kalahari Gemsbok National Park, their former traditional lands. SASI decided to claim the ǂKhomani lands and made Elsie record a message in the ǂKhomani language addressed to the Mandela government. Perhaps there was no one in the world who would understand her words but, in Afrikaans, she explained: "The time has come for the Bushmen to recover their lands and their lost language. The Boers have to move aside and let the Bushmen live again in their real home."

SASI began a search for ǂKhomani survivors, looking also for speakers of the language and, in 1998, they found a ǂKhomani family consisting of four women—three sisters and their cousin—in their late sixties and early seventies. They were Bushmen, they said, and they spoke their language.

>

[17] UNESCO (2003).
[18] Brody (2000), 5.
[19] Brody (2000), 5.
[20] Brody (2000), 5.

> They listened to Elsie's tape. They were amazed and delighted and recorded a message in reply. Yes, they said, they too spoke "Boesmantal". And yes, they said, the time had come to fight to get back their lands and to save their language.
>
> The search for the ‡Khomani diaspora continued and 15 speakers of the language were eventually found. They met, they talked, they shared hopes. And they became the centre of the land claim. In early 1999, then Deputy President Thabo Mbeki met with them and, at a formal ceremony, an agreement was signed, giving the ‡Khomani rights to some 50,000 hectares of land within the Kalahari Gemsbok Park and 40,000 hectares outside the park.
>
> *Source: Brody (2000), 8-9.*
>
> * The term "Bushman" has today been replaced by the term San. Both are generic terms and each San group has its own distinct name.

In the face of language extinction, some efforts are being made by governments, the international community, civil society organizations, academics and, of course, indigenous peoples themselves, to protect, revitalize and record dying languages. UNESCO, for instance, has a programme on safeguarding endangered languages and, following a recommendation from the Permanent Forum, an expert group met in 2008—the International Year of Languages—to look inter alia at how to eliminate the discrimination against the current use of indigenous languages and develop and support the revitalization and recovery of threatened languages. A Convention for the Protection of Indigenous and Endangered Languages is currently being drafted.[21]

While some indigenous peoples are successfully revitalising languages, many others are fighting a losing battle, where languages are simply no longer passed from one generation to the next. Most governments are aware of this language crisis but funding is often provided only for the recording of languages, while limited funds are diverted to language revitalization programmes.

Although the recording of a language is a valuable effort, it is no substitute for revitalization programmes that produce new speakers and keep a language alive. This is an important distinction to make, given that funds are often diverted from indigenous peoples' efforts at revitalization to academic recording projects. While there are hundreds of languages that face impending extinction, there are thousands of other languages that are not in immediate danger of being lost but may well be in danger of extinction within a generation or two if policies and actions that facilitate the use of minority languages within states are not put into place.[22]

Spirituality and belief systems

Spirituality is the relationship human beings create with the spirit world in order to manage forces that seem overpowering. Indigenous spirituality is intimately linked to the environment in which the people live. For indigenous peoples, the land is the core of all spirituality and this relationship to the spirit of the earth is central to all the issues that are important to indigenous peoples today.

---

[21] See UNESCO (2008), 6 and UNPFII (2008), 12.
[22] For further information, see for example the Report of the International Expert Group Meeting on Indigenous Languages organized by UNPFII (2008).

Spirituality is a term that requires special care in its definition. It is important to recognize the difference between spirituality and religion. Spirituality can be seen as an internal connection to the universe, which includes a sense of meaning or purpose in life, a cosmology or way of explaining one's personal universe and personal moral code. Religion, on the other hand, could be defined as a specific practice and ritual that are the external expression of some people's spirituality.

What is important here is that spirituality is the relationship to the universe. Indigenous spirituality could thus be defined as indigenous peoples' unique relationship with the universe around them.[23] Put another way, spirituality defines the relationships of indigenous peoples with their environment as custodians of the land; it helps construct social relationships, gives meaning, purpose and hope to life. It is not separated but is an integral, infused part of the whole in the indigenous worldview.[24]

> spirituality defines the relationships of indigenous peoples with their environment as custodians of the land; it helps construct social relationships, gives meaning, purpose and hope to life

Religion, from the Latin religare, meaning "to bind fast", has been defined as an institution with a recognized body of communicants who gather together regularly for worship and accept a set of doctrines offering some means of relating the individual to what is taken to be the ultimate nature of reality.[25]

Religion or belief systems have been a feature of cultures throughout human history. Belief systems are also integral to indigenous cultures. They often codify behavior; they also inspire and stimulate the development of artistic expressions, including different kinds of artifacts, paintings, songs, attires, music, dances, etc., used in rituals and sacred ceremonies. But foremost, they respond to human needs for reassurance in times of trouble and for averting misfortune; they also provide rituals that bring spiritual healing and address the major passages and transitions in human life. Hence, the preservation of indigenous communities and their cultures is tightly related to their spirituality and belief systems, which require that the earth, land and natural resources be preserved, and that harmonious relationships with other humans and other beings of the universe be maintained.

Indigenous spirituality and belief systems have often been dismissed as being mere expressions of superstitious and irrational thinking. They have in many cases been violently repressed or forbidden and are under constant assault from the large, dominant religions: Christianity, Islam, Hinduism, etc. In the face of strong pressures for social, cultural and religious assimilation, indigenous peoples have struggled hard to retain not only their lands and natural resources and their institutions and ways of life, but also their spirituality and belief systems. This struggle is on-going, although some advances have been made. These efforts are not necessarily a rejection of Western or world cultures, but rather an affirmation of their own cultures. Indigenous peoples continue

---

[23] Wilson (1999).
[24] Wilson (1999).
[25] See Reese (1980).

to explicitly and informally defend their worldviews as they not only want to survive as legal and political entities, but wish to do so within the spiritual and philosophical understandings of their forebears. In other words, indigenous peoples want to continue to be informed by indigenous peoples' worldviews, values and philosophies.[26]

Recognising the role of indigenous spirituality

For many indigenous people, having a healthy sense of spirituality is just as important as other aspects of mental, emotional and physical health. It is important to realize that a healthy spirit is essential for indigenous people to live a healthy life. Mainstream society is beginning to realize that spirituality is an element that must be taken into serious consideration when dealing with indigenous communities. The importance of integrating spirituality into health care, for instance, has been recognized by WHO. Other areas, for example, within rehabilitation and re-education of indigenous prison inmates, have also begun to accept that spirituality is an integral part of indigenous peoples and therefore an important issue that cannot be overlooked.

Sources: Wilson (1999); WHO (1998).

At the same time, however, indigenous peoples around the world are concerned about the on-going appropriation of their spirituality. In many countries, people who appropriate indigenous peoples' spirituality have a desire to (re)-spiritualize themselves (and possibly others) by using the sacred traditions of indigenous cultures. These people see indigenous cultures and spirituality as emphasising values that are missing from their own societies, such as environmental friendliness, solidarity and reciprocity. They also view indigenous societies as free from technology and industrialization. These attributes combine to create a fantasy of indigenous life.

Many indigenous peoples see the appropriation of their spirituality as a continuation of colonialism because it does not appreciate the political understandings that accompany and reinforce indigenous belief systems.[27] Important aspects that are often overlooked or not understood when appropriation takes place include, for example, the fact that spiritual leaders in indigenous communities have their own training and their own experiences; they have knowledge about aspects of spirituality and philosophical thought and often do not enter into disputes in their communities, nor do they seek disciples or converts. They also have, in general, a direct relationship with the sacred and keep their experiences and their knowledge to themselves. Indigenous peoples' spirituality and understandings, on the other hand, are imbued throughout life;

> [a healthy spirit is essential for indigenous people to live a healthy life]

---

[26] Champagne (2007), 328-329.
[27] Welch (2002).

their spirituality and beliefs are not static, but are socially constructed according to changing circumstances in the world or immediate environment and do not necessarily form a set of rules maintained and enforced by a religious hierarchy.[28] Hence, appropriation of indigenous peoples' spirituality is generally done without respect and tends to reinforce a fixed and static colonial understanding of indigenous peoples, thereby denying them the dynamism of cultural growth.

Social institutions

Social institutions determine the way people in a given society organize themselves in order to function as distinct communities, differentiated from others by specific rules, obligations and patterns of behaviour. Relationships to the land, social relationships, kinship rights and obligations constitute some of the social institutions that enable indigenous peoples to organize and relate to each other both as individuals and as sub-categories, such as men, women, youth or elders, or as occupational groups of hunters, herders, farmers, smiths, midwives, etc., and thereby meet their needs as communities.

Indigenous social institutions reflect indigenous peoples' unique and holistic worldviews, as well as their collective perspective, and this includes, for most of them, an interactive relationship between the community, nature and ancestors. Most of the activities of daily life are accompanied by rituals and cultural practices aimed at maintaining that relationship with, for example, the ancestors or nature. Cultural practices relating to ancestors are particularly important because of the reciprocity existing between living and deceased persons. The community depends on the goodwill and help of ancestors through dreams and spiritual paths, and the ancestors need to be honoured through appropriate ceremonies and maintenance of their burial places. Other cultural practices relate to nature and intend to maintain the relationship with the forces in nature on which their success as farmers, hunters or pastoralists will depend.[29]

Social institutions also determine relations of production, and whether those relations produce egalitarian or centralized polities. Most indigenous communities are organized around individuals who have specific roles, but the degree of specialization varies from culture to culture. In some cultures, anyone wishing to specialize in a particular task can do so, while this is not possible in others. Specialization can also be done through age or gender categories whereby women/youth/men/elders have prescribed roles within the society. This brings in the issue of sex and gender, whereby sex refers to the biological differences between male and female, while gender refers to the social classification of masculine and feminine, the attributes of which are defined and patterned by culture. In many societies, including most indigenous societies, women and men have well-differentiated roles, and women usually have a subordinate position in relation to that of men.

It is within social institutions that communities realize economic and political arrangements. In indigenous societies, there usually exists a wide range of social institutions for reciprocity and mutual aid,[30] sharing food and other resources, resolving conflicts and administering justice, and for managing commonly held resources. All indigenous communities traditionally also had people whom they respected and by whose suggestions they frequently chose to abide. These leaders had a significant say in civil matters and in decision-making regarding the use of local resources, and who represented the community in discussions with outsiders. Public policy was always based on extensive consultation and discussion among the group members, with all adults, and sometimes children, having the opportunity to participate. Decision-making was generally done on the basis of

---

[28] Champagne (2007), 330-331.
[29] Gomez (2007). See also Kenrick (2000).
[30] Schwab (1995); Martin (1995).

consensus. Upholding these social institutions—and thus the organization of the local community—was to adhere to a generally accepted system of customs and mores or customary law.[31]

Along with colonization and the spread of non-indigenous institutional structures, indigenous social institutions have largely been replaced and subordinated to the modern state structures. Centralized systems of governance are now the norm, and these have been replicated from the capital to the local level, leaving little power or influence to traditional leaders. Customary laws have been forbidden or subordinated to the formal mainstream legal system; social institutions related to family, education, health and economy have disappeared, changed in accordance with mainstream norms, or been weakened to the extent of losing their significance. The process of losing what has been called "the necessary frame of reference for any culture to thrive"[32] has left many indigenous societies severely disrupted culturally and socially—more so in cases where the process has been accompanied by the loss of land, territories and natural resources.

The weakening of their traditional institutions has challenged indigenous peoples' distinct identities. When indigenous peoples therefore claim the right to maintain their social organization in the face of the pressures of the wider society, they are actually appealing for the preservation of their culture.[33] This explains the importance given by indigenous organizations to the issue of self-government.

> culture should be integrated as a prerequisite and a basis for development project design in order to build 'development with identity', respecting people's way of life and building sustainable human development

In many countries, there has been a push for de-centralization of political power to create more consensus in decision-making and for indigenous peoples to be included in policy-making and legislative reforms on issues that affect them. In numerous instances, indigenous organizations have even been able, through negotiations and treaties, constitutional reform or special legislation, to establish agreements with states regarding this right to self-government. In other cases, however, this has not yet been possible, and national or regional-level governmental units still take it upon themselves to administer the affairs of indigenous communities. [34]

At the international level, on the other hand, the right of indigenous peoples to their own institutions has been enshrined in ILO Convention No. 169 (articles 2.2b and 8.2) and in the Declaration on the Rights of Indigenous Peoples, which, in Article 35, states

> "Indigenous peoples have the right to promote, develop and maintain their institutional structures and their distinctive customs, spirituality, traditions, procedures, practices and, in the cases they exist, juridical systems or customs, in accordance with international human rights standards."

---

[31] Stavenhagen (2005).
[32] Stavenhagen (2005).
[33] Stavenhagen (2005).
[34] Stavenhagen (2005).

As indigenous peoples have further strengthened their own systems, they have also given thought to what and how development should be pursued in their territories. There are various terms and concepts which they have evolved to differentiate their paradigm of development from the mainstream model. The ones currently being used are self-determined development, life projects, development with identity, autonomous development and ethno-development.[35] The Programme of Action for the Second International Decade of the World's Indigenous Peoples uses the term "Development with identity" when recommending "that culture should be integrated as a prerequisite and a basis for development project design in order to build 'development with identity', respecting people's way of life and building sustainable human development".[36]

Several funding agencies and development organizations are also acknowledging the importance of respecting indigenous institutions—not only because of their value for indigenous communities, but because they are now seen as a source of inspiration and a way of ensuring sustainable results.

Development with identity

A new paradigm within development—"Development with identity"—has recently been promoted by several UN agencies, including IFAD, Inter-American Development Bank (IDB) and UNESCO. In its Operational Policy on Indigenous Peoples and Strategy for Indigenous Development adopted in 2006, IDB defines "Development with identity" as referring "to a process that includes strengthening of indigenous peoples, harmony and sustained interaction with their environment, sound management of natural resources and territories, the creation and exercise of authority, and respect for the rights and values of indigenous peoples, including cultural, economic, social and institutional rights, in accordance with their own worldview and governance."

The challenge for the strategy lies in supporting and promoting development initiatives and organizational systems unique to indigenous peoples in order to improve their living conditions through their own leadership and in a manner consistent with each community's specific socio-cultural situation and vision. This means greater access, with gender equality, to socioeconomic development opportunities that strengthen identity, culture, territoriality, natural resources and social organization, and reduce material poverty and marginalization.

Source: IDB (2006).

Culture and traditional knowledge

Indigenous traditional knowledge refers to the complex bodies and systems of knowledge, know-how, practices and representations maintained and developed by indigenous peoples around the world, drawing on a wealth of experience and interaction with the natural environment and transmitted orally from one generation to the next.

Traditional knowledge tends to be collectively owned, whether taking the form of stories, songs, beliefs, customary laws and artwork or scientific, agricultural, technical and ecological knowledge and the skills to implement these technologies and knowledge. Not only does traditional knowledge provide indigenous

---

[35] Tauli-Corpuz (2008).
[36] See United Nations A/60/270 (2004).

peoples with tremendous possibilities for their daily life and sustainable and collective development as peoples, it also reflects indigenous peoples' holistic worldviews, which are considered as a most important source of the world's cultural and biological diversity.[37]

Indigenous knowledge is embedded in community practices, institutions, relationships and rituals and is inextricably linked to indigenous peoples' identity, their experiences with the natural environment and hence their territorial and cultural rights. Indigenous peoples therefore place a great deal of importance on passing this knowledge on to future generations—not only for the sake of preserving the knowledge, but also for preserving their own cultures and identities.

The transmission of traditional knowledge

Tom Mexsis Happynook belongs to what he calls a hereditary whaling family that comes from Cha-cha-tsi-us, which is part of the Huu-ay-aht First Nation on the west coast of Vancouver Island, British Columbia, Canada. He recalls the following:

> As a child, I was fortunate to be raised and taught by my grandfather, two great-grandmothers and two great-aunts. I am still being taught by my grandmother, who has turned 85. She was taught by her grandmother, who died in 1958 at the age of 108. I am still receiving the teachings from the mid-1800s.

> What did they teach me? I was taught that there is a natural law of nature which we must live by; that we are only one component in the web of life; that we are not dominant over the environment but, in fact, related; that we take only what we need and utilize all that we take; that everything is inter-connected, and when one component in the environment or ecosystem is over-exploited and not protected, the balance is lost.

Source: Happynook (2000), 64.

[
traditional knowledge tends to be collectively owned
]

Traditional knowledge is also directly linked to the concept of self-determination in the sense that indigenous peoples have the right to manage their own heritage, knowledge and biodiversity and, in order to do so, their rights to their territories and resources must be fully recognized and protected. In other words, "the right to self-determination requires that [indigenous peoples] must be able to freely dispose of their wealth and resources, and they must not be deprived of their means of subsistence".[38]

---

[37] SPFII (2005), 4.
[38] See, e.g., the UN Human Rights Committee Observations on Norway and Canada (1999).

Traditional knowledge among hunter-gatherers and pastoralists in Africa

Traditional knowledge and traditional resources have been managed by indigenous and local communities since time immemorial, using customary law embedded in spiritual cosmology. Such is the case of the Baka, Efe and Mbuti of Central Africa who spend long periods of time in the forest, hunting for meat, gathering plant foods and collecting honey. Everything they own has to be carried when they move to a new hunting camp, so there is considerable advantage in having few possessions. What they do have in abundance is an intimate knowledge of the forest: the ability to read animal tracks, to know the flowering and fruiting cycles of plants, to locate a bee's nest from the flight of a bee. They know the individual properties of thousands of plants and make use of them to eat, to make poisons, to dull pain, heal wounds and cure fever. Most of them engage in rituals which involve asserting their relationship with the forest and with the spirits of the forest. Song is central to these rituals, and may last all night with the intention of establishing a peaceful state of mind in everyone, establishing co-operation among the whole camp, and improving the hunt through re-establishing a good relationship with the forest.

Another example is that of the Maasai pastoralists from Kenya and Tanzania. For them, rainfall and drought are the most critical climatic features, as they have a significant impact on the productivity of their animals. The Maasai have a number of techniques for monitoring the onset of rains—the flowering of specific trees, the shape of the moon, special sounds from a bird, etc.—and for predicting water availability in their rangelands, looking, for example, for the presence of butterflies or certain trees. Maasai communities also assess both quality and quantity of grazing by observing plant vigour, biomass production, vegetation cover and botanical composition. They also have a wealth of indigenous knowledge in the diagnosis of animal diseases and the therapeutic nature of plants on which they depend for the everyday treatment of their animals. This indigenous knowledge has proven to be important in matters of wildlife and environmental management and conservation. Evidence in indigenous Kenya indicates that the Maasai peoples peacefully co-existed with wildlife, that there were more wild animals in their territory before national parks and game reserves were established in those areas, and that the way they managed rangelands was beneficial to the wildlife.

Sources: Kenrick (2000), 11-24; FAO/LINKS (2005).

A great deal of traditional knowledge, including customary laws and folklore, has been undermined and destroyed by colonizers and post-colonial states who imposed their own systems of law, knowledge and worldviews on indigenous people. Today, there is an increasing appreciation of the value and potential of traditional knowledge. International law, for instance, recognizes that such knowledge forms an integral part of indigenous cultures and, as a consequence, to deprive indigenous peoples of their traditional knowledge and folklore violates those peoples' human rights.[39] Besides the Declaration on the Rights of Indigenous Peoples, ILO Convention No. 169, for example, includes several provisions regarding the need to respect and protect "customs and traditions" as well as "handicrafts, rural and community-based industries and traditional activities".[40] Article 8(j) of the Convention on Biological Diversity (1992) is particularly clear in its language and provides that contracting Member Parties shall *"respect, preserve and maintain knowledge, innovations and practices of indigenous and local communities embodying traditional lifestyles relevant for the conservation and sustainable use of biological diversity and promote their wider application with the approval and involvement of the holders of such*

---

[39] Åhrén (2002), 66.
[40] See ILO Convention No.169, articles 2.2b and 23.1.

knowledge, innovations and practices and encourage the equitable sharing of the benefits arising from the utilization of such knowledge innovations and practices".

The Declaration on the Rights of Indigenous Peoples and traditional knowledge

Article 31

1. Indigenous peoples have the right to maintain, control, protect and develop their cultural heritage, traditional knowledge and traditional cultural expressions, including human and genetic resources, seeds, medicines, knowledge of the properties of fauna and flora, oral traditions, literatures, designs, sports and traditional games and visual and performing arts. They also have the right to maintain, control, protect and develop their intellectual property over such cultural heritage, traditional knowledge, and traditional cultural expressions.

2. In conjunction with indigenous peoples, States shall take effective measures to recognize and protect the exercise of these rights.

In 2002, UNESCO launched its Local and Indigenous Knowledge Systems (LINKS) Programme, which aims at empowering local and indigenous peoples in various aspects of environmental management by advocating recognition and mobilization of their unique knowledge. It also contributes to the safeguarding of traditional knowledge within indigenous communities by reinforcing their inter-generational transmission.

UNESCO has also adopted two conventions of relevance for indigenous cultures and traditional knowledge: the Convention for the Safeguarding of Intangible Cultural Heritage (2003), and the Convention on the Protection and Promotion of the Diversity of Cultural Expressions (2005). However, UNESCO has been criticized for having neither consulted nor included indigenous peoples in the drafting of the two conventions. Furthermore, neither convention adequately acknowledges the fact that a large part of the "cultural heritage" and "cultural expressions" they refer to is the heritage of indigenous peoples and indigenous cultures.[41]

[there is an increasing appreciation of the value and potential of traditional knowledge]

At the same time, researchers, scholars and development practitioners and other stakeholders are demanding changes in attitude and approaches on the part of governments and donor agencies, stressing the need to incorporate indigenous knowledge into development policies and projects—not only for its cultural value to indigenous communities, but because it is adapted to local

---

[41] See chapter VII "Emerging Issues" in this publication.

conditions and therefore more apt to give sustainable results. A case in point are indigenous agricultural practices, which reflect the store of experience and knowledge accumulated over literally thousands of years and are based on a sound understanding of soils, plants and the environment. This knowledge is revealed through various practices that are used in crop/plant diversity, mixed cropping, land fallowing, and others associated with soil and crop management. For centuries, farmers deliberately influenced the natural processes of mutation by carefully selecting seeds and, thanks to their sophisticated knowledge, developed an intricate range of crop variability. In many places, however, this knowledge was neglected and eventually lost when the Green Revolution was introduced in the late 1960s. This transfer of technology involved widespread use of new (hybrid) seeds, chemicals fertilizers, pesticides and irrigation. While it did increase food production, it is now evident that it also entailed lasting costs, such as high soil erosion and the loss of plant genetic materials that were resistant to pests and diseases.

The traditional knowledge of indigenous women

The traditional knowledge of indigenous women is often not recognized or is undervalued. However, examples from many indigenous communities worldwide show that women are the repositories of knowledge and know-how that are of vital importance for the survival of their community. One example among many is that of indigenous women in Nepal and Bhutan who are known to play a crucial role in decisions regarding what to plant and which seeds to use. In other seed-related activities, women also supersede men: They select good seeds for the next season, basing their decisions on taste, colour, resistance to diseases and insect pests and adaptation to soil and agro-climatic conditions, and preserve them with a variety of traditional methods. Indigenous women also exchange seeds, and in some ethnic groups, grandmothers and mothers pass seed selection skills on to their daughters. Their special knowledge of the value and diverse uses of plants for nutrition, food security, health, and income determines which plant varieties should be conserved based on their usefulness to the family and community. Women take into consideration a plant's multiple uses, providing a balance to the market-oriented pressures that emphasize high yields and uniformity.

Source: Gurung (1998).

It is also now emerging that indigenous peoples' overall health, well-being and cultural continuity is directly related to their ability to consume their traditional foods[42] and continue their traditional food practices.[43] This realization has led to calls to governments to incorporate culture into the development of sustainable agriculture, food systems and related practices, policies and programmes that respect and support the well-being of indigenous peoples.

Threats and challenges

While this increased recognition of the importance of indigenous cultures and indigenous traditional knowledge is a positive development, at the same time, indigenous peoples realize that they have to struggle ever more

---

[42] During the African Regional Conference on Indicators held in November 2006, it emerged that a main element of well-being is having access to traditional foods. See UNPFII (2007a).

[43] In February 2006, the International Indian Treaty Council submitted a framework and summary of key issues for the development of cultural indicators for food security and sustainable development in preparation for the Second Global Consultation on the Right to Food and Food Security for Indigenous Peoples. See International Indian Treaty Council (2006).

in order to protect their cultures and traditional knowledge from a number of threats and challenges.

Misappropriation of indigenous knowledge

There is an increasing appreciation amongst academics and scientists, as well as industrial and agricultural corporations, of the value of traditional knowledge. Entrepreneurs, too, have been quick to see the market potential, and many Western companies are patenting traditional medicines without granting due recognition to the indigenous communities whose knowledge systems went into identifying the active ingredients as useful for particular ailments.[44]

Traditional medicinal plants and prescription drugs

Researchers state that of the more than 130 clinically useful major prescription drugs that are derived from plants, over 70 per cent of them came to the attention of pharmaceutical companies because of their use in traditional systems of medicine. Examples include the medicinal properties of the sacred Ayahuasca plant (processed by indigenous communities in the Amazon basin for centuries), and a pesticidal extract from the neem tree used in India for its antiseptic properties since ancient times. They further noted that most of the plants from which these drugs are derived are found in tropical forests. Although tropical forests constitute only 7 per cent of the earth's surface, they contain an estimated two-thirds of its plant species.

A study in 2000 concluded that 7,000 patents had been granted for the unauthorized use of traditional knowledge or the misappropriation of medicinal plants.

Sources: Rossi (1980), 4; Human Development Report (2004).

[many Western companies are patenting traditional medicines without granting due recognition to the indigenous communities]

A growing number of widely used consumer products, pharmaceutical drugs, cosmetics and handicrafts are derived from traditional knowledge and indigenous cultural expressions. There are also high hopes for further advances based on traditional knowledge in the fields of biotechnology, medicine and agriculture.

For centuries, indigenous peoples have readily shared their knowledge with non-indigenous people, seeing their knowledge not as private property to be protected, but as collective goods to be shared for the benefit of all. However, in more recent times, as they have seen how their traditional knowledge is being

---

[44] See supra note 2, 4.

ever more used for profit, indigenous peoples increasingly demand that their traditional knowledge be protected and recognized.

The respect—or rather, the lack of respect—accorded to indigenous peoples in terms of their identity and cultural expressions is an ongoing issue. The idea that indigenous peoples "own" their own cultures as well as the spiritual and cultural meanings of their lives and surroundings is an issue that many institutions are reluctant to concede. Previously, indigenous peoples' knowledge systems and cultural expressions were seen as the property of academics, governments, scientists, museums and art galleries. For example, many indigenous sites are today considered to have cultural and scientific as well as aesthetic and public value and therefore the potential of becoming World Heritage sites that "belong to all the peoples of the world, irrespective of the territory on which they are located".[45] The connection and relationships between these sites and living indigenous communities who want to protect their cultural heritage and assert their custodianship is still an issue that the wider society finds difficult to understand and accept.

The impact of globalization

Cultures have never been static, constrained and homogeneous, even though this belief is still common throughout the world. Cultures do not have rigid borders. On the contrary, they are open to multiple influences, and changes are happening at an accelerated speed, with cultural information and people flowing more freely across borders than ever before.

The interaction between cultures is a complex process of negotiation. New ideas are confronted, contested, integrated or rejected within historical and cultural contexts. The telephone, internet and global media bring realities of life across the globe into people's living rooms, making them aware of the many products available for consumption.

For indigenous peoples, globalization is a mixed blessing. It both constitutes an unprecedented opportunity for empowerment and an unprecedented threat to the autonomy of their cultures.[46] Globalization has made it easier for indigenous peoples to organize, raise funds and network with other groups around the world. It has also made it possible to alert and mobilize the international community in times of crisis, raise awareness about human rights abuses and have greater political reach and impact than before.

Globalization has also meant easier access for multinationals to exploit the lands and natural resources on which indigenous peoples depend; it has opened up markets and found new ways of commoditifying indigenous cultures. Globalization makes indigenous cultures available to a wider audience and thus provides access to cultural practices to outsiders who consider that "public" property can be "borrowed" at will. At the same time, it has also allowed an influx of cheap manufactured goods that indigenous cottage industries and handicraft production find difficult to compete with.

Another major reason why indigenous peoples feel threatened by globalization is the way national governments and international institutions promote national growth through exploiting resources on indigenous peoples' lands while at the same time talking about protecting indigenous peoples' identities, traditions and cultural expressions. Indigenous peoples find that the two things are at odds and could potentially lead to a conflictive

---

[45] See World Heritage site at http://whc.unesco.org/en/about. See also Chapter I "Indigenous Peoples: Poverty and Well-being" in this publication.
[46] Smith et al. (2000).

situation. They believe that many issues are being overlooked, such as their spiritual connections to their lands and territories, their concerns for the impact on their cultural identity and economic livelihood, and their unfair exclusion from decision-making processes, including the process of free and informed prior consent and the lack of adequate compensation when the resources on the lands are exploited.[47]

For all these reasons, indigenous peoples tend to see globalization as a threat to their territories, their traditions and cultural expressions, their cultures and identities, compelling them to fight harder on a variety of fronts to ensure their cultural survival, as well as to find a new way to assert their rights and autonomy.[48]

Commodification of indigenous cultures

The commodification of indigenous cultures has taken on considerable dimensions with globalization. The exploitation of indigenous arts, designs, stories, performance and other art forms, as well as the proliferation of products on the market that imitate, misrepresent and profit from the alleged associations with indigenous cultures continue to be of major concern.

The use of indigenous peoples' names and images on sports mascots, commercial products, ventures or enterprises is an ongoing issue because it is most often designed to profit non-indigenous people. Further, the images are often derogatory, offensive and disrespectful to indigenous peoples. Owners of products explain their choice of mascot, name or logo by contending that their choice is motivated by a desire to show respect for indigenous peoples. However, it appears the real motive is profit, as there is little, if any, concern for the harm and suffering it has caused indigenous peoples. One example is the use of Native American names and mascots as symbols for college and school sports teams in the United States. Native American rituals, too, have been used for entertainment purposes at half-time during games. Native Americans have held protests for many years to eliminate the use of names and mascots from sporting teams, and in 1993, the National Congress of American Indians denounced "the use of any American Indian name or Artifice associated with Indian mascots" and called "upon all reasonable individuals in decision making positions to voluntarily change racist and dehumanising mascots".[49] Similar positions were expressed by the National Coalition on Racism in Sports and the Media, KOLA, the American Indian Movement and the Institute of American Indian Arts.

> indigenous peoples tend to see globalization as a threat to their territories, their traditions and cultural expressions, their cultures and identities

---

[47] Human Development Report (2004).
[48] Human Development Report (2004).
[49] See National Congress of American Indians (1993), Resolution MID-GB-93-58.

Governmental support for discontinuing the use of stereotypical American Indian images

In 2001, the United States Civil Rights Commission issued a statement that said, in part

The use of stereotypical images of Native Americans by educational institutions has the potential to create a racially hostile educational environment that may be intimidating to Indian students. American Indians have the lowest high school graduation rates. The perpetuation of harmful stereotypes may exacerbate these problems.[50]

Source: Wisconsin Indian Education Association "Indian" Mascot and Logo Taskforce at http://www.indianmascots.com

Stereotyping indigenous cultures as static "voices from the past" lies at the heart of cultural appropriation. The misuse of indigenous peoples' images, designs, music, etc., denies the complex realities of indigenous societies whereby rights to lands, stories, music and designs connects peoples to places and cannot be separated from indigenous peoples' identity. The selective borrowing of indigenous spiritual belief systems by outsiders is a corruption of the truths of indigenous peoples and their connection to their lands and to the laws that govern the use and transmission of their spiritual and cultural systems.

Tourism

As indigenous peoples and their cultures and territories are increasingly seen as desirable tourist attractions, tourism has opened the further commodification of indigenous cultures—something that affects many indigenous communities.

Tourism is undeniably an immensely important industry, with almost 900 million visitors generating US$856 billion in 2007. Understandably, governments have recognized tourism as an important opportunity for income generation.[51] But as a profit-driven industry, tourism tends to view landscapes and people as consumer products to be bought and sold. Particularly when imposed from outside the community, the negative impacts of tourism may include disrupted lifestyles and ecosystems, poorly distributed or inconsistent profits, the pressure to turn cultural traditions into products, greenwashing,[52] and unequal participation in the planning of projects dominated by foreign or government interests. Many critics have pointed out that the tourist industry is dominated by outsider interests, which retain most of the benefits and leave the host destinations to suffer the costs.[53]

The rise of ecotourism has particularly been promoted as a viable development model for indigenous peoples. Tourism, including ecotourism, is frequently not environmentally friendly. It takes vast amounts of fossil fuel to transport 900 million individuals to their destinations, and the expansion of tourism in the relatively pristine areas where indigenous peoples live brings a great deal of waste and disruption to local environments, economies and cultures. With ecotourism, indigenous peoples have experienced eviction from traditional lands, overuse of habitat related to increased tourist demand and the destruction of habitat to create tourism infrastructure.[54]

---

[50] Kraatz (n.d.).
[51] Hinch and Butler (1996). 4.
[52] Greenwashing is the unjustified appropriation of environmental virtue by a company, an industry, a government, a politician or even a non-governmental organization.—Ed.
[53] Hinch and Butler (1996), 4.
[54] Tourism Concern (2002).

In fact, the driving forces of ecotourism—clean untouched nature and authentic indigenous cultures—are often severely compromised by the influx of tourism.

Tourism has been both a contributor and a motivating force when it comes to exposure to and renewal of indigenous cultures. But like most other local populations, indigenous peoples frequently do not benefit from tourism-related activities, but they do bear the costs, which can and often are devastating, economically as well as culturally. The urge to see "real, genuine and authentic indigenous peoples" is a strong motive for many tourists. But this can be problematic, as the tourists may not be looking for in-depth exposure. Hence, the cultural practices and activities of indigenous peoples are often transformed into demonstrations, souvenirs and experiences for the consumption of the visitors. Indigenous heritage is reduced to trinkets and spectacles devoid of their original spiritual meaning and valued only as commodities to be sold. At the same time, traditional modes of sustenance are abandoned, leaving indigenous peoples dependent on outside visitors as a fickle and unreliable source of livelihood.

Indigenous peoples involved in the tourist industry and who incorporate cultural elements in their tourist products are constantly faced with the challenge of sharing their culture without compromising its integrity. This situation often results in indigenous peoples and their communities having to face difficult decisions and potential dissent. The issue of whether outsiders can participate in ceremonies and other spiritual activities, for example, varies from place to place. However, in most instances, indigenous elders are unequivocal in their belief that indigenous peoples' spirituality is not for sale, and that there is no place for spiritual ceremonies in tourism products.[55]

At the same time, tourism is not inherently negative for indigenous peoples and can certainly be an important source of revenue and job creation, provided that indigenous peoples themselves are directly involved in all decision-making processes regarding tourism on their lands. Over the past two decades, community-based approaches to tourism have gained popularity. This form of ecotourism is often presented as an important contribution to sustainable development that generates employment and revenues, improves local infrastructure and generally contributes to a positive interaction between visitor and local communities, thereby promoting increased cultural awareness and respect. In this context, it is crucial to adhere to the principle of free, prior and informed consent, ensuring that indigenous peoples are fully aware of planned tourism activities on their lands, that they themselves authorize and approve these activities and benefit from them.

> [the tourist industry is dominated by outsider interests, which retain most of the benefits and leave the host destinations to suffer the costs.]

---

[55] Notzke (2004).

Intellectual property rights and indigenous peoples

Many indigenous peoples feel they should be able to stop the commodification of some aspects of their culture, especially of objects that are sacred to their communities.

The dominant model for recognising and protecting knowledge and cultural expressions is the intellectual property rights regime. This regime, which is based on Western legal and economic parameters as well as on Western property law, emphasizes exclusivity and private ownership, reducing knowledge and cultural expressions to commodities that can be privately owned by an individual or a corporation. The intellectual property rights regime is widely recognized as the primary mechanism for determining ownership and property rights over knowledge, processes, innovations, inventions, and even naturally occurring phenomena such as plants, animals and genetic material. This form of ownership is protected by states and promoted by the World Trade Organization (WTO) and the World Intellectual Property Organization (WIPO).

The intellectual property rights (IPRs) regime and the worldview it is based on stand in stark contrast to indigenous worldviews, whereby knowledge is created and owned collectively, and the responsibility for the use and transfer of the knowledge is guided by traditional laws and customs.[56] What is often overlooked by the wider society is the fact that, within indigenous societies, there are already laws governing the use and transmission of their knowledge systems that often do not have any formal recognition in the wider legal system. These internal regimes have operated within indigenous communities since time immemorial and have been developed from repeated practices, which are monitored and enforced by the elders, spiritual and community leaders. The international property rights regime, however, often fails to recognize indigenous customary law.

There are therefore concerns that the IPRs regime, grounded in Western concepts of individualism and innovation, does not have the ability to protect the collective or perpetual interests of indigenous forms of cultural expression.

> The international property rights regime, however, often fails to recognize indigenous customary law

How indigenous peoples' rights to their knowledge differ from conventional IPRs

- ❖ Indigenous peoples have collective rights, often vested in clan, family or other socio-political groups

- ❖ Indigenous peoples' cultural heritage and expressions often cannot be associated with a single, identifiable individual creator, author or producer

---

[56] The United Nations Permanent Forum on Indigenous Issues, at its Fifth Session, appointed Mick Dodson, Member of the Forum, to prepare a study on customary laws pertaining to indigenous traditional knowledge. This study was presented to the Permanent Forum at its Sixth Session. See UNPFII (2007b).

> ◆ Cultural heritage, objects and expressions are managed and owned in accordance with customary rules and codes of practice, and are usually not sold or alienated in ways that conventional IPRs can be
>
> ◆ Indigenous rights include all forms of traditional knowledge, such as intangible cultural products and expressions, none of which are protected under conventional IPRs laws
>
> ◆ Indigenous peoples' knowledge is transmitted orally, and is therefore not subject to the same requirements regarding material forms that pertain to conventional IPRs laws
>
> ◆ Indigenous traditional knowledge is usually held by the owners and their descendents in perpetuity, rather than for a limited period
>
> *Source: Davis (1997).*

Yet, in many instances, indigenous peoples are compelled to turn to the (IPRs) regime to find ways to clarify and protect their rights. Some indigenous peoples, typically artists and craftsmen, have used IPR legal systems to achieve copyright protection for tangible arts and crafts objects such as wood carvings, silver jewellery and sculptures, or have used trademarks to identify traditional art, food products and clothing. But on the whole, indigenous traditional knowledge and folklore usually do not meet the criteria of novelty and originality generally required for work to be protected under IPRs legal systems. Intellectual property protection is of limited time duration and does not apply to "old" creations already in the public domain (i.e., the indigenous community); moreover, it is normally impossible to identify individual creators behind traditional knowledge.[57] The IPRs regime therefore leaves most indigenous traditional knowledge and folklore vulnerable to appropriation, privatization, monopolization and even biopiracy by outsiders.

The Hoodia case

A celebrated case regarding the appropriation of indigenous traditional knowledge involves the San of southern Africa. In 1937, an anthropologist noticed that the San ate the Hoodia cactus to stave off hunger and thirst. Based on this knowledge, in 1995, the South African Council for Scientific and Industrial Research (CSIR) patented the Hoodia cactus's appetite-suppressing element (P57). By 1998, revenues from the licensing fee for developing and marketing P57 as a slimming drug had risen to US$32 million. When the San alleged biopiracy and threatened legal action in 2002, the CSIR agreed to share future royalties with the San.

Source: Human Rights Report 2004.

This has prompted organizations such as WIPO to identify the needs and expectations of traditional knowledge holders and explore current and future possibilities of protecting traditional knowledge (TK), genetic resources (GR) and traditional cultural expressions (TCEs), or folklore.

In 2000, an Intergovernmental Committee (IGC) on Intellectual Property, TK, GR and TCEs was established. Indigenous representatives participate in its meetings,[58] and the IGC is currently considering the protection

---

[57] Åhrén (2002), 65.
[58] WIPO created, in 2005, a fund that supports the participation of indigenous representatives.

of TK and TCEs through several related and complementary processes, including a draft set of Objectives and Principles.[59]

Indigenous peoples have emphasized that such protection must ensure that their heritage is safeguarded for the use of future generations, and that it is not to be misappropriated or commercialized "without the free, prior and informed consent of the custodians of the culture, knowledge and biodiversity."[60] Indigenous peoples also feel that there are still arguments for a new legal regime specifically designed for indigenous peoples enabling them to protect and benefit from their cultural expressions and traditional knowledge, and that support should be given to develop systems and standards that allow them to fully negotiate terms in relation to the commercial use of their cultural expressions.[61]

The issue, then, is to find ways to reconcile the provisions of different international intellectual property regimes in order to protect traditional knowledge for the benefit of the indigenous community and promote its appropriate use within wider society.

Concluding Remarks

All over the world, there are clashes between state and indigenous peoples' cultures and systems of livelihood (pastoralism, hunting and gathering, and shifting cultivation). It is a clash between the desire of many indigenous peoples to live on traditional lands, and the general thrust of government policies aimed at using indigenous peoples' lands for other purposes. Whether this is the establishment of natural reserves or mega-projects such as hydro-electric dams or infrastructure development, indigenous peoples are frequently portrayed as an obstacle to national development plans.

Governments and developers have employed the dominant development paradigms to manufacture stereotypes that are negative and that depict indigenous peoples as "backward", "uncivilized" and "uncultured". While the Western culture and way of life is presented as modern and "civilized", that of the indigenous peoples is depicted as an embarrassment to modern states. As a result, indigenous peoples have been discriminated against and marginalized by the processes of economic modernization and development.

Although indigenous peoples are often portrayed as a hindrance to development, their cultures and traditional knowledge are also increasingly seen as assets. It is argued that it is important for the human species as a whole to preserve as wide a range of cultural diversity as possible, and that the protection of indigenous cultures is vital to this enterprise. The twenty-first century is already witnessing growing recognition of the right of indigenous peoples to decide for themselves what should happen to their ancient cultures and their ancestral lands.

In recent years, the world has become more aware of the role of indigenous cultures in development processes. Many United Nations agencies and countless civil society organizations continue to make the case for the central role that indigenous peoples play in the preservation of cultural diversity. For development to be socially and economically sustainable, it must take into account and draw upon the values, traditions and cultures of the people in the countries and societies it serves. Indigenous peoples, perhaps more than any others, are aware of these relationships between culture and development.[62]

---

[59] Åhrén (2002); Traditional Knowledge Bulletin (2008).
[60] Tauli Corpuz (2005).
[61] Janke (1999).
[62] Supra note 2, p.4

Such campaigns are bringing influence to bear on policy makers, development practitioners and the public, who have become increasingly aware of the important role that indigenous peoples' traditional knowledge systems (TKS) can play in promoting sustainable development in the economic and spatial spheres they occupy.[63]

However, much remains to be seen in the practical world of development because indigenous peoples' cultures have not yet had the desired influence on development institutions, which are located far from the often remote areas in which indigenous people live.[64]

In the face of increasing losses through globalization, discrimination or pressures to assimilate, there is also evidence indicating the resurgence of indigenous cultures, knowledge and languages. The increasing number of people acknowledging their indigenous status is contributing to the increased numbers and expansion of indigenous peoples and to the recovery of languages and indigenous knowledge systems. Efforts are being made toward recovering some of the endangered languages and cultures. This change is largely attributed to an increased knowledge of indigenous cultures and their potential. It is now an established fact that indigenous peoples' cultures are self-sustaining and can guarantee indigenous peoples a sense of well-being.[65]

This resurgence is particularly evident at the international level, where the global indigenous movement grows ever stronger while indigenous peoples' organizations keep growing in size and sophistication. The indigenous peoples' movement has made significant strides in fighting for the recognition and protection of the collective rights of indigenous peoples, as highlighted by the adoption of the United Nations Declaration on the Rights of Indigenous Peoples on the part of the United Nations General Assembly in 2007, and indigenous peoples are increasingly present and visible at various international fora. These new achievements are heralding a new era in promoting the protection and development of indigenous cultures around the world.

---

[63] Supra note 2, p.4
[64] Supra note 2, p.4
[65] Peterson (1996).

List of references

Aboriginal Law Bulletin. 1993. Mabo – "The High Court Decision on Native Title" Extracts from the Commonwealth Government's Discussion Paper – June 1993 Available online at http://www.austlii.edu.au/au/journals/AboriginalLB/1993/18.html#Heading3

Agreements, Treaties and Negotiated Settlements Project. 2007. Alexkor Limited v. The Richtersveld Community and Others Case CCT10/03. Available online at http://www.atns.net.au/agreement.asp?EntityID=3895

Åhrén, Mattias. 2002. "An introduction to the WIPO Intergovernmental Committee on Intellectual Property, Genetic Resources, Traditional Knowledge and Expressions of Folklore". Indigenous Affairs, International Processes: Perspectives and Challenges, 1/02:64-70. Copenhagen: IWGIA. Available online at http://www.iwgia.org

Anaya, James & Claudio Grossman. 2002. The Case of Awas Tingni v. Nicaragua: A New Step in the International Law of Indigenous Peoples. Arizona Journal of International and Comparative Law. Vol. 19, No.1.

Bello, Alvaro. 2007. "Indigenous migration in Chile: trends and processes". Indigenous Affairs, Migration, 3/07: 6-17. Copenhagen: IWGIA. Available online at http://www.iwgia.org

Brody, Hugh. 2000. "Taking their words from their mouths". Indigenous Affairs, Hunters and Gatherers, 2/2000: 4-9. Copenhagen: IWGIA. Available online at http://www.iwgia.org

Champagne, Duane. 2007. Social Change and Cultural Continuity among Native Nations. Lanham, New York; Toronto; Plymouth, UK: Altamira Press.

Current Law Journal. 2005. Kerajaan Negeri Selangor & others v. Sagong Tasi & others. CLJ Bulletin 39/2005 Available online at http://www.cljlaw.com/public/cotw-051007.htm

Daes, Erika-Irene. 1995. Draft principles and guidelines for the protection of the heritage of indigenous peoples. Elaborated by the Special Rapporteur for the Sub-Commission on the Promotion and Protection of Human Rights. UN Doc. E/CN.4/Sub.2/1995/26, Annex.

Davis, Michael. 1997. Indigenous Peoples and Intellectual Property Rights. Research Paper No. 20, 1996-97. Canberra: Information and Research Services, Department of the Parliamentary Library.

FAO/LINKS. 2005. The Utilization of Indigenous Knowledge in Range Management and Forage Plants for Improving Livestock Productivity and Food Security in the Maasai and Barbaig Communities (Nelson Kilongozi, Zabron Kengera, Samwel Leshongo). Available online at http://www.fao.org/sd/LINKS/documents_download/Nelson_41.pdf

Friedl, J. and Pfeiffer, J.E.. 1977. Anthropology, New York: Harper's College Press.

Gomez, Nieves. 2007. "Healing Hidden Wounds", Cultural Survival Quarterly, Issue 31.3, October 2007.

Gurung, Jeannette. 1998. Gender Dimensions of Biodiversity Management: Cases from Bhutan and Nepal. Newsletter No. 31 Biodiversity Management in the Hindu Kush-Himalayas. International Centre for Integrated Mountain Development (ICIMOD)

Happynook, Tom Mexsis. 2000. "Indigenous whalers and traditional resource management knowledge". Indigenous Affairs, Hunters and Gatherers, 2/2000: 64-71. Copenhagen: IWGIA. Available online at http://www.iwgia.org

Hinch, Thomas and Richard Butler, eds. 1996. Tourism and Indigenous Peoples. Toronto: International Thomsen Business Press.

Human Development Report. 2004. Chapter V "Globalization and Cultural Choice". Washington, D.C.: UNDP.

Inter-American Development Bank (IDB). 2006. Operational Policy on Indigenous Peoples and Strategy for Indigenous Development Operational Policy on Indigenous Peoples. Washington, D.C.: IDB. Available online at http://idbdocs.iadb.org/wsdocs/getdocument.aspx?docnum=1442299

International Indian Treaty Council. 2006. "Cultural Indicators for Food Security, Food Sovereignty and Sustainable Development". Paper prepared for the Second Global Consultation on the Right to Food and Food Security for Indigenous Peoples, Bilwi (Nicaragua), 7-9 September 2006. Available online at http://www.treatycouncil.org/new_page_52412242132.htm

International Labour Organization (ILO). 1989. ILO Convention concerning Indigenous and Tribal Peoples in Independent Countries (No. 169). Available online at http://www.ilo.org/ilolex/english/index.htm

International Work Group on Indigenous Affairs (IWGIA). 2004. Indigenous Affairs 4/04. Copenhagen: IWGIA.

Janke, Terri. 1999. Our Culture, Our Future. A Report on Australian Indigenous Cultural and Intellectual Property Rights.

Kenrick, Justin. 2000. "The Forest Peoples of Africa in the 21st Century". Indigenous Affairs, Hunters and Gatherers, 2/2000: 10-24. Copenhagen: IWGIA. Available online at http://www.iwgia.org

Kraatz, Chris. n.d. "The Truth about American Indian Mascots". Available online at http://www.aics.org/mascot/truth.html

Martin, D. 1995. "Money, business and culture: issues for Aboriginal economic policy", CAEPR Discussion Paper No. 101. Canberra: Centre for Aboriginal Economic Policy Research, the Australian National University.

Martínez Cobo, José. 1986/7. "Study of the Problem of Discrimination against Indigenous Populations". UN Doc. E/CN.4/Sub.2/1986/7 and Add. 1-4. Available online at http://www.un.org/esa/socdev/unpfii/en/second.html

National Congress of American Indians. 1993. Resolution MID-GB 93-58: Denouncement of the Use of any American Indian Name or Artifice Associated with Team Mascots by any Professional/Non-professional Sport Teams. Available online at http://www.aistm.org/ncai1993.htm

Notzke, Claudia. 2004. "Indigenous Tourism Development in Southern Alberta, Canada: Tentative Engagement", Journal of Sustainable Tourism, Vol.12, No. 1. Available online at http://www.multilingual-matters.net/jost/012/0029/jost0120029.pdf

Peterson, N. 1996. "Cultural issues", in The 1994 National Aboriginal and Torres Strait Islander Survey: Findings and Future Prospects, ed. J.C. Altman and J. Taylor. CAEPR Research Monograph No. 11, Centre for Aboriginal Economic Policy Research. Canberra: The Australian National University.

Reese, William L. 1980. Dictionary of Philosophy and Religion: Eastern and Western Thought. Atlantic Highlands, N.J.: Humanities Press

Rossi, I., ed. 1980. People in Culture: A Survey of Cultural Anthropology. New York: Praeger.

Schwab, R.G. 1995. "The calculus of reciprocity: principles and implications of Aboriginal sharing", CAEPR Discussion Paper No. 100, Centre for Aboriginal Economic Policy Research. Canberra: The Australian National University.

Skutnabb Kangas, Tove. 2000. Linguistic Genocide in Education – or worldwide diversity and human rights? Mahwah, N.J.: Lawrence Erlbaum Associates.

Smith, Claire, Burke, Heather and Ward, Graeme K.. 2000. "Globalisation and Indigenous Peoples: Threat or Empowerment?" In Indigenous Cultures in an Interconnected World, ed. Graeme Ward and Claire Smith. St Leonards, N.S.W.: Allen & Unwin.

Secretariat of the Permanent Forum on Indigenous Issues (UNPFII). 2005. Background note prepared by the Secretariat of the Permanent Forum for the International Workshop on Traditional Knowledge, Panama City, 21-23 September 2005. Doc. PFII/2005/WS.TK. Available online at

http://www.un.org/esa/socdev/unpfii/documents/workshop_TK_background_note.pdf

South African Legal Information Institute. 2006. Sesana and Others v Attorney General (52/2002) [2006] BWHC 1 (13 December 2006) Available online at http://www.saflii.org/bw/cases/BWHC/2006/1.html

Stavenhagen, Rodolfo. 2005. Indigenous Peoples: An Essay on Land, Territory, Autonomy and Self-Determination. Available online at Land Research Action Network (LRAN) website http://www.landaction.org

Tauli-Corpuz, Victoria. 2005. Biodiversity, Traditional Knowledge and Rights of Indigenous Peoples. IPRs Series No. 5. Presented at the International Workshop on Traditional Knowledge, Panama City, 21-23 September 2005. Available online at http://www.un.org/esa/socdev/unpfii/documents/workshop_TK_taulicorpuz.pdf

Tauli-Corpuz, Victoria. 2008. "Indigenous peoples' concept of development with culture and identity". Paper presented at the UNESCO/IASG/UNPFII round-table discussion on "Indigenous Peoples: Development with Culture and Identity" held in Paris 15 September, 2008.

Tourism Concern. 2002. "Why Tourism Concern is cautious about the International Year of Ecotourism." Press release 25.01.2002. Available online at http://tourismconcern.org.uk

Traditional Knowledge Bulletin. 2008. Available online at http://tkbulletin.wordpress.com

Tylor, E.B. 1924 [orig. 1871]. Primitive Culture. Researches into the Development of Mythology, Philosophy, Religion, Language, Art and Custom. 2 vols. 7th ed. New York: Brentano's.

UNESCO. 2003. "Language Vitality and Endangerment." Document submitted by Ad Hoc Expert Group on Endangered Languages to the International Expert Meeting on UNESCO Programme Safeguarding of Endangered Languages, UNESCO Paris, 10–12 March 2003.

UNESCO. 2008. Background paper for "Thematic Debate: Protection Indigenous and Endangered Languages and the Role of Languages in promoting EFA in the Context of Sustainable Development" prepared for the 180th session of the Executive Board. Doc. 180 EX/INF.8.

United Nations Human Rights Committee (CCPR). 1999. Concluding Observations of the Human Rights Committee, Norway, U.N. Doc. CCPR/C/79/Add.112/1999.

United Nations Human Rights Committee (CCPR). 1999. Concluding Observations of the Human Rights Committee, Canada, UN Doc. CCPR7797Add.105/1999.

United Nations Organization. 2004. Draft Programme of Action for the Second Decade. UN Doc. A/60/270. Available at UNPFII website http://www.un.org/esa/socdev/unpfii

United Nations Permanent Forum on Indigenous Issues (UNPFII). 2007a. Report of the African Regional Expert Working Group on Indicators of Wellbeing and Indigenous Peoples. Presented at the Sixth Session of the UNPFII. UN Doc. E/C.19/2007/CRP.3.

United Nations Permanent Forum on Indigenous Issues (UNPFII). 2007b. Report of the Secretariat on Indigenous Traditional Knowledge. Presented at the Sixth Session of the UNPFII. UN Doc. E/C.19/2007/10.

United Nations Permanent Forum on Indigenous Issues (UNPFII). 2007c. Report on the Sixth Session. UN Doc. E/2007/43.

United Nations Permanent Forum on Indigenous Issues (UNPFII). 2008. Report of the International Expert Group Meeting on Indigenous Languages presented at the Seventh Session of the UNPFII UN Doc. E/C.19/2008/3.

University of Saskatchewan online library. 2008. Calder v. Attorney-General of British Columbia. Available online at http://library2.usask.ca/native/cnlc/vol07/091.html

Welch, Christina. 2002. "Appropriating the Didjeridu and the Sweat Lodge: New Age Baddies and Indigenous Victims?" Journal of Contemporary Religion, Vol.17, No.1, 2002.

Wesley-Esquimaux, Cynthia C. 2007. "The intergenerational transmission of historic trauma and grief". Indigenous Affairs, Social Suffering, 4/2007: 6-11. Copenhagen: IWGIA. Available online at http://www.iwgia.org

Wilson, Shawn. 1999. "Recognizing the importance of spirituality in indigenous learning". Available online at http://www.acea.org.au/Content/1999%20papers/Shaun%20Wilson%20%20paper.pdf

Working Group on Indigenous Populations (WGIP). 1996. Working Paper by the Chairperson-Rapporteur, Mrs. Erica-Irene A. Daes, on the concept of "indigenous people". UN Doc. E/CN.4/Sub.2/AC.4/1996/2 10 June, 1996.

World gathering of nomadic & transhumant pastoralists. 2007. Pastoralism, Genetic Erosion and Biodiversity. Available online at http://www.nomadassegovia2007.org/documentosDescarga/Appendix%202.pdf

World Health Organization (WHO). 1998. Review of the Constitution of the World Health Organization: Report of the Executive Board special group. WHO Doc. EB101.R2, 22 January 1998.

Young, Elspeth. 2000. "Harvesting from 'country': contemporary indigenous subsistence in Australia's native title era". Indigenous Affairs, Hunters and Gatherers, 2/2000: 56-63. Copenhagen: IWGIA. Available online at http://www.iwgia.org

CHAPTER III

ENVIRONMENT

By Neva Collings

*Western science may have invented the words "nature", "biodiversity" and "sustainability",
but it certainly did not initiate the concepts. Indigenous, traditional and local communities
have sustainably utilized and conserved a vast diversity of plants, animals and ecosystems
since the dawn of homo-sapiens. Furthermore, human beings have molded environments
through their conscious and unconscious activities for millennia – to the extent that it is often
impossible to separate nature from culture.*

Source: Posey (1999), 7.

Introduction

Throughout the world, there are approximately 370 million indigenous peoples occupying 20 per cent of the earth's territory. It is also estimated that they represent as many as 5,000 different indigenous cultures, and the indigenous peoples of the world therefore account for most of the world's cultural diversity, even though they constitute a numerical minority.[1] The areas they inhabit often coincide with areas of high biological diversity, and a strong correlation between areas of high biological diversity and areas of high cultural diversity has been established.[2]

Indigenous peoples have always identified themselves by the importance of the bond with their lands and their distinct cultures.[3] Indigenous peoples share a spiritual, cultural, social and economic relationship with their traditional lands, and their customary laws, customs and practices reflect both an attachment to land and a responsibility for preserving traditional lands for use by future generations.[4] A critical issue for indigenous peoples around the world is therefore access to, as well as the protection and preservation of, their lands and territories and the natural resources pertaining to these lands.

Although indigenous peoples have demonstrated that their close relationship with the environment also makes them its best guardians, the strong environmental movement that emerged after World War II made no reference to indigenous peoples, and for a long time, efforts focused more on how nature could be protected from damaging interventions by human activities[5] than on what impact environmental degradation had on human beings.

Thus, it was first in 1972, with the UN Conference on the Human Environment,[6] that "the protection and improvement of the human environment" was seen as a major issue "which affects the well-being of peoples...."[7] Conference documents, however, made no mention of indigenous peoples and their critical situation, and it was to take

---

[1] Gray (1991), 8.
[2] See, e.g., WWF-International and Terralingua (2000).
[3] Gray (1991), 8.
[4] OHCHR (2008).
[5] IUCN (International Union for Conservation of Nature and Natural Resources) was founded in 1948 as an organization dedicated to natural resource conservation; WWF (standing, at that time, for World Wildlife Fund), was established in 1961 for the conservation, research and restoration of the natural environment.
[6] Also known as the Stockholm Conference. One of the outcomes of this conference was the decision to create an environmental agency - the United Nations Environment Programme (UNEP).
[7] See Declaration of the Conference on the Human Environment at http://www.unep.org

15 years and the Brundtland report on sustainable development (1987)[8] before indigenous peoples were mentioned in an environmental document.

The real breakthrough occurred during the 1992 United Nations Conference on Environment and Development (UNCED, often called the Earth Summit), when indigenous peoples were included as a "major group" that their specific relationship with the environment was recognized and some of their concerns taken into consideration. This was, among other things, the result of efforts made by the international indigenous movement prior to the Earth Summit. The indigenous movement had by then gained strength and recognition within the UN system, notably with the creation of the Working Group on Indigenous Populations (1982) and the adoption of ILO Convention No. 169 (1989).

UNCED was therefore seen as an opportunity to inform the international community about the environmental issues indigenous peoples were facing and how their traditional ecological knowledge and practices could contribute to resolving the global environmental problems.

Indigenous peoples prepared for UNCED as thoroughly and extensively as any state. Prior to the Earth Summit, indigenous peoples held their own summit at Kari Oca, near Rio de Janeiro, to develop their own Declaration and Charter on sustainable development. The Kari Oca Summit was instrumental in formulating the basic documents for indigenous peoples on issues related to sustainable development at a global level and for influencing the official and civil society summits.

> this Declaration recognizes in its preamble that "respect for indigenous knowledge, cultures and traditional practices contributes to sustainable and equitable development and proper management of the environment

All these efforts were reflected in some of the documents that came out of the Summit, including the Convention on Biological Diversity. Since then, indigenous concerns, knowledge and expertise have been taken increasingly into account by the numerous international initiatives related to the environment and by the ensuing documents and policies. Indigenous peoples have also gained some recognition from a number of large environmental organizations such as WWF and IUCN,[9] which have taken this step to work with indigenous peoples in their conservation activities.

At the same time, the inherent rights of indigenous peoples to their lands and resources and to their full and effective participation in decisions relating to their lands, resources and livelihoods have been reflected in a number of

---

[8] See Our Common Future (also known as the Brundtland Report), Report of the World Commission on Environment and Development (1987).

[9] In 1996, WWF (now standing for World Wide Fund for Nature) issued a Statement of Principles on Indigenous Peoples and Conservation, intended to guide partnerships between WWF and indigenous peoples' organizations in conserving biodiversity within indigenous peoples' lands and territories and in promoting sustainable use of natural resources. This statement was last updated in 2008. The IUCN's World Conservation Congress has passed several resolutions on indigenous peoples (e.g. in 1996) in relation to issues such as protected areas, traditional biodiversity knowledge, forests, marine and coastal areas, and mining.

international documents and mechanisms, most recently in the UN Declaration on the Rights of Indigenous Peoples, adopted by the General Assembly in 2007. This Declaration recognizes in its preamble that "respect for indigenous knowledge, cultures and traditional practices contributes to sustainable and equitable development and proper management of the environment", and although it does not create any new rights, it responds to the urgent need to respect and promote indigenous peoples' right to self-determination and thereby, among other things, their inherent rights in relation to political, economic, social, cultural, spiritual as well as environmental and natural resource management[10].

Inherent rights of indigenous peoples

The right of self-determination established in the UN Declaration on the Rights of Indigenous Peoples essentially implies the following inherent rights of indigenous peoples in relation to natural resource management:

◈ to their ancestral land, territories and resources, as a collective and individual right;

◈ to exercise control and management of their right to lands, territories and resources;

◈ to self-government by their own institutions and authorities within their lands and territories;

◈ to self-development (meaning the right to their own decision-making on conservation and development options for their lands, territories and resources);

◈ to fair and equitable benefit sharing from conservation and development actions involving their lands, territories, resources, and people;

◈ to conserve, develop, use and protect their traditional knowledge.

These remarkable advances do not mean, however, that the struggle of indigenous peoples for their rights and concerns when it comes to lands and natural resources is over. At the international level, indigenous peoples' voices are still often marginalized, and vital indigenous interests not taken into consideration at the moment of formulating policies. But it is at the national and local levels that indigenous peoples face the most overwhelming challenges in protecting their environmental rights from structural discrimination, corporate interests, globalization, etc., and in adapting their livelihoods to climate changes.

This chapter examines a number of issues on the topic of indigenous peoples and the environment. After identifying some of the environmental problems confronting indigenous peoples, the chapter looks at the existing international law and mechanisms for environmental protection and how indigenous peoples make use of these instruments. It finally identifies some of the implementation gaps and challenges indigenous peoples still face in the struggle for their environmental rights.

---

[10] Joffe (2008), 2.2.

Major issues

The environmental challenges faced by indigenous peoples today are manifold. The dispossession of lands and natural resources and the impact of large-scale development projects are issues that indigenous peoples have confronted for decades, if not centuries. In addition, there is a range of new challenges that have to do with science-based technology and development in general, such as genetic resources, biopiracy and intellectual property rights, as well as the environmental problems faced by the increasing number of indigenous peoples living in urban areas. And, finally, there is the global challenge of climate change, which will have a great impact on most indigenous peoples, since they often live in physically isolated, fragile and harsh environments which may be "especially vulnerable to climate change due to their latitude, topography, distance from the sea, soils quality, etc."[11]

Common to all these challenges is their close connection with indigenous peoples' rights to land and their lack of self-determination.

Land dispossession

Dispossession of traditional lands and territories is one of the major problems faced by indigenous peoples all over the world. This process has been going on for centuries, first as a result of the intrusion of colonial systems and the ever-growing search for rich agricultural areas and natural wealth; today, as a result of development policies and globalization.

> indigenous peoples feel that many development policies are either directly or indirectly geared toward weakening or eradicating their traditional modes of production

In many regions, the experience of indigenous peoples has been "that inadequate legal frameworks resulted in disruption to their traditional land tenure and use patterns, fragmentation and loss of traditional land, changes in settlement patterns, privatization of communal lands, degradation of land and/or resources, lack of recognition of territorial rights, insufficient and inequitable land allocation, lack of effective mechanisms for conflict resolution, inefficient official land registers, and difficult procedures for land demarcation and titling. These factors have generated local tensions over land tenure and lack of access to productive lands, which impact on the economic and socio-cultural stability of indigenous peoples and their communities."[12] Only a few countries recognize indigenous peoples' land rights, but even in those countries, land titling and demarcation procedures have often not been completed, suffer delays or are shelved because of changes in political leadership and policies. The right to natural resources, on the other hand, is usually restricted, especially when it comes to sub-soil resources. Even where indigenous peoples have legal title deeds to their lands, these lands are often leased out by the state as mining or logging concessions without consultation of indigenous peoples, let alone

---

[11] Macchi (2008), 21.
[12] Working Group on Article 8J (2007d).

their free and prior informed consent. The lack of legal security of tenure remains a crucial issue for indigenous peoples almost everywhere.

In many countries, dominating development paradigms undermine the modes of production of indigenous peoples, such as hunting and gathering, pastoralism and shifting agriculture, which are often perceived as primitive, non-productive and not in line with the modernization aspirations of present-day states. Indigenous peoples feel that many development policies are either directly or indirectly geared toward weakening or eradicating their traditional modes of production.[13] The promotion of new technologies such as improved seeds, chemical fertilizers and pesticides, etc., the introduction of cash-crop cultivation and large plantation schemes have caused environmental degradation and destroyed self-sustaining eco-systems, affecting many indigenous communities to the point of forcing them to resettle elsewhere.

A general trend of promoting individual land ownership at the expense of collective land rights is another threat to indigenous communities. This results in the privatization of land and resources and, more seriously, in land being sold to non-indigenous individuals and business interests—ultimately leaving the landless indigenous people with few options other than to take up menial jobs or migrate to urban areas.[14]

Land privatization in Kenya

Since the end of the 1960s, the Government of Kenya, supported by the World Bank, has promoted the transformation of Trust Lands into group ranches and then individual ownership, thus limiting the land available for traditional transhumant grazing, which forms the basis of indigenous pastoralists' livelihood. Based on the idea that individual titles, through a "willing buyer-willing seller" approach, would improve the prospects for investment and economic growth, this policy in fact encouraged land grabbing and the massive sale of pastoralist land, particularly in areas neighbouring urban centres.

Source: Stavenhagen (2007), Para 29.

Large-scale development projects

Economic policies, promoted by international agencies and triggered by free-trade agreements and globalization, have resulted in a proliferation of large-scale development projects on indigenous lands and territories.

Such projects cover a wide array of activities: the large-scale exploitation of natural resources, including subsoil resources; the establishment of plantations and industrial plants; tourist developments; and the construction of ports, transportation networks, multipurpose dams, military bases or toxic waste dumps.[15]

Evidence shows that indigenous peoples bear the costs of the resource-intensive projects disproportionately, and the human rights effects include loss of traditional territories and land, eviction, migration and eventual resettlement, depletion of resources necessary for physical and cultural survival, destruction and pollution of the traditional environment, social and community disorganization, long-term negative health and nutritional impacts as well as, in some cases, harassment and violence.[16]

---

[13] "Indigenous Peoples and Land Rights" at http://www.iwgia.org/sw231.asp
[14] See, e.g., Stavenhagen (2004).
[15] Stavenhagen (2003), 5.
[16] Stavenhagen (2004), 5.

Large-scale developments and displacements of indigenous peoples

The Bakun Dam in Malaysia is reported to have caused the forced displacement of 5,000-8,000 indigenous persons from 15 communities by clear-cutting 80,000 hectares of rainforest. Indigenous peoples in Manipur, India, were reported to have suffered a similar fate caused by the building of 25 hydroelectric dams. Thousands of families of the Santhal Adivasi people in Jharkhand province of India have reportedly been displaced as a result of extraction of minerals, without proper compensation or economic security. In Thailand, several highland communities, including the Karen people, have reportedly been moved out of national parks against their will, while tourist development in Hawaii has resulted in the displacement of indigenous people and their increasing poverty.

Asian indigenous representatives informed the Working Group on Indigenous Populations (WGIP) at its eighteenth session in 2000 that "conflict and development interventions had resulted in large-scale displacements, internal and external, and serious consequences for [indigenous] children and youth resulting from the implementation of inappropriate and non-consultative development projects".

Source: Stavenhagen (2003), Para. 22

economic policies, promoted by international agencies and triggered by free-trade agreements and globalization, ave resulted in a proliferation of large-scale development projects on indigenous lands and territories

The forest issue

The example of indigenous forest-dwellers is illustrative. For many indigenous peoples, the forest plays an essential part in ensuring their physical, cultural, spiritual and economic well-being by giving them access to secure means of subsistence, medicinal plants and the ability to practice their customs. However, all this is in severe jeopardy as their forest refuge is increasingly being degraded, destroyed or placed off-limits.

Logging is the most prominent cause of deforestation, but agri-business, large-scale infrastructure projects such as hydroelectric dams and gas and oil pipelines, oil exploration and mining operations are also taking their toll.

Oil palm plantations in Indonesia

Indonesia is experiencing the biggest rate of increase in terms of forests converted into oil palm plantations. In a period of 30 years (1967-1997) oil palm plantations have increased 20 times with 12 per cent average annual increases in crude palm oil (CPO) production. From 106,000 hectares in 1960 this has increased to 6 million hectares, although there were around 18 million hectares of forests cleared purportedly for oil palm in 2006. It

> appears that loggers used oil palm plantations as a justification to harvest the timber. The government announced new plans under the Kalimantan Border Oil Palm Mega-Project (April 2006) to convert an additional 3 million hectares in Borneo, of which 2 million will be on the border between Kalimantan and Malaysia. It is understood that the area deemed suitable for oil palm includes forests used by thousands of people who depend on them for their livelihoods.
>
> *Source: Tauli-Corpuz and Tamang (2007), Para. 20.*

According to latest estimates, the net forest loss over the period 2000-2005 was 7.5 million ha of forest per year.[17] In order to counter this development and save the last large forest systems, efforts have been made over the past few decades to establish national parks, game reserves and other forms of protected areas.

But whether logging, large-scale development schemes or conservation are being considered, indigenous peoples have, for the most part, paid a high price. As the plants and wildlife disappear along with the trees, the subsistence base of forest-dwellers disappears too, and forces them to abandon their traditional ways of life based on hunting and gathering. The same happens when their forests are turned into protected areas and they are no longer allowed to reside there or gain access to the forest's natural resources. Whether evicted, involuntarily displaced or forced to find their subsistence elsewhere, these indigenous peoples become landless squatters living on the fringes of settled society. They receive no compensation or other reparation for their losses, and in order to survive, they are forced to farm the lands of others in arrangements that are often functionally equivalent to bonded labour. Many of them eventually end up in urban slums.

The case of the Twa "Pygmies" of Democratic Republic of Congo

The expulsion of the Twa from the Kahuzi-Biega forest (later to become a gorilla reserve) has deprived them of their sources of meat, honey and wild tubers from the forest. Their traditional relationships with non-Twa farmers, which involved exchanges of meat, honey, medicines, etc., were disrupted. They can no longer obtain the plants that used to serve them as medicine for curing illnesses.... Most of their religious activities and rites, for example the initiation of males, which can be performed only in the forest, have become impossible because of their new environment. For the Twa, nothing can substitute or compensate for the loss of the forest, as no other environment can provide them with the same spiritual and material benefits.

Source: Barume (2000), 81.

The experience of most indigenous peoples is that national forest policies and legislation have generally been designed without, or with very little, input and involvement from them. Very few countries have included considerations regarding forest-related traditional knowledge in their forest policies. There are critical problems of an overlap of logging concessions with traditional territories, as well as problems of illegal logging on indigenous peoples' lands.[18] In other instances, indigenous peoples have been arrested and jailed for carrying out customary activities on lands that were declared conservation forest.[19]

---

[17] Tauli-Corpuz and Tamang (2007), para.20.
[18] Working Group on Article 8J (2007g),15.
[19] Working Group on Article 8J (2007c), 37.

Illegal logging

Illegal logging has become a growing problem in the world's rainforests. Recent estimates for Peru suggest that 90 per cent of the timber being extracted in the Peruvian Amazon is illegal and originates from protected areas belonging to indigenous communities or set aside for indigenous peoples who live in voluntary isolation. Apart from the environmental destruction such illegal logging causes, it also puts these isolated people at risk of contracting contagious diseases if contacted by loggers.

Source: Stavenhagen (2004), 9-10.

Protected areas—a story of evictions and abuses

The creation of protected areas has been a central element of conservation policies since the end of the nineteenth century. Between 1872, when Yellowstone National Park was established in the United States, and the early 1960s, some 10,000 protected areas were created. In 2003, the total number of protected areas stood at 102,102, covering more than 18.8 million square kilometres.[20] It should moreover be noted that there is a growing number of privately owned protected areas across the world.

From their inception, most protected areas were designed as areas of land taken over by the state, without the consent and the consideration of indigenous peoples and their land use patterns, and primarily for the enjoyment of outsiders.[21] Applying the so-called Yellowstone model, which consisted of establishing and managing national parks for the benefit of future generations, but to the exclusion of indigenous residents, national parks in many parts of the world have denied indigenous peoples their rights, evicted them from their homelands, and provoked long-term social conflict. This model of "colonial conservation" caused, and continues to cause, widespread human suffering and resentment among indigenous peoples.[22]

Today, a new model of conservation can also be discerned based on respect for the rights of indigenous peoples and their traditional knowledge. "Protected area" has become a cover term and includes many different categories with varying purposes ranging from scientific research to tourism and recreation. In the late 1980s and early 1990s, for instance, a new trend promoting community-based conservation and community-based natural resource management emerged as a way of integrating conservation and development and securing the livelihoods

> national parks in many parts of the world have denied indigenous peoples their rights, evicted them from their homelands, and provoked long-term social conflict

---

[20] See UNEP-World Conservation Monitoring Centre at http://www.unep-wcmc.org/protected_areas/UN_list/index.htm
[21] Borgerhoff Mulder and Coppolillo (2005).
[22] Colchester (2004).

of indigenous peoples.[23] And today, there is some acceptance that conservation can and must be achieved in collaboration with indigenous peoples and based on respect for their internationally recognized rights.

In a number of Latin American countries, where the total size of protected areas has nearly doubled over the past 10 years, there is some progress at the national level in terms of recognising the role of indigenous peoples in the conservation of biodiversity and protected areas management.[24] A number of indigenous communal reserves or indigenous protected areas have been established, for instance, in Peru and Brazil, and the participation of indigenous peoples in the management of other types of protected areas has increased. Nevertheless, co-management of protected areas is still limited, and difficult relationships have often been reported to exist between indigenous communities and the management of protected areas. This has been attributed to limitations imposed on the use of resources in the protected areas and to a lack of formal recognition of land and resource rights within such areas.[25]

In Australia, the Indigenous Protected Area Programme commenced in 1997 with the development of the first Indigenous Protected Area at Nantawarrina, in South Australia.[26] There are now approximately 23 declared Indigenous Protected Areas covering close to 17 million ha, or 23 per cent of Australia's National Reserve System. Indigenous Protected Areas (IPAs) are voluntary agreements entered into by the Traditional Owners of the land and the Commonwealth government. The primary objectives of IPAs are to promote biodiversity and cultural resource conservation on indigenous-owned land.

However, protected areas on the ground often still continue to be imposed according to the colonial model, calling into question the extent to which there is a real commitment to giving conservation a human face.[27] In some countries in Africa, for instance, the authorities responsible for the national parks and protected areas have often displaced indigenous communities, expropriated their lands and denied them access to the natural resources critical for their livelihoods and survival.[28] In Tanzania and Kenya, for example, the expulsions of Maasai from their ancestral territories, which started during the colonial era, are continuing today. The creation of the national parks of Manyara, Tarangire, Ngorongoro, Serengeti and Mkomazi in Tanzania, and of Amboseli, Maasai Mara and others in Kenya, has each time led to the eviction of indigenous Maasai from their ancestral land without compensation—supposedly in the national interest.[29]

Another disconcerting development is that the discussion of "natural" alliances between conservationists and indigenous peoples and the need to work closely also seem on the wane among the big conservationist NGOs, who appear once more to be focussing on large-scale conservation strategies in which science matters more than social realities.[30]

While there is a lack of overall statistics as to how many indigenous peoples have been evicted and displaced to make way for large-scale projects—whether agricultural schemes, infrastructural development, natural resource extraction or protected areas—the consequences of these impositions of development on indigenous peoples' livelihoods have been better documented, and common experiences include:

---

[23] See, e.g., Hitchcock (2001), 38-49.
[24] Valente (2007).
[25] Working Group on Article 8J (2007d), 12.
[26] Commonwealth of Australia (2007).
[27] Colchester (2004).
[28] Nairobi Declaration (2004).
[29] Working Group on Article 8J, (2007a)
[30] Chapin (2004), 20. See also Dowie (2005).

1. Landlessness (expropriation of land assets and loss of access to land)
2. Joblessness (even when the resettlement creates some temporary jobs)
3. Homelessness (loss of physical houses, family homes and cultural space)
4. Marginalization (social, psychological and economic downward mobility)
5. Food insecurity (malnourishment, etc.)
6. Increased morbidity and mortality
7. Loss of access to common property (forests, water, wasteland, cultural sites)
8. Social disarticulation (disempowerment, disruption to social institutions)[31]

It should be added that forced evictions and the dispossession of lands have particularly severe impacts on indigenous women, who, as a result, often have an increased workload as they must walk long distances to find alternative sources of water or fuel wood, or are driven out of income-earning productive activities and into a situation of economic dependence on men.[32]

When indigenous peoples have reacted and tried to assert their rights, they have suffered physical abuse, imprisonment, torture and even death.

Indigenous protests result in human rights abuses

Indigenous peoples in Penan (Malaysia) have reportedly been arrested because they were blockading roads, trying to stop loggers destroying their traditional forests. Philippine indigenous peoples have allegedly been physically abused and detained by mining companies and the police in the process of peaceful picketing against mining activities on their traditional lands. Sometimes, the strict enforcement of environmental conservation laws prevents indigenous farmers, hunters, fishermen or gatherers from using their traditional land or resources, thus turning them into offenders who may be jailed for attempting to subsist. According to a recent report, oil workers in the Upper Pakiria River region of South-eastern Peru forced the Kugapakori to move deep into the Amazon and threatened to arrest and decimate the community with diseases if they refused to leave their home.

Source: Stavenhagen (2004), 9.

Being deprived of their traditional lands and natural resources has, however, also had other consequences. One has been a loss of traditional knowledge and cultural diversity; another, the impoverishment of thousands of indigenous peoples and their migration to urban areas.

Indigenous traditional knowledge – erosion, loss and threats

The bond between nature and the culture of indigenous peoples is manifested in traditional knowledge, which forms the basis of their spiritual growth and reflects their intimate connection with the land. Until recently, conservation policies and practices failed to fully understand and appreciate the rights and roles of indigenous peoples in the management, use and conservation of biodiversity.[33] Today, however, indigenous peoples' traditional knowledge

---

[31] Cernea (2005).
[32] UN-Habitat and OHCHR (2005), xix.
[33] IUCN (2008).

and practices, which were formerly undervalued and ignored, are considered important and necessary contributions to the conservation of biodiversity. Yet this knowledge is under severe threat of being eroded, lost or misappropriated.

Dispossession or forced removal from traditional lands and sacred sites has eroded the relationship between indigenous peoples and their environment. Without access to their land and natural resources, people can no longer carry out their cultural activities or use and develop their traditional knowledge. When forced to migrate and resettle in new environments, indigenous peoples find that their traditional knowledge and practices have to be adapted to new and often difficult circumstances. This has put the cultural diversity and traditional knowledge of indigenous peoples under tremendous pressure.

> indigenous peoples' traditional knowledge and practices, which were formerly undervalued and ignored, are considered important and necessary contributions to the conservation of biodiversity

Traditional knowledge may also sometimes be lost as the result of language extinction. In one century, the world has lost around 600 languages. At current rates, 90 per cent of all languages will be lost in the twenty-first century—most spoken by indigenous and traditional peoples.[34] Since the traditional knowledge accumulated by indigenous peoples is contained in languages that often have no script, this knowledge is passed on to other groups and new generations orally, making it difficult to retrieve once a language becomes extinct. The survival and vitality of indigenous languages is therefore a key to maintaining traditional knowledge. [35]

Poverty is another threat to traditional knowledge. Poverty will often drive the users of bio-diverse environments to over-exploit the resources in their territories to the point of no return in terms of sustainability. It is often the case that when people are poor, conservation is not a high priority, and they will take out of the environment whatever is needed for their survival. As noted in a regional report on threats to traditional knowledge, "even if people have knowledge about sustainable harvesting regimes, when they are poor, this knowledge is ignored".[36] Livelihood diversification must therefore be a key consideration in the process of addressing people's livelihoods and its link to the preservation of traditional knowledge systems recognized.[37]

A more recent threat that is raising growing concern is the misappropriation of indigenous knowledge in the form of biopiracy. It has been stated that "developments in science-based technologies, especially biotechnology and genetic engineering, have broadened the economic utility of natural resources and increased the economic value of biodiversity".[38] As indigenous communities often inhabit areas with the highest biodiversity, "they are coming under increasing pressure from biodiversity prospectors and corporations interested

---

[34] UNHCHR (2008).
[35] Working Group on Article 8J (2007j), para. 42.
[36] Working Group on Article 8J (2007a) para. 54.
[37] Working Group on Article 8J (200ja), para. 54.
[38] Simpson (1997), 50-51.

in privatising and commercialising aspects of their biological knowledge".[39] Furthermore, "in recent decades, developed countries have expanded intellectual property rights to include biological material and 'new' life forms, such as new plant varieties, transgenic animals and human genetic diversity, thereby raising serious ethical questions about ownership and the environmental impacts of these 'new' life forms. In many instances, the knowledge and biological resources that are collected and 'developed' in the laboratories of developed countries are derived from indigenous peoples and their territories".[40] Needless to say, few indigenous peoples have ever received any kind of benefit from these technological developments.

Climate change and indigenous peoples

Assessments of climate change[41] have consistently reported and confirmed that the Earth's climate is changing. According to the most recent reports of the United Nations Intergovernmental Panel on Climate Change (IPCC), there is unequivocal evidence that the Earth's climate is warming and that this is most likely due to anthropogenic (human-induced) greenhouse gas emissions (GHG).[42] Human activity has undermined the ecological integrity of the Earth by using the atmosphere as a dumping ground for GHGs.

The greenhouse effect

Climate change is a negative response currently experienced in the world as a result of the growth of greenhouse gas emissions due to the burning of fossil fuels, mainly for industrial activities and motor transportation. As a result of this "smoke" from cars and machines, carbon dioxide gas is built up in the air and increases the level of heat in the world. This phenomenon is known in as the "greenhouse effect".

Source: Laltaika (2008).

Since the mid-nineteenth century, annual global temperatures have increased by approximately 0.74 per cent.[43] Temperatures are predicted to rise further and indigenous peoples in some regions will be more severely affected than others.[44]

The impact of these temperature changes includes:

◈ diminishing polar sea ice and rising of sea levels, threatening low-lying coastal areas, notably many small islands in the Pacific;

◈ greater exposure to natural disasters, such as floods, and to frequent and intense extreme weather events;

---

[39] Simpson (1997), 50-51.

[40] Simpson (1997), 50-51.

[41] Climate change is defined as a variation either in the mean state of the climate or in its variability, persisting for an extended period, typically decades or longer. It encompasses temperature increases, sea-level rises, changes in precipitation patterns and increases in the frequency of extreme weather events.

[42] Greenhouse gases that are covered by the Kyoto Protocol include carbon dioxide (CO_2), nitrous oxide, methane, sulphur hexachloride, HFCs (hydrofluorocarbons) and PFCs (perfluorocarbons).

[43] IPCC (2007a).

[44] Whilst the IPCC predicts the Earth's air temperatures will increase by 2.0 to 4.5 degrees by the end of the century, predicted temperatures in the Arctic are projected to rise 5 to 7 degrees in the same period. See IPCC (2007a).

◈ degradation of wetlands due to changing freeze-thaw cycles;

◈ glacial melts in high-altitude regions and subsequent inundations of valleys and hill areas;

◈ increased fires in tropical rainforests;

◈ changes in precipitation and desertification.

Despite having contributed the least to GHG, indigenous peoples are the ones most at risk from the consequences of climate change because of their dependence upon and close relationship with the environment and its resources.[45] Although climate change is regionally specific and will be significant for indigenous peoples in many different ways, indigenous peoples in general are expected to be disproportionately affected. Indigenous communities already affected by other stresses (such as, for example, the aftermath of resettlement processes), are considered especially vulnerable.[46]

Some of the consequences of climate change can already be felt, and indigenous peoples across the world have experienced changes in:

◈ the migratory pattern of fish, birds and mammals;

◈ the timing of many life-cycle events, such as blooming, migration and insect emergence;

◈ the population size of certain plants and animals;

◈ the availability of water resources;

◈ the availability of grazing areas, the size of crop yields, etc.

These changes or even losses in the biodiversity of their environment will adversely affect or disrupt:

◈ the traditional hunting, fishing and herding practices of indigenous peoples, not only in the Arctic, but also in other parts of the world;

◈ the livelihood of pastoralists worldwide;

◈ the traditional agricultural activities of indigenous peoples living in mountainous regions;

◈ the cultural and ritual practices that are not only related to specific species or specific annual cycles, but also to specific places and spiritual sites, etc.;

◈ the health of indigenous communities (vector-borne diseases, hunger, etc.);

◈ the revenues from tourism.

The Arctic has been called "the world's climate change barometer" and indigenous peoples "the mercury in that barometer"—especially vulnerable to the impacts of climate change.[47] As noted by the IPCC Fourth Assessment

---

[45] Nilsson (2008), 9.
[46] IPCC (2007b), 11.
[47] IPCC (2007b), 56.

Report, the resilience of indigenous populations is being severely challenged when combined with demographic, socio-economic and lifestyle changes.[48]

The Arctic region is predicted to lose whole ecosystems, which will have implications for the use, protection and management of wildlife, fisheries, and forests, affecting the customary uses of culturally and economically important species and resources. Arctic indigenous communities—as well as First Nations communities in Canada[49]—are already experiencing a decline in traditional food sources, such as ringed seal and caribou, which are mainstays of their traditional diet. Some communities are being forced to relocate because the thawing permafrost is damaging the road and building infrastructure. Throughout the region, travel is becoming dangerous and more expensive as a consequence of thinning sea ice, unpredictable freezing and thawing of rivers and lakes, and the delay in opening winter roads (roads that can be used only when the land is frozen).[50]

Changes in animal populations have also had an impact, and some indigenous communities are observing new species moving into their territories ("climate refugees") as well as a decline in both the health and number of existing species that are staple foods and also have traditional economic value.[51] The resources available to indigenous peoples to counter these threats are limited.

In Africa, climate change projections indicate that some areas may become drier, whereas others may become wetter. Nomadic indigenous pastoralist communities in sub-Saharan and Eastern Africa, who live mainly in semi-arid lands, have started experiencing frequent droughts that are destroying vegetation and livestock. Climate change will also have significant implications in the use of the traditional knowledge, innovations and practices of African indigenous communities. Thus, it is important that climate change adaptation and mitigation measures of change take into consideration the traditional knowledge, innovations and practices of African indigenous communities.[52]

In the Pacific region, indigenous peoples live in sensitive zones where the effects of climate change-induced rising sea levels and coast erosion are most devastating. The challenges faced are a loss of territories, forced migration from low-lying islands and relocation of these migrants to other indigenous peoples' traditional territories. Such relocations of indigenous "environmental refugee" communities are already taking place and are having, and will continue to have, a number of adverse social, spiritual, cultural and economic implications for the affected communities.[53]

> the Arctic region is predicted to lose whole ecosystems, which will have implications for the use, protection and management of wildlife, fisheries, and forests, affecting the customary uses of culturally and economically important species and resources

---

[48] IPCC (2007b), 63.
[49] Working Group on Article 8J (2007e) .
[50] IPCC (2007b).
[51] Centre for Indigenous Environmental Resources (2007), 16.
[52] Working Group on Article 8J (2007a), 39.
[53] UNEP/CBD/WG8J/4/4 (2005).

Climate change impacts on a Pacific island

Lateu is one of the northernmost islands of the Vanuatu archipelago that is particularly vulnerable to the effects of climate change. The increasing frequency of spring tide events, tidal waves and cyclones, together with sea-level rise, has led to coastal erosion and created permanent flooding or standing pools of water. Over the past 20 years, the coastline has eroded 50 metres. In August 2005, the residents living in Lateu were forced to relocate to higher ground 600 metres from the coast to a new settlement named Lirak.

Source: Working Group on Article 8J (2007i) and SCBD (2006).

International treaties, laws and declarations related to environmental protection

Over the past decades, a growing international awareness of the degradation and destruction of the global environment, the loss of biodiversity and the foreseen impact of climate change has generated a plethora of international laws and mechanisms addressing environmental protection and related issues.[54]

At the same time, however, the current treaty-based framework of international environmental law is seen to be poorly equipped to accommodate indigenous peoples as non-state players with rights equivalent to states within the area of international environmental law.[55] International law is built on the Westphalian premise of state sovereignty. This is reiterated throughout international treaties, such as the Convention on Biological Diversity, which reaffirms that "states have sovereign rights over their own biological resources". On the international and domestic stages, the challenge for indigenous peoples is to assert their sovereign rights as peoples to natural resources, decisions concerning resources, and the way in which states engage with them.

> the challenge for indigenous peoples is to assert their sovereign rights as peoples to natural resources, decisions concerning resources, and the way in which states engage with them

Indigenous peoples are not only affected by these instruments, they have also been able to play an important part both in the processes that have led up to the formulation of conference declarations and documents and to the establishment of related mechanisms, as well as in the follow-up processes.

---

[54] Regarding environmental protection, there exist almost 60 legally binding agreements encompassing a wide variety of issue-areas, from nature conservation and terrestrial living resources to atmospheric pollution, hazardous substances and nuclear safety.
[55] L. Westra Environmental Justice and the Rights of Indigenous Peoples: International and Domestic Legal Perspectives (2008) EarthscanPress, UK at p. 9 citing Metcalf (2004)

International law and indigenous land rights

Environmental protection cannot be discussed from an indigenous perspective without first looking at indigenous peoples' rights to lands and territories and the natural resources pertaining to these lands, and the international treaties dealing with these rights.

ILO Convention Nos. 107 and No. 169

The first international treaty to specifically deal with indigenous rights was ILO (International Labour Organization) Convention No. 107 Concerning the Protection and Integration of Indigenous and other Tribal and Semi-Tribal Populations in Independent Countries, adopted in 1959. This Convention recognized the indigenous peoples' right, among other things, of ownership, collective or individual, of the lands they traditionally occupy (Article 11).

Criticized for its assimilationist approach, Convention No. 107 was replaced in 1989 by Convention No. 169 Concerning Indigenous and Tribal Peoples in Independent Countries. This Convention also recognizes indigenous peoples' land rights, defining territory as including "the total environment of the areas which the peoples concerned occupy or otherwise use".[56] It establishes their right to "the natural resources pertaining to their lands, including the right to participate in the use, management and conservation of these resources".[57] Article 15.2 specifically provides rights to fair consultation, participation in the benefits, and compensation for any damages sustained as a result of exploration and exploitation of sub-surface resources. It also establishes their right to be consulted and to freely participate at all levels of decision-making "in bodies responsible for policies and programmes which concern them",[58] and to control their own institutions, ways of life and economic development.

The United Nations Declaration on the Rights of Indigenous Peoples also provides new international guidelines, such as the right to develop strategies for the development or use of indigenous peoples' lands and resources. Going beyond ILO 169 on this matter, the Declaration affirms that states not only have to consult indigenous peoples about projects that affect them, but have "to obtain their free and informed consent" prior to the projects' approval, particularly in connection with the development, use or exploitation of mineral, water or other resources.

The Earth Summit (1992)

As already mentioned, the 1992 Rio Conference on Environment and Development (UNCED), commonly referred to as the Earth Summit, was a turning point for indigenous peoples. Not only were they recognized as a "major group" of civil society but, for the first time, they were able to participate in and influence processes relating to the environment.

UNCED led to the adoption of some of the most important treaties on the environment, namely, the 1992 Convention on Biological Diversity and the 1992 United Nations Framework Convention on Climate Change. In addition, several non-binding documents were adopted: the Declaration on Environment and Development—known as the Rio Declaration; Agenda 21; and the non-legal, non-binding Forest Principles. Most of these documents contain provisions on indigenous concerns.

---

[56] ILO Convention No. 169, Article 13.2
[57] ILO Convention No. 169, Articles 14.1 and 15.1.
[58] ILO Convention No. 169, Article 6.1.

The Rio Declaration, Agenda 21 and the Convention on Biological Diversity all recognize the unique relationship indigenous peoples[59] have with their traditional lands and establish international legal standards that go toward protecting indigenous peoples' rights to their traditional knowledge and practices in the area of environmental management and conservation.

Agenda 21 and indigenous peoples' role in sustainable development

Agenda 21 is perhaps the most ambitious document to have come out of the UNCED process. A 300-page plan for achieving sustainable development in the twenty-first century, it is divided into four sections, 40 chapters and more than 100 programmes, and it covers all areas of the world in which environment and development intersect and major social groups are affected. The third section, "Strengthening the Role of Major Groups", gives extensive and formal recognition to indigenous peoples and recommends the incorporation of indigenous peoples' rights and responsibilities into national legislation. Agenda 21 recognizes that, with respect to indigenous peoples, "[t]heir ability to participate fully in sustainable development practices on their lands has tended to be limited as a result of factors of an economic, social and historical nature. In view of the interrelationship between the natural environment and its sustainable development and the cultural, social, economic and physical well-being of indigenous people, national and international efforts to implement environmentally sound and sustainable development should recognize, accommodate, promote and strengthen the role of indigenous people and their communities".

Source: Agenda 21 (1992), chapter 26.1.

The Convention on Biological Diversity

The objectives of the UN Convention on Biological Diversity (CBD) "are the conservation of biological diversity, the sustainable use of its components and the fair and equitable sharing of the benefits arising out of the utilization of genetic resources...."[60] In its preamble, the Convention recognizes "the close and traditional dependence of indigenous and local communities" on biological diversity, and, in Article 8 on In-situ Conservation, which mainly deals with the establishment of protected areas,[61] paragraph (j) recommends that a Party shall,

> subject to its national legislation, respect, preserve and maintain knowledge, innovations and practices of indigenous and local communities embodying traditional lifestyles relevant for the conservation and sustainable use of biological diversity and promote their wider application with the approval and involvement of the holders of such knowledge, innovations and practices and encourage the equitable sharing of the benefits arising from the utilization of such knowledge, innovations and practices.[62]

Other relevant articles are Article 10(c) on customary sustainable use and Article 15 on access and sharing of the benefits arising out of the utilization of genetic resources.

---

[59] It should be noted that these documents do not refer to "indigenous peoples" but to "indigenous people and their communities" or "indigenous and local communities".

[60] Convention on Biological Diversity (1992), Article 1.

[61] CBD, Article 8 reads: "Each contracting party shall... (a) establish a system of protected areas or areas where special measures need to be taken to conserve biological diversity".

[62] CBD, Article 8(j).

With 191 Parties,[63] the CBD is one of the most widely adopted international agreements in history and is proving to be a relatively effective forum for indigenous and local communities to seek recognition of their rights.

UN Framework Convention on Climate Change

The United Nations Framework Convention on Climate Change (UNFCCC) adopted in 1992 is aimed at stabilising greenhouse gas concentrations in the atmosphere at a level that would prevent dangerous anthropogenic interference with the climate system. The text of the Convention does not explicitly discuss indigenous peoples in relation to climate change, although Article 4 is interpreted as describing the urgency that various social groups are facing in relation to climate change. Further, developed countries are urged to support social groups living in developing countries through the transfer of knowledge and technology in order to strengthen their resilience to the adverse effects of climate change on their livelihoods.[64]

Since 1988, indigenous peoples have been participating at UNFCCC Conferences of the Parties (COP) and have released a number of statements and declarations expressing concerns on the implications of climate change policies on their livelihoods and cultures. Since 2001, indigenous peoples' organizations have been acknowledged as a constituency in climate change negotiations within the UNFCCC. At the same time, however, indigenous peoples are still waiting for the approval of an ad hoc Working Group on Indigenous Peoples and Climate Change by the UNFCCC, allowing them to actively participate in the meetings of the Conference of Parties. [65]

With no mandatory limits on GHG for individual nations and no enforcement provisions, the Convention is considered legally non-binding. However, it includes provisions for updates or "protocols" that can set mandatory emission limits. The Kyoto Protocol, adopted in 1997, thus commits ratifying countries to reduce their emissions of carbon dioxide and five other greenhouse gases. As with the UNFCCC, the Kyoto Protocol does not mention indigenous communities.

The Forest Principles

The Statement of Principles for the sustainable management of forests is also non-legally binding. However, it has paved the way for a number of mechanisms, and Principle 12(d) recommends recognising, respecting, recording, developing and, as appropriate, introducing in the implementation of programmes "indigenous capacity and local knowledge regarding the conservation and sustainable development of forests". It further states that "benefits arising from the utilization of indigenous knowledge should therefore be equitably shared with such people".

The United Nations World Summit on Sustainable Development (WSSD)

As stipulated in the Rio Declaration, a first assessment of Agenda 21 was made in 1997. This assessment concluded that, despite some positive developments, many of the trends and problems that faced leaders in Rio remained unabated or had worsened. In 2002, a second summit was convened in Johannesburg, South Africa, where the international indigenous movement participated actively.

Assembled in Kimberley (South Africa), 20-24 August 2002, more than 300 indigenous peoples' leaders and organizations from all over the world attended the Indigenous Peoples' International Summit on Sustainable

---

[63] These 191 Parties include 190 states and the European Union. 168 states signed the Convention in 1992.
[64] Macchi (2008), 11.
[65] Ibid, p. 12

Development. Two documents were adopted at the Summit: the "Kimberley Political Declaration", which highlighted, among other things, the fact that the commitments made to indigenous peoples in Agenda 21, including their full and effective participation, had not been implemented because of a lack of political will, and the Plan of Implementation on Sustainable Development. This Plan sets forth commitments and visions addressing the future role of indigenous peoples in working toward a sustainable future and insists that sustainability on a global scale cannot be achieved if governments and corporations continue to ignore the rights and unique capabilities of indigenous communities.

From the Kimberley Political Declaration, 2002

We continue to pursue the commitments made at the Earth Summit as reflected in this political declaration and the accompanying plan of action. The commitments which were made to Indigenous Peoples in Agenda 21, including our full and effective participation, have not been implemented due to the lack of political will....

As peoples, we reaffirm our rights to self-determination and to own, control and manage our ancestral lands and territories, waters and other resources....

We have the right to determine and establish priorities and strategies for our self-development and for the use of our lands, territories and other resources. We demand that free, prior and informed consent must be the principle of approving or rejecting any project or activity affecting our lands, territories and other resources.

Source: For the full text of the Kimberley Political Declaration , see IWGIA Web site at http://www.iwgia.org/sw217.asp

---

The Kimberley summit was able to contribute substantially to the WSSD. A major achievement was to get the sentence "We reaffirm the vital role of indigenous peoples in sustainable development" incorporated into the official Political Declaration as Paragraph 25. This meant that for the first time ever, the United Nations had accepted the term "indigenous peoples", with an "s", signifying its acceptance of indigenous peoples as peoples and not just as individuals.

The Johannesburg Plan of Implementation also reflects indigenous peoples' concerns.[66] It reaffirms the potential of indigenous peoples to be "stewards" of national and global natural resources and biodiversity, their important role in sustainable development, and the value of their traditional knowledge and practices in a variety of areas (forest and agricultural management systems, medicine, biodiversity, etc.).

Indigenous peoples and the international mechanisms

A number of mechanisms and bodies have been set up by Agenda 21 and the various conventions to ensure the implementation of their objectives. As one of the "major groups",[67] indigenous peoples have increasingly become involved in the work of these bodies. This entails an impressive workload: indigenous representatives participate in numerous preparatory regional workshops, intersessional meetings and official sessions of the

---

[66] Johannesburg Plan of Implementation (2002) Full text available from www.un.org/esa/sustdev/documents/WSSD_POI_PD/English/POIToc.htm

[67] The Major Groups have a homepage at http://www.un.org/esa/sustdev/mgroups/mgroups.htm

governing bodies of the Conventions—the Conference of the Parties (COP); they elaborate background papers and documents, present statements, organize side events, lobby and promote indigenous issues. Prior to and during the official sessions, an indigenous caucus is usually organized so that indigenous representatives can meet to strategize, discuss and follow up on the debates taking place in the plenary meetings.

In order to ensure a better coordination of their efforts and have access to specialized expertise, indigenous peoples have formed several networks and bodies where representatives from indigenous governments, indigenous NGOs, scholars and activists meet to organize the pending tasks, which are often quite technical and demanding. The International Indigenous Forum on Biodiversity (IIFB), for instance, has, since 1996, organized indigenous representatives around the Convention on Biological Diversity (CBD) and its COP meetings, as well as other important international environmental meetings to help coordinate indigenous strategies, provide advice to government parties, and influence the interpretations of government obligations to recognize and respect indigenous rights to their knowledge and resources. It has also established an open-ended sub-group—the Indigenous Peoples Committee on Conservation (IPCC)—which is made up of a core of several dozen indigenous leaders and activists and a few support groups.

UNEP

The level of indigenous involvement depends, to a large extent, on the various bodies' commitment to the indigenous cause, and it is often an uphill battle not to be marginalized in these international fora. It is, for instance, only recently (2007) that indigenous peoples—as a major group—have been able to gain accreditation with the Governing Council/Global Ministerial Environment Forum (GC/GMEF) of the UN Environment Programme (UNEP). This gives them the opportunity to comment on draft papers being considered by the governments, to participate as observers, and to make oral statements to the GC/GMEF, as well as to take part in the Global Civil Society Forum (GCSF), which is the main entry point for civil society organizations to the GC/GMEF. UNEP is currently working on a draft strategy that will include a broader consultation process among indigenous peoples' representatives.

The Commission on Sustainable Development (CSD)

The Commission on Sustainable Development—established by Agenda 21 in 1992— has been very consistent in promoting the participation of the Major Groups, and indigenous peoples have been very active in this Forum. CSD is the high-level forum for sustainable development within the United Nations system and is responsible for reviewing progress in implementing Agenda 21 and the Rio Declaration on Environment and Development. It is also responsible for providing policy guidance to follow up on the Johannesburg Plan of Implementation at the local, national, regional and international levels. The CSD meets annually in New

> indigenous representatives participate in numerous preparatory regional workshops, intersessional meetings and official sessions of the governing bodies of the Conventions—the Conference of the Parties (COP); they elaborate background papers and documents, present statements, organize side events, lobby and promote indigenous issues.

York in two-year cycles, with each cycle focusing on clusters of specific thematic and cross-sectoral issues. Through, among other things, its multi-stakeholder dialogue sessions, the CSD provides direct interaction between governments and civil society and thus gives indigenous peoples the possibility of directly voicing their concerns and suggestions.

The Convention on Biological Diversity - COPs and Working Groups

For indigenous peoples, the Conference of the Parties (COP) of the CBD is particularly important because it has established seven thematic programmes of work that correspond to some of the major biomes, or ecological communities, on the planet. Each programme establishes a vision for and basic principles to guide future work. The COP has also initiated work on cross-cutting issues and set up a number of bodies and working groups to work toward achieving the commitments made in the Convention in, among other things, Article 8(j) (Ad Hoc Open-Ended Working Group on Article 8[j] and related provisions - WG8J), Article 25 (Subsidiary Body on Scientific, Technical and Technological Advice - WGSBSTA), Articles 15 and 8(j) (Ad Hoc Open-ended Working Group on Access and Benefit-sharing - WGABS), and on protected areas (Ad Hoc Open-Ended Working Group on Protected Areas - WGPA).

> for indigenous peoples, the Conference of the Parties (COP) of the CBD is particularly important

The CBD has also developed specific mechanisms such as, for example, financial support through the recently established Voluntary Fund to facilitate the full and effective participation of indigenous peoples in meetings under the Convention, including the meetings of its governing body—the Conference of the Parties (COP). This has allowed indigenous peoples to be very active and to be represented in, among other groups, the Advisory Group/Steering Committee, where it assists with the completion of the composite report on the status and trends regarding traditional knowledge relevant to biological diversity. However, it is within the Working Groups that the role of indigenous peoples has been particularly crucial for the promotion of indigenous views and interests.

This is particularly the case with WG8J, the Working Group under Article 8(j) and related provisions. Its programme of work and plan of action "for the retention of traditional knowledge, innovations and practices" were adopted in 2000 and form the main instruments that Parties to the Convention have given themselves to achieve the commitments in Article 8(j) to "respect, preserve and maintain the knowledge, innovations and practices of indigenous and local communities embodying traditional lifestyles relevant for the conservation and sustainable use of biological diversity, to promote their wider application with the approval and involvement of the holders of such knowledge, and encourage the equitable sharing of the benefits arising from the utilization of such knowledge".[68]

One of the main achievements of WG8J has been the Akwe: Kon Voluntary Guidelines, developed in cooperation with indigenous peoples. The name of the

---

[68] See http://www.cbd.int/traditional

Guidelines is a Mohawk term meaning "everything in creation" and was adopted in 2004 by COP7 as decision VII/16 F.[69] The Guidelines provide a collaborative framework ensuring the full involvement of indigenous peoples in assessing the cultural, environmental and social impact of proposed developments on sacred sites and on lands and waters they have traditionally occupied. Moreover, guidance is provided on how to take into account traditional knowledge, innovations and practices as part of the impact-assessment processes and promote the use of appropriate technologies.

The objectives of the Akwe: Kon Voluntary Guidelines

The specific objectives of the Akwe: Kon Guidelines are to

- ◈ support the full and effective participation of indigenous peoples in screening, scoping and development planning exercises;

- ◈ take into account the cultural, environmental and social concerns and interests of indigenous peoples;

- ◈ take into account the traditional knowledge of indigenous peoples with due regard to the ownership of the need for its protection; promoting the use of technologies associated with TK;

- ◈ identify and implement appropriate measures to prevent or mitigate any negative impacts of proposed developments; and

- ◈ take into consideration the interrelationships between cultural, environmental and social elements.

Given that most indigenous peoples live in areas where the vast majority of the world's biological and genetic resources are found, the voluntary Akwe: Kon Guidelines are an important tool that can be used in development assessment processes to ameliorate the potential long-term negative impacts of developments on the livelihoods and traditional knowledge of indigenous peoples who have used biological diversity in a sustainable way for thousands of years and for whom living cultural traditions and knowledge are deeply rooted in the environment on which they depend.

The WG8J has also, more recently, undertaken the important task of developing elements of sui generis systems (laws within national legal systems) for the protection of traditional knowledge as well as draft elements of an Ethical Code of Conduct to Ensure Respect for the Cultural and Intellectual Heritage of Indigenous Peoples. This work will make a substantial contribution to the work being conducted by indigenous peoples in another working group—the Ad Hoc

> the voluntary Akwe: Kon Guidelines are an important tool that can be used in development assessment processes to ameliorate the potential long-term negative impacts of developments on the livelihoods and traditional knowledge of indigenous peoples

---

[69] See full text at http://www.cbd.int/doc/publications/akwe-brochure-en.pdf

Open-ended Working Group on Access and Benefit-Sharing—on the elaboration and negotiation of an international regime on access and benefit-sharing. Such a regime is of great interest to indigenous peoples and their organizations, given the significant impact that a legal instrument of this kind could have on the genetic resources found on their territories and on their associated traditional knowledge and the fair and equitable sharing of benefits arising from their utilization.

WIPO and the IGC

A growing concern with regard to traditional knowledge is the issue of protecting it from misappropriation and misuse. In this regard, the Intergovernmental Committee on Intellectual Property and Genetic Resources, Traditional Knowledge and Folklore (the IGC) under the World Intellectual Property Organization (WIPO) is relevant for indigenous peoples. WIPO was established by the WIPO Convention of 1967. It is a multifaceted, specialized UN agency that has among its many activities that of providing a forum for international policy debate and development of legal mechanisms and practical tools concerning the protection of traditional knowledge (TK) and traditional cultural expressions (TCEs) from misappropriation and misuse, and the intellectual property rights (IPRs) aspects of access and benefit-sharing of genetic resources. The ICG was established in 2001 to identify the needs and expectations of the holders of TK and cultural expressions.

> a growing concern with regard to traditional knowledge is the issue of protecting it from misappropriation and misuse

While WIPO has a role to play in protecting TK, there is a belief among some indigenous peoples that it is not an appropriate forum to set standards because it is limited by its mandate to promoting intellectual property rights (IPRs) as the only viable path to protecting traditional knowledge. Indigenous peoples have consistently called on WIPO, governments and other multilateral organizations to explore other ways of protecting and promoting indigenous and traditional knowledge outside of the traditional IPRs regime.[70] The IGC is currently consolidating on-going work on two sets of draft provisions that outline policy objectives and core principles relating to the protection of TK and TCEs from misappropriation. The close involvement of indigenous peoples has been essential to this process.[71]

United Nations Forum on Forests (UNFF)

As one of the Major Groups, indigenous peoples also participate in the work of the United Nations Forum on Forests (UNFF). The UNFF is a subsidiary body of ECOSOC and was established in 2000, together with the Collaborative Partnership on Forests (CPF), comprising forest-related UN agencies and international and regional organizations, institutions and instruments.

---

[70] See The Kimberley Political Declaration, Kimberley, South Africa, August 2002.
[71] See Chapter II, this publication; Traditional Knowledge Bulletin (2008) at http://tkbulletin. wordpress.com

The mandate of the UNFF has been to facilitate and promote the implementation of the Proposals for Action set up by the UN Intergovernmental Panel on Forests (IPF) and the Intergovernmental Forum on Forests (IFF).[72] In 2007, the Forum adopted the Non-Legally Binding Instrument on All Types of Forests (NLBI), and a Multi-Year Programme (2007-2015) with four measurable and time-bound global objectives to achieve sustainable forest management.[73]

NLBI is the first ever inter-governmental instrument on sustainable forest management. It covers issues ranging from protection and use of traditional forest-related knowledge and practices in sustainable forest management to the need for enhanced access to forest resources and relevant markets to support the livelihoods of forest-dependent indigenous communities living inside and outside forest areas.[74]

Although UNFF recognizes the role of indigenous peoples in achieving sustainable forest management, indigenous peoples' organizations and civil society have generally been disappointed by the UNFF, which does not build on the open and progressive practices of the IPF/IFF and CSD.[75] They have also widely criticized NLBI for failing to recognize, respect and support the implementation of customary rights of indigenous peoples who live in and depend on forests and for failing to comply with best practices in environment management.[76]

UNCCD and UNFCCC

Indigenous peoples also participate in the COPs of the Convention on Desertification (UNCCD) and the Framework Convention on Climate Change (UNFCCC). However, they are admitted only as observers, not as peoples. In the case of the UNFCCC, for instance, they have participated since 1988 in the COPs and have released a number of statements and declarations expressing concerns regarding the implications of climate change policies on their livelihoods and cultures. Since 2001, indigenous peoples' organizations have been acknowledged as a constituency in climate change negotiations within UNFCCC. At the same time, however, indigenous peoples are still waiting for UNFCCC's approval of an Ad Hoc Working Group on Indigenous Peoples and Climate Change, which would allow them to actively participate in the meetings of the Conference of Parties in the same way they are able to under the Convention on Biological Diversity.[77]

Implementation gaps and challenges

Indigenous peoples today are increasingly attempting to exert greater control over their natural resources as well as over their economic and political life. They are acutely aware of the environmental damage that accompanies most development programmes and the toll that these efforts impose on peoples and their ecosystems.[78] They also realize that the rapid pace of human-induced environmental change calls for decisive action not only at the international level but also at the national and local levels in order to fill the implementation gap and fully respect indigenous peoples' environmental rights. However, while indigenous peoples have, since 2002, experienced increased recognition of their environmental rights at the international level, translating this political

---

[72] IPF was set up by the CSD in 1995. It was succeeded by the IFF in 1997, which, in turn, gave way to the UNFF in 2000.
[73] For full text of NLBI, see UN Doc. A/C.2/62/L.5 (2007).
[74] NLBI Article 6 (f) and (y).
[75] See, e.g., Forest Peoples Programme (2004a).
[76] See, e.g., Forest Peoples Programme (2007a).
[77] See indigenous peoples' statements made at various COPs on the web site of the International Alliance for Indigenous and Tribal Peoples of the Tropical Forests at http://www.international-alliance.org
[78] Barkin (2006).

recognition into concrete advances at the national and local levels remains a major challenge. Many decisions made at the international level are not always respected or implemented at the national level, and indigenous peoples' voices are all too often marginalized, if heard at all.

Several factors contribute to this situation: structural discrimination of indigenous peoples at all levels in many countries, a lack of political will to prioritize indigenous issues and provide funds to address them, the low level and efficacy of indigenous participation in national policy formulation and implementation, and a lack of awareness of international commitments amongst government officials as well as among indigenous peoples themselves (except for a minority who work in leading indigenous organizations).

Indigenous land rights

A main challenge still facing most indigenous peoples is the right to their traditional lands and resources. There are a number of other instruments that allow for broader recognition and protection of indigenous peoples' rights to lands and territories. In 1997, the UN Committee on the Elimination of Racial Discrimination, in its General Recommendation No. 23 on Indigenous Peoples, called on states-parties to "recognize and protect the rights of indigenous peoples to own, develop, control and use their communal lands, territories and resources and, where they have been deprived of their lands and territories traditionally owned or otherwise inhabited or used without their free and informed consent, to take steps to return these lands and territories." The Committee further called "upon state-parties with indigenous peoples in their territories to include in their periodic reports full information on the situation of such peoples, taking into account all relevant provisions of the Convention".[79] In recent years, in its comments on country reports, CERD has made several observations on the issue of indigenous peoples' right to land.[80]

In Africa, indigenous peoples can refer to Articles 21 and 22 of the African Charter, which enshrine the right of peoples to freely dispose of their wealth and natural resources and provide for the right of peoples to economic, social, and cultural development. Similar provisions are contained in other instruments adopted by the African Union, such as the African Convention on the Conservation of Nature and Natural Resources, which is intended "to preserve the traditional rights and property of local communities and request the prior consent of the communities concerned in respect of all that concerns their access to and use of traditional knowledge". These provisions have been used by the African Commission on Human and Peoples' Rights (ACHPR) to enhance protection of indigenous peoples' rights to lands. The African Commission has also received land-related communications, for example, from the Endorois, indigenous peoples of Kenya, regarding their claims to ancestral lands around Lake Bogoria. [81]

> while indigenous peoples have, since 2002, experienced increased recognition of their environmental rights at the international level, translating this political recognition into concrete advances at the national and local levels remains a major challenge

---

[79] CERD (1997) General Recommendation No.23: Indigenous Peoples.
[80] See, for instance, CERD (2003) Concluding Observation on Uganda.
[81] Barume (forthcoming 2009).

There have also been recent examples where, after exhausting national remedies, indigenous peoples of the Americas took their complaints to the Inter-American Human Rights System. A series of landmark decisions resulted: *Awas Tingni v. Nicaragua*, 2001; *Yakye Axa v. Paraguay*, 2005; and *Sawhoyamaxa v. Paraguay*, 2006. In ruling on these cases, the court affirmed the validity of the United Nations (then) Draft Declaration and OAS Proposed Declaration on the Rights of Indigenous Peoples, even though neither had been finally approved at the time of the verdict.[82]

This raises the hope that, with the adoption of the Declaration, indigenous peoples' rights to land and to self-determination may appear on the domestic agenda of many countries.

Biological diversity and traditional knowledge

The Convention on Biological Diversity is a commitment to achieving a significant reduction in the current rate of biodiversity loss at the global, regional and national level by 2010. The current rate is estimated to be up to 100 times the natural rate. This unprecedented biodiversity loss is being exacerbated by the negative impact of climate change. According to the IUCN Red List of Threatened Species, between 12 and 52 per cent of species within groups such as birds or mammals are threatened with extinction,[83] and up to 30 per cent of all known species may disappear before the end of this century because of climate change.[84]

> the rate of erosion of traditional ecological/ environmental biodiversity-related knowledge has never been as high as in the current generation

Parties to the Convention on Biological Diversity have also made a commitment to ensure the protection of indigenous peoples' traditional knowledge as established by Article 8(j), which states that "each contracting party shall as far as possible and as appropriate, subject to national legislation, respect, preserve and maintain knowledge, innovations and practices of indigenous and local communities embodying traditional lifestyles relevant to the conservation and sustainable use of biological diversity."

Yet, the rate of erosion of traditional ecological/environmental biodiversity-related knowledge has never been as high as in the current generation.[85] Although efforts are being made, for instance by the UNESCO programme LINKS,[86] to encourage the use and inter-generational transfer of innovations and practices in biodiversity-related traditional knowledge innovations and

---

[82] Alwyn (2006).

[83] See full list at http://www.greenfacts.org/glossary/ghi/iucn-red-list.htm

[84] Statement by Executive Secretary of the SCBD (2008). For full text, see http://www.cbd.int/doc/speech/2008/sp-2008-06-16-ias-en.pdf

[85] For detailed summaries of the threats to traditional knowledge, see Working Group on Article 8(j) (2005). For measures and mechanisms to address the decline of traditional knowledge, see Working Group on Article 8(j) (2007f).

[86] LINKS specifically seeks to maintain the vitality of local knowledge within communities by strengthening ties between elders and youth in order to reinforce the transmission of indigenous knowledge and know-how.

practices, more incentive measures tailored to ensure the survival of traditional knowledge within and beyond this current generation, urgently need to be developed.

Implementation of the goals related to biodiversity and traditional knowledge requires both political will and economic support. Most indigenous peoples are highly dependent on the states in which they live.[87] However, they rarely enjoy sufficient national legislative support or any degree of self-governance, both of which are needed for maintaining their biodiversity-related practices and knowledge and for ensuring the successful implementation of Article 8(j).[88] They also face constraints in the exercise of customary laws relevant to the management, conservation, and sustainable use of biological diversity. The outcome of the work being done in WG8J and WGABS is therefore of special interest to indigenous peoples.

In ratifying the Convention on Biological Diversity, developed countries have also committed themselves to providing financial resources to ensure that developing countries can implement the Convention. In adopting the Declaration on the Rights of Indigenous Peoples, states have recognized a similar obligation to "establish and implement assistance programmes for indigenous peoples for such conservation and protection without discrimination".[89]

This funding, which can be made through bilateral, regional or multilateral donations, is channelled through the Global Environment Facility (GEF), the financial mechanism of the UN environmental conventions and the largest funder of projects to improve the global environment.[90] Indigenous peoples' involvement in the GEF policy processes is limited, although they participate in the GEF assembly and council meetings and have their own focal point within the NGO network that is part of the GEF structure.[91]

Although the GEF is an independent financial body, its projects and programmes are implemented through agencies, such as the UNDP and the World Bank, some of which have their own policies on indigenous peoples. Several indigenous organizations have been able to access project funding, and the CBD Conference of the Parties has specifically requested that GEF finance projects strengthening the involvement of indigenous peoples in conserving biological diversity and in maintaining the sustainable use of its components, and in supporting the priority activities identified in the WG8j's programme of work.

Protected areas

Although 12 per cent of the earth's land surface now consists of protected areas, they do not cover all biomes and species requiring protection, and so the objectives of the Convention on Biological Diversity (CBD) are not being fulfilled. In order to address these gaps, a Programme of Work on protected areas was developed at the CBD Conference of Parties in 2004. The objective of this Programme is to

> *Support the establishment and maintenance by 2010 for terrestrial and by 2012 for marine areas of comprehensive, effectively managed, and ecologically representative national and regional protected areas that collectively contribute to achieving the 2010 target.*[92]

---

[87] Working Group on Article 8(j) (2007b).

[88] Working Group on Article 8(j) (2007b).

[89] United Nations (2007), Article 29.

[90] The GEF has, since 1991, assisted countries in meeting their obligations under the conventions that they have signed and ratified, such as the Convention on Biological Diversity (CBD), the United Nations Framework Convention on Climate Change, the UN Convention to Combat Desertification (UNCCD), etc. GEF provides grants for projects related to the following six focal areas: biodiversity, climate change, international waters, land degradation, the ozone layer and persistent organic pollutants. See http://thegef.org

[91] See, e.g., Forest Peoples Programme (2007b).

[92] Convention on Biological Diversity (2004), COP 7 Decision VII/28.

However, prioritising the expansion of protected area networks without issues of equity and participation at the forefront may lead to an unjust implementation of the Programme of Work by excluding social, cultural and justice aspects while focusing on quantitative targets. A WWF report from 2004 identified indigenous peoples' participation in management decision-making as a weakness in protected area management and concluded, "one depressingly consistent problem is a failure to manage relations with people. Problems are evident in terms of effectively channelling the input of indigenous peoples and securing their voice and participation in management decisions".[93]

Only by adhering to the goals of the Programme of Work on Protected Areas, in particular Goal 2 on Equity and Benefit Sharing, can the Parties ensure that a number of outcomes are realized in the process of achieving the 2010 biodiversity targets and representative biomes in protected areas. This can be done by

◈ adjusting policies to avoid and mitigate negative impacts and, where appropriate, compensate costs & equitably share benefits in accordance with the national legislation;

◈ recognising and promoting a broad set of protected area governance types, which may include areas conserved by indigenous and local communities; and,

◈ using social and economic benefits generated by protected areas for poverty reduction, consistent with protected-area management objectives;

◈ enhancing and securing the involvement of indigenous and local communities and relevant stakeholders.[94]

The UN Declaration on the Rights of Indigenous Peoples also provides guidance with regard to protected areas. As mentioned above, one of the problems with protected areas is that indigenous peoples are forcibly removed from lands or excluded from accessing lands and the resources contained therein. Article 10 of the Declaration states that

Indigenous peoples shall not be forcibly removed from their lands or territories. No relocation shall take place without the free, prior and informed consent of the indigenous peoples concerned and after agreement on just and fair compensation and, where possible, with the option of return.

At the CBD Working Group on Protected Areas, convened in preparation for COP 9 (2008), indigenous peoples stated their disappointment at the lack of progress in the implementation of Element 2 of the Programme of Work on governance, equity, participation and benefit-sharing:

Despite all the hard work to contribute to the development of the Programme of Work and our efforts at the national level to implement its activities directly relevant to the indigenous peoples and local communities, we have met many obstacles and in many cases Parties have preferred to continue with the establishment of protected areas without taking into account our rights and without ensuring our full and effective participation.[95]

They therefore recommended that the Programme of Work proceed in accordance with the following:

---

[93] WWF (2004), 4.
[94] Workgin Group on Article 8(j) Programme of Work, Goal 2.1 and Goal 2.2. at http:/www.cbd.int/protected/pow.shtml?prog=p2
[95] Indigenous Statement (2008).

◈ recognize the customary practices and legal system related to the sustainable use and conservation of biodiversity;

◈ recognize the rights of indigenous peoples to their territories, lands and resources and the rights of Free Prior Informed Consent;

◈ review and reform national protected area policies and laws that contravene the goals and targets of Element 2 of the programme; and,

◈ train protected area managers and personnel in participatory approaches and to recognize and respect indigenous rights.[96]

At COP 9 (May 2008), the Parties decided to promote the establishment of "effective processes for the full and effective participation of indigenous and local communities, in full respect of their rights and recognition of their responsibilities, in the governance of protected areas, consistent with national law and applicable international obligations".[97] This would include building capacity for indigenous and local communities to enable their participation in establishing and managing protected areas and preserving and maintaining traditional knowledge for the conservation and sustainable use of biodiversity in the management of protected areas.[98]

Forest issues

Policy commitments developed at the international level urge states to promote, support, protect and encourage the use of traditional knowledge and customary practices of indigenous peoples in the management and use of forest resources. These policy commitments can be found in specific instruments such as Agenda 21 (e.g., Chapter 11 on Combating Deforestation), the Convention on Biological Diversity, the non-legally binding Forest Principles and the Millennium Development Goals (Goal No.7 on Environmental Sustainability).

Since UNCED, the international community has made significant progress in the development of international forestry policy focused on sustainable forest management. However, there is much concern that progress on the ground is poor, and there is no effective monitoring system. Whilst there are state reports to the UNFF and CBD, and national strategy documents such as National Forest Plans (NFPs), National Forest Action Programmes (NFAPs), and National Biodiversity Strategy and Action Plans (NBSAPs) have been produced, information on effective implementation in laws and policies and related actions on the ground is far more difficult to obtain.[99]

Regarding the Non-Legally Binding Instrument on all Types of Forests (NLBI), indigenous peoples have pointed out that it is not clear whether such an instrument would better conserve forests and provide better protections of the rights of indigenous peoples because states seem to be unwilling to deal with social justice and human rights issues and instead prefer to strengthen state power and sovereignty over natural resources. A recurrent concern is that UNEP and UNFF, when defining "forests", do not make the distinction between natural forests and forest plantations (of oil palms, for instance). This means that countries that expand the area for tree plantation can claim that they are achieving MDG 7 because one of its indicators is "proportion of lands covered by forests".[100]

---

[96] Indigenous Statement (2008).
[97] Convention on Biological Diversity (2008a), 165: Decision IX/18, 6(d).
[98] Convention on Biological Diversity (2008a), 165: Decision IX/18,12.
[99] See Newing (2004).
[100] Tauli-Corpuz and Tamang (2007).

The efforts being made to improve commercial forest management through a certification process that ensures that the social, economic and ecological needs of present and future generations that are being met are more positive. One example is the Forest Stewardship Council (FSC), whose principles and criteria for certification include "respect of human rights with particular attention to indigenous peoples" and "identification and appropriate management of areas that need special protection, (e.g., cultural or sacred sites, habitat of endangered animals or plants)". Currently, more than 100 million ha of forest worldwide have been certified to FSC standards. These forests are distributed over 79 countries and represent the equivalent of 7 per cent of the world's productive forests. In most cases, these forests are inhabited by indigenous peoples who are actively involved in mapping, management and other related activities.[101]

Environmental impact assessment

As keepers of life-sustaining resources, indigenous peoples have proven to be successful in developing mechanisms and techniques in harmony with their environment. Although indigenous knowledge is different from the Western paradigm of development, the knowledge of indigenous peoples is of particular interest for environmental assessment because it is systemic and comprehensive and offers an all-encompassing understanding of a territory that is utilized and known in its entirety. In contrast, Western scientific expertise has a tendency to move toward increasing levels of specialization, rendering a holistic vision difficult, if not impossible. Indigenous peoples' traditional ecological knowledge and management systems are therefore the subject of increasing attention because they can be used to improve development planning in regions inhabited by indigenous peoples. There are an increasing number of texts advocating the articulation of environmental assessment and indigenous knowledge (e.g., Agenda 21, Convention on Biological Diversity, the Akwe: Kon Voluntary Guidelines and the Declaration on the Rights of Indigenous Peoples).

> the knowledge of indigenous peoples is of particular interest for environmental assessment because it is systemic and comprehensive and offers an all-encompassing understanding of a territory that is utilized and known in its entirety

But beyond statements of good intent, there are still questions as to whether real progress has been made toward bringing indigenous knowledge into environmental assessment, and the extent to which environmental impact assessment and land use planning and decision-making reflect the above mentioned texts is highly variable throughout and within regions. So far, most national reports submitted by the Parties to the Convention on Biological Diversity indicate that the *Akwe: Kon Guidelines* have not been implemented.

In several cases, indigenous peoples have tried to have traditional knowledge integrated into environmental impact assessments conducted for climate change response measures. It was, for instance, recommended by the Arctic International Expert Meeting on Responses to Climate Change for Indigenous Communities and the Impact on their Traditional Knowledge Related to Biological

---

[101] See, e.g., Lewis and Nelson (2006).

Diversity, which also noted the relevance of the Akwe: Kon Guidelines. It also recommended that processes be developed to link local-level adaptation to national planning.[102]

In many parts of the world, the "environment" is still not a priority when dealing with difficult development decisions, and cultural factors are almost always absent from decision-making processes. In the case of extractive industries in Latin America, for instance, there is insufficient evaluation of their impacts on traditional knowledge and practices, even if it is argued that such impacts, especially indirect impacts, are of considerable magnitude. [103]

In 2005, indigenous peoples living in the Russian Federation protested against the oil industry, demanding the implementation of an "ethnological impact assessment" in addition to the environmental impact assessment. In 2007, the Committee of Nationalities Affairs of the Russian State Duma drafted a federal law "[o]n the protection of the environment, traditional way of life, and traditional natural resource use of the small numbered indigenous peoples in the Russian Federation". Such a law would have made ethnological impact assessments a reality and secured traditional lands and natural resource management for the indigenous peoples' communal enterprises. The Department of Nationalities Affairs has, however, reacted negatively to the draft law and the general feeling is therefore that it will not be passed by Duma, even though several regional administrations have stressed the need for such a law.[104]

Climate Change – adaptation and mitigation

For many indigenous peoples, climate change is already a reality, and they are increasingly realising that climate change is clearly not just an environmental issue, but one with severe socioeconomic implications. The World Bank, among other things, also sees climate change as having the potential to hamper achievement of the Millennium Development Goals, including those on poverty eradication, child mortality, combating malaria and other diseases, as well as environmental sustainability. For indigenous peoples, already vulnerable and marginalized, climate change therefore represents a major challenge to which the only answer so far seems to be adaptation and mitigation.

Adaptation

Indigenous peoples have survived many kinds of environmental changes and are therefore often seen as having a special capacity to adapt. As Nuttall observes, however, "adaptive capacity and resilience depend on the strength of culture, of human-environment relations, cohesiveness of community, identity, and of strong social relationships… Adaptation may well begin at the local level in individual, household and community decisions, but it also requires strong policy measures

> for many indigenous peoples, climate change is already a reality, and they are increasingly realising that climate change is clearly not just an environmental issue, but one with severe socioeconomic implications

---

[102] Convention on Biological Diversity (2008b).
[103] Working Group on Article 8(j) (2007g).
[104] IWGIA (2008), 40.

that, for example, support traditional practises of hunting, fishing and pastoralism, agricultural production, food security, resource management, infrastructure development, and education".[105] In many instances, adaptation to new conditions requires additional financial resources and a transfer of technological capacity, which most indigenous communities do not possess.

On the other hand, indigenous peoples may have valuable lessons to offer about successful and unsuccessful adaptations which could be vital in the context of climate change. There is increasing recognition of the "untapped resource of indigenous peoples' knowledge about past climate change"[106] that could be used to inform adaptation options,[107] as well as scientific research, as was the case during the Arctic climate impact assessment.

Incorporating indigenous knowledge and Western science

Indigenous observations of climate change contribute to understanding climate change and associated changes in the behaviour and movement of animals. Over many generations and based on the direct, everyday experience of living in the Arctic, they have developed specific ways of observing, interpreting, and adjusting to weather and climate changes. Based on careful observations, on which they often base life-and-death decisions and set priorities, indigenous peoples have come to possess a rich body of knowledge about their surroundings. Researchers are now working with indigenous peoples to learn from their observations and perspectives about the influences of climate change and weather events on the Arctic environment and on their own lives and cultures. These studies are finding that the climate variations observed by indigenous people and by scientific observation are, for the most part, in good accord and often provide mutually reinforcing information.

Source: Arctic Climate Impact Assessment (2005), 992.

Taking indigenous peoples' knowledge into account when designing climate change policies could also lead to the development of effective adaptation strategies that are cost-effective, participatory and sustainable.[108] It is also important to emphasize that any attempt to enhance and support the adaptive capacity of indigenous peoples will be successful only if integrated with other strategies, such as disaster preparation, land-use planning, environmental conservation and national plans for sustainable development.

Coping with climate changes in the Arctic

Living in the north-eastern corner of Siberia, the Nutendli peoples have witnessed the disappearance of lakes, severe flooding and the rapid new erosion of the banks of the Kolyma River. In order to survive the changes that modernity, and now climate changes, impose on them and their world, the Nutendli community acts to prioritize the survival of traditional knowledge, spirituality and language. This effort manifests itself in a unique attempt to provide education to the children of the community by means of a nomadic school. The community believes that it is able to build a relationship with the rapid changes of the land as long as its knowledge and beings survive.

Source: Convention on Biological Diversity (2008b), 17.

---

[105] Nuttall (2008), 6.

[106] IPCC (2007b), 523, citing Rose (1996), Lewis (2002) and Orlove (2003).

[107] IPCC (2007b), 523, citing Webb (1997) and Hill (2004).

[108] IPCC (2007b), 865, citing Robinson and Herbert (2001).

Although indigenous peoples are experts in adapting to changing conditions, adapting to simultaneous changes in their homeland that affect, for instance, their land tenure, their access to natural resources, their health situation, etc., indigenous communities may start to show signs of stress and may be unable to cope when a rapidly changing climate accelerates the degradation of their ecosystem and impinges upon their ability to maintain their livelihoods.[109]

It should also be mentioned, however, that indigenous groups, in some regions of the world, see economic opportunities in climate change. In Greenland, for instance, the Home Rule Government reckons that a warmer climate will make mining and hydrocarbon development possible and potentially open the path for lucrative industrial development.[110] In other regions, opportunities may be found in having wind and solar power generated on traditional lands. In Australia, in June 2007, ConocoPhillips, a giant new natural gas refinery, and Aboriginal landowners agreed to offset 100,000 tons of the refinery's own greenhouse emissions over a period of 17 years. The Aboriginal landowners in question will use traditional fire management practices, which have been scientifically shown to reduce greenhouse emissions as compared to naturally occurring wildfires.[111]

Mitigation efforts

Current mitigation efforts include a whole gamut of initiatives that all have the objective of reducing the emission of CO_2 and other gases. These initiatives include bio-fuel plantations, hydropower dams, geothermal plants, etc., and a series of projects to deal with emission reductions in general and the reduction of emissions from deforestation and forest degradation in particular.

> indigenous peoples also point to an increase in human rights violations, evictions and conflicts due to expropriation of ancestral lands and forests for afforestation and reforestation or biofuel plantations

Many indigenous peoples adopt a defensive position in view of these efforts as they fear they will lead to expropriation of their lands, displacement or loss of biological diversity. In Australia and New Zealand, for instance, "large-scale" participation of indigenous lands in the mitigation effort is anticipated.[112] The IPCC Fourth Assessment Report recommends that more research is required regarding adaptation options for Australian indigenous and New Zealand Maori communities, particularly those on traditional lands that may be targeted for mitigation schemes.[113] At the Conference of the Parties of UNFCCC in 2005, the International Alliance of Indigenous and Tribal Peoples of Tropical Forests was critical of the fact that the modalities and procedures for activities under the Clean Development Mechanism (CDM) did not respect or guarantee indigenous peoples' right to lands, territories and self-determination. There is a view that CDM and carbon sinks projects do not contribute to climate change mitigation and sustainable development.

---

[109] See, e.g., ACIA (2005), 676.
[110] Nuttall (2008), 45.
[111] Mugarura (2007).
[112] See also the The Garnaut Climate Change Review (2008).
[113] IPCC (2007b), 531.

Indigenous peoples also point to an increase in human rights violations, evictions and conflicts due to expropriation of ancestral lands and forests for afforestation and reforestation or biofuel plantations (soya, sugar cane, jatropha, oil palm, corn, etc.). Such projects affect whole eco-systems, placing demands on water supply, changing the face of the landscape upon which indigenous peoples depend and bringing about an associated declined in food security.[114]

The World Bank and the carbon market

According to the World Bank, the resources needed to tackle climate change are unprecedented compared to existing development and global public goods financing,[115] and together with GEF, the World Bank Group (WBG) has become the leading agency in developing funding facilities aimed at adaptation and mitigation efforts. The first fund—the Prototype Carbon Fund (PCF)—became operational in 2000 and, since then, two more carbon funds have been created. The Bank also administers several funds on behalf of individual donor countries, including Italy, the Netherlands and Spain.

More recently, the World Bank has developed a new range of funding facilities, such as the Climate Investment Funds,[116] the Transformation Fund for Sustainable Development[117] and the Forest Carbon Partnership Facility (FCPF). Such initiatives potentially represent billions of dollars in funding for activities related to the mitigation of global climate change and for adaptation to changing climatic conditions.

The Forest Carbon Partnership Facility (FCPF) was developed by the Bank in 2006 and 2007, together with a larger proposal for a Global Forest Partnership (GFP) which, if adopted, will have major implications for forests and forest peoples.[118] Both were launched at the UNFCCC COP 13, in Bali, in 2007, and were met with massive criticism from indigenous peoples.

According to a survey conducted by the Forest Peoples Programme,[119] the general concerns expressed by indigenous peoples regarding the FCPF included, among other things

◈ the FCPF fails to take into account the UN Declaration on the Rights of Indigenous Peoples and does not provide any other form of effective protection for the rights of indigenous peoples, their lands and territories;

◈ the draft proposals for "emission reduction programmes" include a variety of areas of great concern to indigenous peoples, including expansion of protected area systems, expansion of plantations, strong emphasis on law enforcement and patrolling of lands;

◈ the proposed FCPF governance structures privilege the interests of governments and business over those of indigenous peoples, and there is a fear that indigenous peoples will be marginalized by a top-down implementation process, as well as by the centralized forest-policy planning and design process;

◈ affected indigenous communities would have few avenues for redress in the event of conflict or violation of rights stemming from activities supported by the FCPF.[120]

---

[114] Working Group on Article 8(j) (2007a).
[115] See World Bank (2007).
[116] Two trust funds are to be created under the CIF: the Clean Technology Fund and the Strategic Climate Fund.
[117] This is a British-funded initiative administered by the Bank.
[118] Forest Peoples Programme (2008), 5.
[119] Forest Peoples Programme (2008), 4.
[120] Forest Peoples Programme (2008), 4.

Regarding the Global Forest Partnership (GFP), concerns included, among others things, that

◈ the GFP does not recognize indigenous peoples as rights holders;

◈ it risks undermining or impoverishing indigenous forest-based livelihoods and traditional practices in forests by supporting conventional protected area systems;

◈ it would enable activities that could lead to the expropriation of indigenous peoples' forest lands;

◈ it would deliver only minimal or token benefits to indigenous peoples and forest communities;

◈ it would marginalize indigenous peoples through top-down implementation processes, as well as by its centralized planning and design structure;

◈ a lack of transparency and accountability in its governance arrangements does not provide indigenous peoples and affected communities with avenues for effective involvement or representation.[121]

Indigenous peoples were also critical of the fact that they had been excluded from the FCPF/GFP process in spite of the fact they are the main stakeholders in tropical and subtropical regions. In response, the World Bank held consultations with indigenous peoples in Asia, Latin America and Africa in early 2008.

Many people, including indigenous peoples in developing countries, have questioned the logic of having a multilateral bank that has been and continues to be involved in funding the drivers of deforestation and climate change (fossil fuel energy extraction, mining, industrial logging, industrial plantations and infrastructure— including dams, roads, oil and gas pipelines and coastal developments) fund mitigation and adaptation efforts. These critics have called upon the Bank to cease the funding of fossil fuel activities and to prevent its projects from resulting in deforestation.[122]

REDD

At the COP meeting, a programme on Reducing Emissions from Deforestation and Forest Degradation (REDD) was launched by the Norwegian government, which pledged to spend NOK 3 billion annually to support developing countries in fighting deforestation and reducing global CO_2 emissions. The REDD programme, too, has met with criticism. It makes no reference to indigenous peoples' rights, and it is argued that it will reinforce a centralized, top-down management of forests and undermine indigenous rights.

The concerns regarding the Forest Carbon Partnership Facility and REDD were also raised at the Seventh Session of the UN Permanent Forum on Indigenous Issues in May 2008, where the theme was Climate Change. Recommendations related to adaptation and mitigation initiatives were made, and it was emphasized that all actions to be taken should be implemented with the participation or consent of indigenous peoples and in accordance with the UN Declaration. In particular, it was recommended that

> [i]ndigenous peoples should be effectively involved in the design, implementation and evaluation of the Forest Carbon Partnership Facility. Displacement and exclusion of indigenous peoples from their forests, which may be triggered by projects funded by the Partnership Facility, should

---

[121] Forest Peoples Programme (2008), 4.
[122] Forest Peoples Programme (2008), 16

be avoided at all costs. Indigenous peoples or their representatives should have a voice in and a vote on the decision-making body of the Partnership Facility and of other climate change funds that will have impacts on them. In the case of those who opt not to participate in reducing emissions from deforestation and degradation or in the projects supported by the Partnership Facility, their choice should be respected. The Forum calls on all parties to ensure that the United Nations Declaration on the Rights of Indigenous Peoples is implemented when undertaking these processes.[123]

Concluding Remarks

Since the Earth Summit in 1992, interest in the rights of indigenous peoples in relation to the environment has continued to grow. There is now a better understanding of the importance of traditional lands and natural resources for the economic, cultural and spiritual survival of indigenous peoples, and indigenous values, knowledge and perspectives are increasingly respected as vital contributions to the renewal of society and nature.[124] The creation of a number of mechanisms specifically targeted at indigenous peoples[125] has contributed significantly to this development.

Indigenous peoples have invested enormous efforts in the work related to the different processes within the Committee for Sustainable Development, the Convention on Biological Diversity, the Forest Forum and the Framework Convention on Climate Change. It has been an uphill battle to gain recognition as valuable partners today, but indigenous peoples have become highly visible in international environmental fora.

At the local and national level, however, indigenous land rights, land use and resource management remain critical issues. The environmental damage to indigenous lands and territories has been substantial: flora and fauna species have become extinct or endangered, unique ecosystems have been destroyed, and rivers and other water catchments have been heavily polluted. Commercial plant varieties have replaced the many locally adapted varieties used in traditional farming systems, leading to an increase in industrialized farming methods. In many countries, development projects, mining and forestry activities, and agricultural and conservation programmes continue to displace indigenous peoples. In addition, indigenous peoples are now also facing new challenges, such as biotechnology, intellectual property rights and, not least, the impacts of climate change. For many indigenous peoples, climate change is a potential threat to their very existence and a major issue of human rights and equity.

It has been argued that this situation is the result of the current treaty-based framework of international law, including the Convention on Biological Diversity, which is poorly equipped to accommodate non-state players such as indigenous peoples with rights equivalent to those of states.[126] International law is built on the principle of state sovereignty and Article 3 of the CBD therefore affirms that "States have, in accordance with the Charter of the United Nations and the principles of international law, the sovereign right to exploit their own resources pursuant to their own environmental policies...."

---

[123] UNPFII (2008), para. 49.

[124] Carino (2001), 4.

[125] These mechanisms include the two International Decades of the World's Indigenous People (1995-2004 and 2005-2015); the Permanent Forum on Indigenous Issues (2000); the Special Rapporteur Mechanism on the situation of human rights and fundamental freedoms of indigenous people (2001); the Declaration on the Rights of Indigenous Peoples (2007); and the Human Council's Expert Mechanism on the Rights of Indigenous Peoples (2007).

[126] Westra (2008), 9 citing Metcalf (2004).

However, it has also been argued "that the CBD must be read consistently with the superior authority of the UN Charter whose article 1(3) defines one of the primary purposes and principles of the UN as 'promoting and encouraging respect for human rights and fundamental freedoms for all without distinction as to race, sex, language or religion....' In the exercise of their sovereign will, the vast majority of states have voluntarily accepted this international legal obligation by ratifying international human rights conventions.[127] These and other obligations are not suspended in connection with CBD; Article 22 of the Convention on Biological Diversity specifically states that its provisions 'shall not affect the rights and obligations of any Contracting party deriving from any existing international agreement, except where the exercise of those rights and obligations would cause a serious damage or threat to biological diversity'".[128] The Declaration on the Rights of Indigenous Peoples also refers to international human rights obligations and states in its Article 32 (3) that: its provisions "shall be interpreted in accordance with the principles of justice, democracy, respect for human rights, equality, non-discrimination, good governance and good faith".

But good international policies do not necessarily result in good implementation, and one of the greatest challenges lies at the national level. Many indigenous peoples have a distinct legal status within their countries, are barely recognized as equal citizens, and face multiple constraints when trying to claim the rights that international law grants them. This does not mean that efforts at the international level should not be sustained. On the contrary, because it is here that indigenous peoples, aside from their political aims, can develop a multiplicity of additional relationships, that are critically important for self-realization and the exercise of self-determination[129] and can have the opportunity for face-to-face interactions and dialogues with decision-makers at the national level and thereby the possibility to impact domestic policies.

At both levels, the Declaration can be a useful tool. Indigenous participants in recent CBD meetings on the International Regime on Access to Genetic Resources and Benefit-Sharing pointed out that the Declaration contained articles of direct relevance to the issues under discussion and that any component or provision of the International Regime had to be consistent with the Declaration. At the same time, they also noted among the Parties a widespread recognition of the Declaration as a new framework to be taken into account.[130]

On the international and domestic stages, the challenge for indigenous peoples is therefore to continue to assert their sovereign rights as peoples to access their lands and natural resources, to participate in decisions concerning these resources, and to use their right of free, prior and informed consent.

---

[127] For instance, the International Covenant on Civil and Political Rights (ICCPR), the International Covenant on Economic, Social and Cultural Rights (IESCR), and the International Covenant on the Elimination of Racial Discrimination (ICERD).
[128] Forest Peoples Programme (2004b), 2.
[129] Carino (2001), 5.
[130] IWGIA (2008), 564.

List of references

Agenda 21. 1992. Plan of Action adopted at the Rio Conference on Environment and Development (UNCED). Available online at www.un.org/esa/sustdev/agenda21.htm

Akwe: Kon. 2004. The Akwe: Kon Voluntary Guidelines. Available online at http://www.cbd.int/doc/publications/akwe-brochure-en.pdf

Alwyn, José. 2006. "Land and Resources" in Cultural Survival Quarterly, Issue 30.4, December 2006.

Arctic Climate Impact Assessment. 2005. Cambridge, Mass.: Cambridge University Press. Available online at http://www.amap.no./acia

Barkin, David. 2005. "Incorporating indigenous epistemologies into the construction of alternative strategies to globalization to promote sustainable regional resource management: The struggle for local autonomy in a multiethnic society". Paper at the Workshop on Ethics and Development: The Capability Approach in Practice, Michigan State University, 13 April, 2005. Available online at http://www.ma.caudillweb.com/documents/bridging/papers/Barkin.david.pdf

Barume, Albert K. 2009 (forthcoming). Land Rights in Africa (working title). Copenhagen: IWGIA.

Borgerhoff Mulder, Monique and Coppolillo, Peter. 2005. Conservation: Linking Ecology, Economics, and Culture. Princeton: Princeton University Press.

Brockington, Daniel and Igoe, James. 2006. "Eviction for Conservation: A Global Overview" in Conservation and Society, Volume 4, No. 3, September 2006: 424–470.

Carino, Joji. 2001. "Indigenous peoples and the World Summit for Sustainable Development (WSSD)". Indigenous Affairs, Sustainable Development, 4/2001: 4-6. Copenhagen: IWGIA.

CSD Indigenous Peoples' Caucus. 2001. "Dialogue paper by indigenous peoples". Indigenous Affairs, Sustainable Development, 4/2001: 13-25. Copenhagen: IWGIA.

Centre for Indigenous Environmental Resources. 2007. Climate change impacts on abundance and distribution of traditional foods and medicines – Effects on a First Nation and their capacity to adapt. Available at http://www.cier.ca/WorkArea/showcontent.aspx?id=1296

Cernea, Michael M. 2005. "Concept and method: Applying the IRR model in Africa to resettlement and poverty". In Displacement Risks in Africa: Refugees, Resettlers and their Host Population, ed. I. Ohta and Y.D. Gebre. Kyoto: Kyoto University Press.

Cernea, Michael M. and Schmidt-Soltau, Kai. 2006. "Poverty Risks and National Parks: Policy Issues in Conservation and Resettlement". World Development Vol. 34, No. 10: 1808–1830.

Chapin, Mac. 2004. "A Challenge to Conservationists". World Watch Magazine, November/December 2004.

Colchester, Marcus. 2004. "Conservation Policy and Indigenous Peoples", Cultural Survival Quarterly, Issue 28.1, March 2004.

Committee on the Elimination of All Forms of Racial Discrimination (CERD). 1997. General Recommendation No. 23: Indigenous Peoples. Fifty first session of the CERD, August 1997. Available online at http://www2.ohchr.org/english/bodies/cerd/index.htm

Committee on the Elimination of All Forms of Racial Discrimination (CERD). 2003. Concluding Observations on Uganda. UN Doc. CERD/C/62/CO/11, 2 June 2003. Available online at http://www.unhchr.ch/tbs/doc.nsf/(Symbol)/CERD.C.62.CO.11.En?Opendocument

Commonwealth of Australia. 2007. Growing up Strong – The first 10 years of Indigenous Protected Areas in Australia. Canberra: Commonwealth of Australia. Available online at http://www.environment.gov.au/indigenous/publications/growingupstrong.html

Convention on Biological Diversity (2002). The text of the Convention available online at http://www.cbd.int

Convention on Biological Diversity (CBD). 2004. Report on the Conference of the Parties to the Convention on Biological Diversity on the work of its seventh meeting. UN Doc. UNEP/CBD/COP/7/21 February 2004.

Convention on Biological Diversity (CBD). 2008a. Report of the Conference of the Parties to the Convention on Biological Diversity on the work of its ninth meeting. UN Doc. UNEP/CBD/COP/9/29 October 2008.

Convention on Biological Diversity (CBD). 2008b. Report of the International Expert Meeting on Responses to Climate Change for Indigenous and Local Communities and the impact on their traditional Knowledge Related to Biological Diversity: The Arctic Region. UN Doc. UNEP/CBD/COP/9/INF/43 March 2008.

Dowie, Mark. 2005. Conservation Refugees – When protecting nature means kicking people out. Orion November/December 2005. At http://www.oriononline.org/pages/om/o5-6om/Dowie.html

Forest Peoples Programme. 2004a. Briefing on the United Nations Forum on Forests (UNFF) and Collaborative Partnership on Forests (CPF). Available online at http://www.forestpeoples.org

Forest Peoples Programme. 2004b. Indigenous Peoples' Rights, State Sovereignty and the Convention on Biological Diversity. Available online at http://www.forestpeoples.org

Forest Peoples Programme. 2007a. The UNFF fails indigenous peoples again. Briefing Note. Available online at http://www.forestpeoples.org

Forest Peoples Programme. 2007b. Indigenous peoples' Participation in the Decisions and Policy-making of GEF. Available online at http://www.forestpeoples.org

Forest Peoples Programme. 2008. Some views of indigenous peoples and forest-related organisations on World Bank's "Forest Carbon Partnership Facility" and proposals for a "Global Forest Partnership". A global survey. FPP Briefing. Available online at http://www.forestpeoples.org

Garnaut Climate Change Review. 2008. Final Report. Available online at http://www.garnautreview.org.au/index.htm

Gray, Andrew. 1991. Between the spice of life and the melting pot: biodiversity conservation and its impact on indigenous peoples. IWGIA Document No. 70. Copenhagen: IWGIA.

Hill, R. 2004. Yalanji Warranga Kaban: Yalanji People of the Rainforest Fire Management Book. Cairns: Little Ramsay Press.

Hitchcock, R.K. 2001. "Decentralization, Natural Resource Management, and Community-Based Conservation Institutions in Southern Africa". Indigenous Affairs, Sustainable Development, 4/2001: 38-49. Copenhagen: IWGIA.

Indigenous Statement. 2008. Statement made by the Indigenous Peoples Committee on Conservation during Agenda item 3.1.1 and 3.1.2 at Working Group Meeting on Protected Areas on the Review of the Implementation of the Programme of Work on Protected Areas for the Period 2004-2007 (UNEP/CBD/WG-PA/2/2). Available online at http://indigenousstatement.blogspot.com/2008/02/unepcbdwgpa22.html

IPCC. 2007a. Climate Change 2007: The Physical Science Basis. Contribution of Working Group I to the Fourth Assessment. Report of the Intergovernmental Panel on Climate Change, ed. S. Solomon, D. Qin, M. Manning, Z. Chen, M. Marquis, K.B. Averyt, M. Tignor and H.L. Miller. Cambridge, U.K. and New York, N.Y.: Cambridge University Press.

IPCC. 2007b. Climate change 2007: Impacts, Adaptation, Vulnerability. Contribution of Working Group II to the Fourth Assessment Report of the Intergovernmental Panel on Climate change, ed. M.L. Parry, O.F. Canziani, J.P. Palutikof, P.J. van der Linden and C.E. Hanson. Cambridge, UK.: Cambridge University Press.

IPCC. 2007c. Climate Change 2007: Mitigation. Contribution of Working Group III to the Fourth Assessment Report of the Intergovernmental Panel on Climate Change, ed. B. Metz, O.R. Davidson, P.R. Bosch, R. Dave, L.A. Meyer. Cambridge, U.K. and New York, N.Y.: Cambridge University Press.

IUCN. 1994. WCC Resolution and Recommendations. Available online at http://www.iucn.org/resolutions/index.html

IUCN. 1996. WCC Resolution and Recommendations. Available online at http://www.iucn.org/resolutions/index.html

IUCN. 2008. Indigenous and Traditional Peoples. Available online at http://www.iucn.org/about/work/programmes/social_policy/sp_themes/sp_themes_ip/index.cfm

IUCN-WWF. 1996. IUCN-WWF Principles and Guidelines on Indigenous and Traditional Peoples and Protected Areas. Available at http://www.iucn.org/themes/wcpa/pubs/pdfs/Indig

IWGIA. 2008.The Indigenous World 2008. IWGIA's yearbook. Copenhagen: IWGIA. Available online at http://www.iwgia.org

Joffe, Paul. 2008. UN Declaration: Achieving Reconciliation and Effective Application in the Canadian Context. Paper prepared for the Continuing Legal Education Society of British Colombia, Aboriginal Law Conference 2008, Vancouver.

Johannesburg Plan of Implementation. 2002. Adopted by the World Summit on Sustainable Development in Johannesburg, South Africa. Available online at http://www.un.org/esa/sustdev/documents/WSSD_POI_PD/English/POIToc.htm

Kimberley Political Declaration. 2002. Declaration adopted at the International Indigenous Peoples Summit on Sustainable Development, Khoi-San Territory, Kimberley, South Africa, 20-23 August 2002. Available online at http://www.iwgia.org/sw217.asp

Kyoto Protocol. 1997. Available online at http://unfccc.int/kyoto_protocol/items/2830.php

Laltaika, Eliamani. 2008. "Climate Change Mitigation & Indigenous Peoples' Welfare: Analysis of the International Legal Regime". Mimeo. Kenya: TAPHGO. Accessible at http://www.taphgo.org

Larsen, Peter Bille and Springer, Jenny. 2008. Mainstreaming WWF principles on indigenous peoples and conservation in project and programme management. Gland, Switzerland and Washington, D.C.: WWF.

Lewis, D. 2002. Slower Than the Eye Can See: Environmental Change in Northern Australia's Cattle Lands, A Case Study from the Victoria River District, Northern Territory. Darwin, Northern Territory: Tropical Savannas CRC. Available online at http://savanna.ntu.edu.au/publications/landscape_change.html

Lewis, Jerome and John Nelson. 2006. "Logging in the Congo Basin: What Hope for Indigenous Peoples' Resources and their Environments?" Indigenous Affairs, Logging and Indigenous Peoples, 4/06: 8-15. Copenhagen: IWGIA.

Macchi, Mirjam. 2008. Indigenous and Traditional Peoples and Climate Change. Issues Paper. Gland, Switzerland: IUCN.

Mugarura, Victor. 2007. "Aborigines burn the way to climate control". BBC (18.11.2007) at http://news.bbc.co.uk/2/hi/asia-pacific/6726059.stm

Metcalf, Cherie. 2004. "Indigenous Rights and the Environment: Evolving International Law". 35 Ottawa L. Rev. 103, 105 (2003/-2004).

Nairobi Declaration. 2004. Declaration of the 2nd African Indigenous Women's Conference, Nairobi. Available online at
http://www.indigenous-info-kenya.org/images/issue%208/nairobi%20declaration %20of%20the%202nd%20 african%20indigenous%20women's%20co.pdf

Newing, Helen. 2004. A summary of case study findings on implementation of international commitments on traditional forest related knowledge (tfrk). Available online at
http://www.international-alliance.org/documents/overview-finaledit.pdf

Nilsson, Christiana. 2008. "Climate Change from an Indigenous Perspective: Key issues and Challenges". Indigenous Affairs, Climate Change and Indigenous Peoples, 1-2/08: 8-15. Copenhagen: IWGIA.

Nuttall, Mark. 2008. "Climate change and the warming politics of autonomy in Greenland". Indigenous Affairs, Climate Change and Indigenous Peoples, 1-2/08: 45-51. Copenhagen: IWGIA.

Orlove, B. 2003. How People Name Seasons, ed. S. Strauss and B. Orlove. Oxford: Berg Publishers.

Parry, M.L., Canziani, O.F., Palutikof, J.P., van der Linden, P.J. and Hanson, C.E., eds., 2007. "Cross-chapter case study" in Climate Change 2007: Impacts, Adaptation and Vulnerability. Contribution of Working Group II to the Fourth Assessment Report of the Intergovernmental Panel on Climate Change. Cambridge, UK: Cambridge University Press.

Posey, Darrell A., ed. 2000. Cultural and Spiritual Values of Biodiversity. New York, N.Y.: United Nations Environment Program/London: Intermediate Technology Publications.

Ribis, Nick and Andrea Mascarenhas. 1994. "Indigenous Peoples after UNCED". Cultural Survival Quarterly, Issue 18.1, 1994.

Rio Declaration. 1992. Declaration on Environment and Development adopted at the World Conference on Environment and Development, Rio de Janeiro, 1992. Available online at
http://www.unep.org/documents/default.asp?documentid=78

Robinson, J.B. and D. Herbert. 2001. "Integrating climate change and sustainable development", Int. J. Global Environ., 1, 130-149.

Rose, D. 1996. Nourishing Terrains: Australian Aboriginal Views of Landscape and Wilderness. Canberra: Australian Heritage Commission. Available online at http://www.ahc.gov.au/publications/generalpubs/nourishing/index.html

SCBD. 2003. Interlinkages between biological diversity and climate change. Advice on the integration of biodiversity considerations into the implementation of the United Nations Framework Convention on Climate Change and its Kyoto protocol. CBD Technical Series No. 10. Montreal: Secretariat of the Convention on Biological Diversity. Available online at http://www.cbd.int/doc/meetings/tk/emccilc-01/other/emccilc-01-cbd-ts-10-en.pdf

SCBD. 2006. Guidance for Promoting Synergy Among Activities Addressing Biological Diversity, Desertification, Land Degradation and Climate Change. Technical Series No. 25. Montreal: Secretariat of the Convention on Biological Diversity CBD. Available online at http://www.cbd.int/doc/meetings/tk/emccilc-01/other/emccilc-01-cbd-ts-25-en.pdf

Simpson, Tony. 1997. Indigenous Heritage and Self-Determination. IWGIA Document 86. Copenhagen: IWGIA.

Stavenhagen, Rodolfo. 2003. Report on Large Scale development. Report of the Special Rapporteur on the situation of human rights and fundamental freedoms of indigenous people to the UN Economic and Social Council. UN Doc. E/CN.4/2003/90 21 January 2003.

Stavenhagen, Rodolfo. 2004. Indigenous Peoples in Comparative Perspective – Problems and Policies. Background paper for the Human Development Report Office. UNDP.

Stavenhagen. Rodolfo. 2007. "Mission to Kenya". Report of the Special Rapporteur on the situation of human rights and fundamental freedoms of indigenous people to the UN Economic and Social Council, Addendum 3. UN Doc. A/HRC/4/32/Add.3 26 February 2007.

Tauli-Corpuz, Victoria and Tamang, Parshuram. 2007. Oil palm and other commercial tree plantations: Monocropping impacts on indigenous peoples' land tenure and resource management systems and livelihood. Paper prepared for UNPFII Sixth Session. UN Doc. E/C.19/2007/CRP.6. Available online at UNPFII website http://www.un.org/esa/socdev/unpfii

United Nations. 2007. Declaration on the Rights of Indigenous Peoples. Resolution A/61/L.67, September 2007. Available online at UNPFII Web site http://www.un.org/esa/socdev/unpfii/en/declaration.html

United Nations Convention to Combat Desertification (UNCCD). 1994. Text of Convention available at http://www.unccd.int

United Nations Forum on Forests (UNFF). 2000. See Web site at http://www.un.org/esa/forests

United Nations Framework Convention on Climate Change (UNFCCC). 1992. Text of Convention available at http://unfccc.int/

UN-HABITAT 2005. Indigenous peoples' right to adequate housing: A global overview. Nairobi: United Nations Human Settlements Programme (UN-HABITAT) and Office of the High Commissioner for Human Rights (OHCHR).

UNHCHR. 2008. Leaflet No. 10: Indigenous Peoples and the Environment. Available online at http://www.unhchr. ch/html/racism/indileaflet10.doc

United Nations Permanent Forum on Indigenous Issues (UNPFII). 2008. Report on the Seventh Session (21 April-2 May 2008). UN DOC. E/C.19/2008/13. Available online at http://www.un.org/esa/socdev/unpfii

Valente, Marcela. 2007. "Environment: Conservation expands in Latin America". Inter Press Service (IPS) online at http://ipsnews.net/news.asp?idnews=39493

Webb, E.K. 1997. Windows on Meteorology: Australian Perspective. Collingwood: CSIRO Publishing.

Westra, L. 2008. Environmental Justice and the Rights of Indigenous Peoples: International and Domestic Legal Perspectives. UK: EarthscanPress.

Working Group on Article 8J. 2005. The Revised Phase One and Phase Two of the Composite Report on the Status and Trends Regarding the Knowledge, Innovations and Practices of Indigenous and Local Communities relevant to the Conservation and sustainable use of Biological Diversity. UN Doc. UNEP/CBD/WG8J/4/4 December 2005.

Working Group on Article 8J. 2007a. Revision of the Second Phase of the Composite Report on the Status and Trends Regarding the Knowledge, Innovation and Practices of Indigenous Peoples and Local Communities. Report on Threats to the Practice and Transmission of Traditional Knowledge: Africa. UN Doc. UNEP/CBD/ WG8J/AG/2/2/Add.1 April 2007.

Working Group on Article 8J. 2007b. Revision of the Second Phase of the Composite Report on the Status and Trends Regarding the Knowledge, Innovation and Practices of Indigenous Peoples and Local Communities. Report on Threats to the Practice and Transmission of Traditional Knowledge: Arctic. UN Doc. UNEP/CBD/ WG8J/AG/2/2/Add.2 April 2007.

Working Group on Article 8J. 2007c. Revision of the Second Phase of the Composite Report on the Status and Trends Regarding the Knowledge, Innovation and Practices of Indigenous Peoples and Local Communities. Report on Threats to the Practice and Transmission of Traditional Knowledge: Asia and Australia. UN Doc. UNEP/CBD/WG8J/AG/2/2/Add.3 April 2007.

Working Group on Article 8J. 2007d. Composite Report on the Status and Trends Regarding the Knowledge, Innovations and Practices of Indigenous and Local Communities: Regional Report: Latin America, Central and the Caribbean. UN Doc. UNEP/CBD/WG8J/AG/2/2/Add.4 April 2007.

Working Group on Article 8J. 2007e. Composite Report on the Status and Trends Regarding the Knowledge, Innovations and Practices of Indigenous and Local Communities: Regional Report: North America. UN Doc. UNEP/CBD/WG8J/AG/2/2/Add.6 April 2007.

Working Group on Article 8J. 2007f. Draft Report of Measures and Mechanisms to Address the Underlying Causes of the Decline of Traditional Knowledge. Element D of the Plan of Action for the Retention of Traditional Knowledge, Innovations and Practices of Indigenous and Local Communities. UN Doc. UNEP/CBD/WG8J/ AG/2/4, April 2007.

Working Group on Article 8J. 2007g. Revision of the Second Phase of the Composite Report on the Status and Trends Regarding the Knowledge, Innovations and Practices of Indigenous and Local Communities: Latin America, Central and the Caribbean. UN Doc. UNEP/CBD/WG8J/5/INF/6, July 2007.

Working Group on Article 8J. 2007h. Report on Research on and Implementation of Mechanisms and Measures to Address the Underlying Causes of the Decline of Traditional Knowledge, Innovations and Practices. UN Doc. UNEP/CBD/WG8J/5/INF/9 July 2007.

Working Group on Article 8J. 2007i. Report on Indigenous and Local Communities Highly Vulnerable to Climate Change, inter alia, of the Arctic, Small Island States and High Altitudes, with a focus on causes and solution. UN Doc. UNEP/CBD/WG8J/5/INF/18 July 2007.

Working Group on Article 8J. 2007j. Plan of Action for the Retention of Traditional Knowledge –Section D: Research on and implementation of mechanisms and measures to address the underlying causes of the decline of traditional knowledge, innovations and practices. UN Doc. UNEP/CBD/WG8J/5/3/Add.1 September 2007.

World Bank. 2007. Clean Energy for Development Investment Framework: Progress Report on the World Bank Group Action Plan. Washington, D.C.: World Bank Group. Available online at http://siteresources.worldbank.org/DEVCOMMINT/Documentation/21510693/DC2007-0018(E)CleanEnergy.pdf

World Commission on Environment and Development. 1987. Our Common Future. Report of the WCED (Brundtland Report). UN Doc. A/42/427 1987.

WWF. 1996. Indigenous Peoples and Conservation: WWF Statement of Principles. Gland, Switzerland, World Wide Fund For Nature. Available online at http://assets.panda.org

WWF. 2004. Are protected areas working? An analysis of forest protected areas. Gland, Switzerland: WWF. Available online at http://assets.panda.org

WWF. 2008. Indigenous Peoples and Conservation: Statement of Principles. Principles for partnership between WWF and indigenous peoples' organizations in conserving biodiversity within indigenous peoples' lands and territories, and in promoting sustainable use of natural resources. Gland, Switzerland: WWF. Accessible at website: http://assets.panda.org

WWF - International. 2008. Indigenous Peoples and Conservation: WWF Statement of Principles. Available online at http://assets.panda.org.

WWF-International and Terralingua. 2000. Indigenous and Traditional Peoples of the World and Ecoregion Conservation: An Integrated Approach to Conserving the World's Biological and Cultural Diversity. Switzerland: WWF-International and Terralingua.

CHAPTER IV

CONTEMPORARY EDUCATION

Duane Champagne

Millions of people are denied their right to education because of poverty, marginalization, poor and ill-funded services, geographic isolation and conflicts. Indigenous peoples are particularly affected and, throughout the world, they suffer from lower levels of education than their non-indigenous counterparts.

> indigenous students have lower enrolment rates, higher dropout rates and poorer educational outcomes than non-indigenous people in the same countries

The situation of indigenous peoples is typically characterized by a lack of access to education in general, due to their geographic and politically marginalized status. Too often, education systems and curricula do not respect indigenous peoples' diverse cultures. There are too few teachers who speak their languages and their schools often lack basic materials. Educational materials that provide accurate and fair information on indigenous peoples and their ways of life are particularly rare. It is too common that "…educational programs fail to offer indigenous peoples the possibility of participating in decision-making, the design of curricula, the selection of teachers and teaching methods and the definition of standards." [1] The result is an education gap - indigenous students have lower enrolment rates, higher dropout rates and poorer educational outcomes than non-indigenous people in the same countries.

Education as a fundamental right

Education is recognized as both a human right in itself and an indispensable means of realizing other human rights and fundamental freedoms, the primary vehicle by which economically and socially marginalized peoples can lift themselves out of poverty and obtain the means to participate fully in their communities. Education is increasingly recognized as one of the best long-term financial investments that States can make. Education of indigenous children contributes to both individual and community development, as well as to participation in society in its broadest sense. Education enables indigenous children to exercise and enjoy economic, social and cultural rights, and strengthens their ability to exercise civil rights in order to influence political policy processes for improved protection of human rights. The implementation of indigenous peoples' right to education is an essential means of achieving individual empowerment and self-determination. Education is also an important means for the enjoyment,

---

[1] King & Schielmann (2004), 19.

maintenance and respect of indigenous cultures, languages, traditions and traditional knowledge… Education is the primary means ensuring indigenous peoples' individual and collective development; it is a precondition for indigenous peoples' ability to realize their right to self-determination, including their right to pursue their own economic, social and cultural development.[2]

There are a number of international instruments that establish education as a fundamental human right. The Universal Declaration of Human Rights (1948), and later, the World Declaration on Education for All (1990) and the Dakar Framework of Action (2000), all reiterate the commitment of the international community to providing quality education to all children, youth and adults.

Relating specifically to indigenous peoples in general, International Labour Organization (ILO) Convention No. 169 (1989) on Indigenous and Tribal Peoples encourages state-funded education programmes at all levels to teach in indigenous languages and to produce media and educational materials in local languages.[3] The Convention on the Rights of the Child (CRC 1989) stipulates that the child's own cultural identity, language and values be respected (Article 29.1c) and explicitly addresses the situation of indigenous children by stating, "a child… who is indigenous shall not be denied the right, in community with other members of his or her group, to enjoy his or her own culture, to profess and practise his or her own religion, or to use his or her own language" (Article 30).

During the First International Decade of the World's Indigenous Peoples (1995-2004), the UN General Assembly adopted resolution 48/163 affirming progress at national and international levels toward broader enjoyment of the right to education by indigenous peoples. Indigenous peoples themselves have, in various fora and on various occasions, emphasized the importance they place on education. The Coolangatta Statement (1999) recounts numerous international documents supporting indigenous peoples' right to education in indigenous languages and the teaching of indigenous cultural content, spirituality and policies of self-determination.[4] More recently, and based on the findings of the Special Rapporteur on the situation of human rights and fundamental freedoms of indigenous people,[5] the United Nations Permanent Forum on Indigenous Issues (UNPFII) has recommended that states include indigenous community members in education policy-making and decisions, support indigenous knowledge and languages in primary and secondary schools, and help train additional indigenous people to manage and implement their own education systems.[6]

> indigenous peoples have the right to establish and control their educational systems and institutions providing education in their own languages

---

[2] Expert Mechanism on the Rights of Indigenous Peoples p. 4-5 & 25.

[3] ILO Convention No. 169, articles 26 to 31.

[4] The Coolangatta Statement on Indigenous Peoples' Rights in Education was issued by the World Indigenous Peoples' Conference on Education, held in Hilo, Hawai'i, 6 August 1999.

[5] Stavenhagen (2005a), 19, para. 87.

[6] UNPFII (2005).

Finally, and not least, the recently adopted Declaration on the Rights of Indigenous Peoples (2007) recognizes the importance of adequate education for indigenous peoples, especially in Article 14 which states that indigenous peoples have the right to establish and control their educational systems and institutions providing education in their own languages, in a manner appropriate to their cultural methods of teaching and learning. Articles 12 (1) and 13 (1) also emphasize education, recognizing indigenous peoples' right to manifest, practice, develop and teach spiritual and religious traditions customs and ceremonies and their right to revitalize, use develop and transmit to future generations their histories, languages, oral traditions, philosophies, writing systems and literatures. [7]

The education gap

Despite the numerous international instruments that thus proclaim universal rights to education, indigenous peoples do not fully enjoy these rights, and an education gap between indigenous peoples and the rest of the population remains critical, worldwide.[8]

In most countries, indigenous children have low school enrolments, poor school performance, low literacy rates, high dropout rates, and lag behind other groups in terms of academic achievements nationally.[9] Illiteracy, which is prevalent in indigenous communities is a direct result of educational exclusion in the form of poor access, low funding, culturally and linguistically inadequate education and ill-equipped instructors. Among the H'mong of Viet Nam, one of the most marginalized of the country's indigenous groups, 83 per cent of men and 97 per cent of women are illiterate;[10] in many small communities in Southern Arnhem Land (Australia), up to 93 per cent of the population is illiterate.[11] In Ecuador, the illiteracy rate of indigenous peoples was 28 per cent in 2001, compared to the national rate of 13 per cent[12], while in Venezuela, the indigenous illiteracy rate (32 per cent) is five times higher than the non-indigenous illiteracy rate (6.4 per cent).[13]

Disparity in years of schooling among indigenous and non-indigenous populations

A sizeable gap persists between indigenous and non-indigenous years of schooling. (Average years of schooling, population 15 and older, latest available year)

Country	Non-Indigenous	Indigenous	Schooling gap in years
Bolivia	9.6	5.9	3.7
Ecuador	6.9	4.3	2.6
Guatemala	5.7	2.5	3.2
Mexico	7.9	4.6	3.3
Peru	8.7	6.4	2.3

Source: Hall and Patrinos (2006).

---

[7] United Nations Declaration on the Rights of Indigenous Peoples (2007).

[8] See Vinding (ed.) (2006), 13-16.

[9] See Larsen, Peter Bille (2003), vii, 14-15; The Coolangatta Statement; Abu-Saad (2006), 128-140, and (2003), 103-120; Hays (2005), 27; Lasimbang (2005) 43; Hicks (2005), 9, 13-14; Freeman and Fox (2005), 34, 42-44, 50, 86; Mellor and Corrigan (2004), 2.

[10] UNICEF (2003).

[11] The Age, (November 2005).

[12] UNESCO (2008), p. 96.

[13] ECLAC/CEPAL (2006), 177.

Disparate secondary school graduation rates between indigenous and non-indigenous students

A gap exists between indigenous and non-indigenous rates of high school graduation. (Percentage of the population who graduated high school, latest available year)

Country	Total Population	Indigenous	Percentage Gap
Australia[a]	49	23	26
Canada[b]	65	37	28
New Zealand: Māori[c]	76.1	62.9	13.2
USA: Native American/ Alaska Native[d]	80.4	70.9	9.5
USA: Native Hawaiian/ Pacific Islander	80.4	78.3	2.1

Sources: [a]Australian Bureau of Statistics (2008); [b]Stewart, S.C. (2006); [c]New Zealand Household Labour Force Survey (2008); [d]U.S. Census Bureau (2000).

In a recent ILO study on the MDGs,[14] examples from different indigenous communities around the world showed that primary school enrolment rates in general were low; in the case of a Bolivian Andean community, rates were substantially lower (75 per cent) than the national average (97 per cent); in Cameroon, only 1.31 per cent of the indigenous Baka children in the District of Salapoumbé attended primary school. In 2000, the UN Committee on the Rights of the Child expressed "serious concern regarding the striking disparities in terms of access to education, attendance at primary and secondary levels and drop-out rates [suffered by] children belonging to scheduled castes and tribes [in India]".[15]

Speaking an indigenous or non-official language is a clear marker of disadvantage in terms of schooling. In Mozambique, for example, 43 per cent of people aged between 16 and 49 who speak Portuguese have at least one grade of secondary schooling, while among speakers of Lomwe, Makhuwa, Sena and Tsonga, the rates are between 6 and 16 per cent. In Bolivia, 68 per cent of Spanish speakers aged 16 to 49 have completed some secondary education, while only a third or fewer of Aymara, Quechua and Guaraní speakers have done so.[16] Indigenous girls tend to be more disadvantaged than indigenous boys. In Guatemala, only 54 per cent of indigenous girls are in school, compared with 71 per cent of indigenous boys. By age 16, only a quarter of indigenous girls are enrolled, compared with 45 per cent of boys.[17]

[speaking an indigenous or non-official language is a clear marker of disadvantage]

---

[14] Vinding (ed.) (2006).
[15] UN Committee on the Rights of the Child (CRC) (2000).
[16] UNESCO (2008), p. 96.
[17] UNESCO (2008), p.104-105.

According to census data in Australia, Canada, New Zealand and the United States, the gap between indigenous and non-indigenous peoples' participation in formal education has narrowed in recent years. Nevertheless, there remains a significant gap. In 2006, 21 per cent of 15-year-old indigenous children in Australia were not participating in school education, compared with 5 per cent of non-indigenous children, while indigenous students were half as likely to complete year 12 of primary school education as their non-indigenous counterparts.[18] In the United States, absences from school are higher among indigenous children than other groups.

Estimated probability of primary school dropout, Mexico, 2002 (per cent)

	Indigenous	Non-Indigenous	All
Male	51.8	25.0	28.2
Female	56.6	29.7	32.9
Rural	61.8	47.5	51.4
Urban	24.4	19.2	19.4

Source: Hall and Patrinos (2006).

High dropout rates are due to multiple causes: Parents cannot afford the out-of-pocket costs related to keeping their children in schools, especially in rural areas where children customarily participate in traditional agricultural activities and are valuable contributors to the household economy; they face numerous obstacles (language problems, discrimination, etc.) or, in the case of girls, because they have to help their mothers with domestic chores, take care of siblings or contribute to their families' income, or because they get married.

Probability of a 10-14-year-old child working, Guatemala, 2000 (per cent)

	School only	School and work	Work, no school	No work, no school
Indigenous	47	24	14	15
Non-Indigenous	69	14	8	9

Source: Based on table in Hall and Patrinos (2006), 124.

---

[18] Steering Committee for the Review of Service Provision (2007).

Indigenous education in the United States: some highlights

During the 2005-2006 school year, there were 644,000 Native American and Alaska Natives in the public primary and secondary school system, or about 1 per cent of all public school students, whilst they make up 1.5 per cent of the total population. A larger percentage of Native American and Alaska Native eighth-graders (13-14 years old) were absent from school than any other segment of the population, and only Hispanic youth had higher dropout rates (21 per cent) than Native American and Alaska Native youth (15 per cent).

Native American and Alaska Native students in public schools are less likely to have access to a computer at home than any other group. The number of Native American and Alaska Natives enrolled in college has doubled in the past 30 years, while still lagging behind the total population.

In 2006, there were 32 tribally controlled colleges and universities attended by over 17,000 students. Educational outcomes remain deeply unequal, where Native American and Alaska Natives suffer from significantly higher unemployment rates (16 per cent in 2007) than others (3-12 per cent), whilst the median annual earnings in 2006 for 25- to 34-year-old Native Americans and Alaska Natives was $27,000, compared to the general population's $35,000.

Source: DeVoe, J.F., and Darling-Churchill, K.E. (2008) pp. iii-v.

The state of Aboriginal education in Australia

Despite the improvements in school completion within the indigenous population, indigenous people aged 15 years and over were still half as likely as non-indigenous Australians to have completed school to year 12 in 2006 (23 per cent, compared with 49 per cent). They were also twice as likely to have left school at year 9 or below (34 per cent, compared with 16 per cent). In 2006, around 10,400 young indigenous adults aged 18-24 years (22 per cent) had left school at year 9 or below, compared with 58,100 non-indigenous young people in the same age group (4 per cent). These relative differences have remained unchanged since 2001.[a]

Indigenous people living in rural or remote areas of Australia were less likely than those in urban areas to have completed year 12. In 2006, 31 per cent of indigenous people living in major cities had completed school to this level, compared with 22 per cent in regional areas and 14 per cent in remote areas. With the exception of Queensland, this was reflected across the states and territories, with the Australian Capital Territory (46 per cent) having the largest proportion of indigenous people who had completed year 12, and the Northern Territory the lowest (10 per cent).[a]

While 93 per cent of all Australian students and 83 per cent of Aboriginal students achieved year 3 reading benchmarks, only 20 per cent of indigenous students in remote Northern Territory schools met the standard.[b]

By year 5, 89 per cent of all students and 70 per cent of Aboriginal students nationally achieved the reading benchmark, compared with only 21 per cent of Aboriginal students in remote parts of the NT.[b]

Sources: [a]Australian Bureau of Statistics (2008); [b]Storry, K. (2006)

Why they drop out...

Añú girl, aged 11, from Lagoon Sinamaica (Venezuela):

"I went from first to third grade... but gave up going to school some two months ago because I was working, fetching water, helping my mother, and therefore the teacher took me off the list".

Warao woman, Grade 6 teacher, aged 21, from Nabasanuka (Venezuela):

"They drop out because they get tired of repeating classes... when they repeat, they get discouraged and don't come back".

Source: ECLAC/CEPAL (2006), 182.

Age-Grade Distortion, Guatemala, 2000

(Percentage of students more than one year behind the appropriate grade for their age)

Grade	Indigenous	Non-indigenous
Third	79	75
Fourth	71	63
Fifth	59	54
Sixth	59	50

Source: Hall and Patrinos (2006).

Even in countries where the general level of schooling among indigenous peoples has increased, such as, for instance, several Latin American countries and Canada, the quality gap in schooling persists, resulting in poor education outcomes for indigenous peoples (Table 4.6).[19]

---

[19] ILO/PRO169/IPEC (2006).

Primary education in Latin America (10 countries)

Percentage of population aged 15 to 19 having completed primary education, by ethnicity and sex and gender ratio, based on census data (2000-2002)

Countries and date of census	Percentage of youth aged 15 to 19 that completed primary school						Gender ratio (per 100)	
	Indigenous			Non-Indigenous				
	Total	Men	Women	Total	Men	Women	Indigenous	Non-Indigenous
Bolivia 2001	73.7	79.5	68.4	86.4	86.6	86.3	116.2	100.3
Brazil 2000	63.7	63.0	64.4	78.6	74.6	82.9	97.8	89.9
Chile 2002	93.3	92.5	94.0	95.5	95.1	96.1	98.4	99.0
Costa Rica 2000	55.7	56.1	55.2	86.3	84.5	88.0	101.6	96.1
Ecuador 2001	70.2	74.1	66.7	74.2	72.3	76.2	111.1	94.8
Guatemala 2002	36.3	42.9	30.0	68.7	64.6	72.7	142.9	88.9
Honduras 2001	45.1	42.8	47.6	81.6	77.4	85.6	89.8	90.5
México 2000	68.7	72.4	65.0	90.0	89.7	90.2	111.3	99.4
Panamá 2000	55.8	61.2	50.2	93.3	92.0	94.7	121.8	97.1
Paraguay 2002	21.4	25.6	16.8	82.8	82.0	83.7	151.9	97.9

Source: ECLAC/CEPAL (2006), 61.

Most states focus on access to primary and basic education while under-emphasizing secondary, technical and university education. In countries such as the United States and Canada, where indigenous high school graduation rates are similar to that of non-indigenous groups, indigenous students are often less well-prepared for college and are less well-represented in professional and academic fields.[20] This is clearly illustrated by looking at college enrolment numbers, where in 2001, 3.7 per cent of the Native American and Alaska Native population was enrolled in college in the United States, in comparison to 5.6 per cent of the total population. When looking only at graduate students, the difference is greater yet.[21] A similar trend is also visible in Nepal, where indigenous peoples' literacy rates are as high, if not higher than, those of the non-indigenous population, whilst indigenous graduates and post-graduates are only 8.5 per cent of all graduates and post-graduates, yet they constitute 32.7 per cent of the total population.[22]

---

[20] Taylor and Kalt (2005), 40-43; Greene and Forster (2003), 11-14; Institute of Higher Education Policy (1999), A-2; Indian and Northern Affairs Canada (2003), 3-4.

[21] In 2001, there were 11,200 Native Americans and Alaska Natives enrolled in graduate studies, or 0.26 per cent of the Native American and Alaskan Native population in the United States, while graduate students made up 0.69 per cent of the total population of the country, making them 2.7 times less likely to be graduate students. Taken from United States Census Bureau (2008) American Indian, Alaska Native Tables from the Statistical Abstract of the United States: 2004-2005. Accessed on 24 November 2008, at http://www.census.gov/statab/www/sa04aian.pdf

[22] UNDP (2004), 63.

Formal school systems

Indigenous communities are frequently perceived as disappearing social and cultural forms that are no longer viable and which must be rescued by outside forces through formal education and economic and social development. However, as the Special Rapporteur on the situation of human rights and fundamental freedoms stated in his report on Indigenous Peoples and Education Systems:

> The systems of formal education historically provided by the State or religious or private groups have been a two-edged sword for indigenous peoples. On the one hand, they have often enabled indigenous children and youth to acquire knowledge and skills that will allow them to move ahead in life and connect with the broader world. On the other hand, formal education, especially when its programmes, curricula and teaching methods come from other societies that are removed from indigenous cultures, has also been a means of forcibly changing, and in some cases, destroying, indigenous cultures.[23]

Policymakers have long been aware of the formative socializing qualities of education. During the late nineteenth century and throughout the twentieth century, this knowledge informed decisions in many countries, such as Canada, Australia and the United States, where formal education in missionary and many boarding and residential schools separated children from families. This left a legacy of what is referred to in these countries as the "lost" or "stolen" generations.

Although reliable data are not available on a global scale, it is nevertheless clear that a majority of indigenous children do not enjoy access to education that is specifically designed for their needs, taught in their languages or that reflects their world views. In many indigenous communities, education is inseparable from culture, economy, family and survival.[24]

Most formal education systems do not employ community-based or indigenous approaches such as elders passing on traditional knowledge, or parents and other community members teaching children about the environment and their relationship with it.

> a majority of indigenous children do not enjoy access to education that is specifically designed for their needs, taught in their languages or that reflects their world views

Indigenous education in San communities (Southern Africa)

San communities in Southern Africa have been able to survive in a harsh environment for generations depending upon their intimate knowledge of the environment and the animals that live in it. Such survival skills are not

---

[23] Stavenhagen (2005a), 7, para. 15.
[24] Hicks (2005), 9.

> innate; they are learned, passed down from generation to generation in very specific ways. Generations of San children have had to learn the skills and flexibility necessary to survive in their particular circumstances. San children have also had to learn the appropriate behaviours to be accepted within their community. We can thus understand San communities as educating their children.
>
> *Source: Hays, Jennifer (2004), 243.*

On the contrary, national school curricula tend to have very little (if any) focus on indigenous peoples, their issues and histories. Some national curricula even reinforce negative stereotypes, portraying indigenous peoples as underdeveloped, childlike or uncivilized, in contrast to the population of the modern, developed, mature nation-state.[25]

Formal schools teach specific, defined curricula such as national history, culture, etc., which serve the purpose not only of providing information to students, but also of socializing them, teaching them how to be citizens and ultimately incorporating them into the national society. By learning topics such as history, sociology, geography and even biology or chemistry, school children are introduced to a national discourse that emphasizes specific identities, histories and a sense of place in the world.

> schools with predominantly indigenous students are more likely to cancel classes, hire less-qualified teachers, and be understaffed

By excluding indigenous issues from school curricula, many formal education systems ignore indigenous peoples, their cultures and practices. But when indigenous school children are introduced only to the national discourse at the expense of their native discourse, they are in danger of losing part of their identity, their connection with their parents and predecessors and, ultimately, of being caught in a no man's land whereby they lose an important aspect of their identity while not fully becoming a part of the dominant national society. This makes indigenous school children less inclined to pursue their studies. Indeed, indigenous communities often resist state-provided education that does not show respect for their traditional knowledge, values and livelihoods.[26]

Difficulties encountered while delivering formal education to indigenous communities include lack of respect for indigenous languages and culture, interference in internal community affairs, inadequately trained teachers and the irrelevance of teaching curricula.[27] Education services in indigenous areas are, furthermore, usually under-funded, of low quality and poorly equipped. Poor and indigenous children therefore often attend the worst schools, are served by the least educated teachers, and have too few and often outdated textbooks

---

[25] Stavenhagen (2005b), 4-7; Larsen (2003), vii and 14-15.
[26] Larsen (2003), 17-18.
[27] Kroijer (2005), 17.

and other teaching materials.[28] In the United States, for example, according to the 2001 Bureau of Indian Affairs budget report, many schools on Native American reservations were structurally unsound and/or of insufficient size to accommodate the student population.[29]

Schools with predominantly indigenous students are more likely to cancel classes, hire less-qualified teachers, and be understaffed. The lack of qualified teachers is often due to the low priority given to their training and to inadequate salaries. They are also not sufficiently supported and sometimes abandon their posts. There is relatively little parent, community or school board involvement, and underfunding and poor facilities inhibit the development of strong school programmes for indigenous children.[30]

> indigenous girls, in particular, experience difficult problems related to unfriendly school environments

Indigenous children, moreover, are more likely to arrive at school hungry, ill and tired;[31] they are often bullied, and the use of corporal punishment is still widespread. Ethnic and cultural discrimination at schools are major obstacles to equal access to education, causing poor performance and higher dropout rates. Indigenous girls in particular, experience difficult problems related to unfriendly school environments, gender discrimination, school-based violence and sometimes sexual abuse, all of which contribute to high dropout rates.

Participation in formal schooling can also be more difficult for indigenous students who participate in subsistence hunting and gathering economies and uphold egalitarian ethics and preferences for non-hierarchical social organization. In a community that values equality and non-competitive approaches to learning, those who succeed in a system based upon hierarchy and competition have, at some point, had to contradict the cultural values of their upbringing.[32] Some nomadic indigenous communities see formal education as weakening traditional knowledge, threatening economic livelihoods and disrupting the institutional foundations of identity.[33]

The remoteness of many indigenous communities is one of the main reasons for the gap in schooling between indigenous and non-indigenous people. Many remote schools lack qualified teachers, and especially indigenous teachers who speak indigenous languages and can serve as role models for the younger generations. In some cases, only primary education is available locally, after which children must leave their communities for boarding schools, which are often run by missionaries.[34]

Boarding schools are costly for families for multiple reasons. Indigenous children in boarding schools often suffer from discrimination, misunderstanding

[28] ILO/PRO169/IPEC (2006), 22.
[29] UNICEF (2003).
[30] Pavel et al. (1997), 41-48; St. Germaine (1995); US General Accounting Office (1997), 2.
[31] ILO/PRO 169/IPEC (2006), 22; Hicks (2005).
[32] Hays (2004), 242.
[33] Kaunga (2005), 37-41; Hays and Siegruhn (2005), 27.
[34] UNICEF (2003).

of their indigenous culture, lack of support and, in some cases, even physical and sexual exploitation. Sometimes indigenous children are not allowed to follow their cultural practices, such as wearing traditional dress and hairstyles. Indigenous children are often discouraged from speaking their native languages if not forbidden altogether. Students often feel unwelcome in the school towns; they long for their own village schools and often face emotional difficulties in a foreign learning environment that offers little support.[35] The very idea of separating parents and children is foreign to many indigenous peoples. If separation happens, indigenous children are often unable to adjust, suffer from alienation and drop out.

Boarding schools and other practices have often been aimed at assimilating indigenous children into the dominant culture and society. These policies were partly based on a racist notion that indigenous cultures were inferior and that indigenous children would benefit from being assimilated into the dominant culture, language and society. These assimilationist policies uprooted children from their heritage, tore families apart and decimated whole communities. The victims of these policies were left without a sense of belonging; otsiders in both the dominant society and their own indigenous societies. In recent years, the damage boarding schools have done to indigenous peoples' cultures has been recognized, including by the governments of Canada, the United States and Australia.[36]

On the positive side, formal education has made it possible for some indigenous leaders and civil society organizations representing indigenous peoples to gain access to the state. Formal education has also helped to improve the status of indigenous women, enabling them to become more active participants in decision making that affects their lives.

Education in boarding schools may also work in some countries and not in others. If students are separated from their communities in order to attend boarding schools, vocational schools or universities, then emphasis on affirming identity and cultural community with other indigenous students may help to ameliorate the conditions of isolation. Community centres, active student organizations and cultural events, as well as indigenous issue policy discussions and curricula, can foster student leadership, knowledge, retention and training.[37]

Barriers to education for indigenous children

Most indigenous communities see education as very important, even crucial, for improving their overall situation.[38] However, indigenous children face a number of obstacles to participating in formal education systems. Some of these obstacles have to do with their marginalized situation; others are the direct result of national policies.

Poverty, discrimination and marginalization are the leading causes of low educational performance which further exacerbate indigenous children's vulnerable status. From the moment they are born and throughout their lives, indigenous children are particularly exposed to the effects of marginalization. They are less likely to receive adequate health care because they are often not registered at birth or, in some cases, are denied citizenship by the national state in which they live; they may thus have problems accessing education and other public services.

---

[35] Hays and Siegruhn (2005), 31-32.
[36] Official apologies have recently been made by the Government of Australia (February 2008) and by the Government of Canada (June 2008).
[37] Champagne (2001), 21-28; Champagne and Stauss (eds.) (2002).
[38] Vinding (ed.) (2006), 16.

Indigenous children and the right to birth registration and nationality

Article 7 of the Convention on the Rights of the Child requires that a child be registered immediately after birth. It also recognizes the child's right to acquire a nationality. Many indigenous people have neither. "When a child's birth goes unregistered, that child is less likely to enjoy his or her rights and to benefit from the protection accorded by the state in which he or she was born. Furthermore, the unregistered child may go unnoticed when his or her rights are violated. Later in life, he or she will be unable to vote or stand for election…" These children are also at risk of falling victim to child trafficking and are often easy prey for those who exploit their vulnerability recruiting them as street beggars, domestic servants in slave-like arrangements, or as child soldiers.

Source: UNICEF (2003), 9.

Lack of public funding, too few primary schools, too few teachers, inadequate curricula and high costs for parents all contribute to an insurmountable obstacle for many indigenous students. These problems are particularly acute in rural areas that suffer from poor infrastructure and where schools are often located at considerable distances from the community centres and are poorly equipped and understaffed.[39]

Despite increasing awareness and efforts on the part of governments and civil society, indigenous students and their parents often have to face deeply-rooted discrimination and prejudice, making the school environment unfriendly and uncomfortable. School children also often have to cope with abuse at the hands of school authorities and other students; mainstream cultures frequently have little understanding of the values, cultures and histories of indigenous peoples. In many countries, the issue of the school uniform versus traditional dress is often a contentious one;[40] other issues may have to do with cultural practices (for example, hunting trips or religious rites), which are not taken into consideration by school authorities.

Many indigenous peoples' economies are based on modes of subsistence whereby the whole family is required to work at certain times of the year, making children's labour contributions essential. This, too, is seldom recognized by educational authorities, leading to yet another clash of interests that contributes to dropout rates.

One of the most common requests from indigenous parents is that their children be taught in their own language.[41] Bilingual education is widely recognized as a

> bilingual education is widely recognized as a superior alternative for indigenous students, and bilingual and multi-lingual students have frequently been shown to perform better than monolingual indigenous students

---

[39] Lasimbang (2005), 43.
[40] Vinding (ed.) (2006), 14.
[41] ILO/PRO169/IPEC (2006), 16.

superior alternative for indigenous students, and bilingual and multi-lingual students have frequently been shown to perform better than monolingual indigenous students. Nevertheless, limited resources are devoted to building and expanding existing bilingual and intercultural programmes.[42]

The lack of mother-tongue education, cultural differences between home and school, and work obligations are all factors that keep students away from school. The situation is further exacerbated by monolingual education systems, educational materials that are inadequate to the needs and realities of indigenous children, and teaching that is conducted by non-indigenous teachers.

Even under some of the best circumstances, in which physical isolation, school funding and language are not obstacles, there still often remain challenges. Indigenous students frequently find that the education they are offered by the state promotes individualism and a competitive atmosphere, rather than communal ways of life and cooperation. They are not taught relevant survival and work skills suitable for indigenous economies, and they often return to their communities with a formal education that is irrelevant or unsuitable for their needs. They therefore have limited employment prospects in the indigenous economies; instead, they are forced to seek employment in the national economy, leading to a vicious cycle of social fragmentation, brain drain and a lack of development,[43] especially because the jobs and salaries available to them often will not match their educational achievements. In most countries with indigenous populations, there persists a gap in education and labour market earnings between indigenous and non-indigenous people. The earning gap tends to increase at the higher education levels. This inequality in earnings threatens to discourage indigenous peoples from investing in education and reduces their chances of escaping the cycle of poverty.

Education and gaps in labour earnings

The highest gap in earnings for each additional year of schooling between indigenous and non-indigenous people in Latin America exists in Bolivia. In México, the returns from schooling were higher for non-indigenous than for indigenous peoples at every level except post-secondary—the gap being driven by a decline in the relative earnings of the three population groups that are the most likely to benefit from education gains: young workers, those who have completed secondary education, and those who are employed in the non-agricultural sector. According to the Living Conditions Survey conducted in Ecuador in 1998, the gap in labour earnings increased with education, affecting mostly indigenous skilled workers and professionals. Indigenous people received an earnings gain of 9 per cent from completed higher education, compared to an earnings gain of 15 per cent for non-indigenous people.

Source: Hall and Patrinos (2005)

Culture, community and indigenous education: searching for alternatives

Throughout the world, formal school systems have not provided educational opportunities to indigenous students that adequately prepare them for a life in the wider national society while at the same time fostering and strengthening indigenous cultures, community, interests and goals. Recognizing this, many indigenous

---

[42] Bando et al. (2005), 1, 24.
[43] Kaunga (2005), 38-40; Larsen (2003). vii, 14-15.

communities have demanded greater access and control over their education. Indigenous communities, education scholars and state education policymakers are seeking solutions to provide indigenous students with the skills and knowledge they need to confront the issues of the twenty-first century.

Rural Development Program of the University of Alaska Fairbanks

Indigenous people constitute 100 per cent of the M.A. graduates and over 90 per cent of the B.A. graduates of University of Alaska Fairbanks Rural Development Program, which allows students to pursue their degrees while living and working in their home villages. The program is designed to educate a new generation of community leaders for rural Alaska. Graduates typically take positions with tribal and municipal governments, Native corporations, fisheries, tourism and other private businesses, regional health corporations or non-profits, and state/federal agencies. Students gain understanding of Alaska's relationship to the global economy and an appreciation for sustainable development strategies. They also learn specific tools essential for community leadership, including business plan and grant proposal writing, cultural documentation, project management and evaluation techniques. They learn about land/renewable resources, rural health, community visioning and planning processes, and tribal and local government administration. Graduate students gain a broader theoretical understanding of development processes in Alaska and the circumpolar north.

Source: Rural Development News (2006).

The goal for indigenous education is not only to recover culture and strengthen communities and identities, but also to acquire economic and political skills to successfully manage local indigenous affairs and economies within national and international contexts.[44] The burden of providing an array of multicultural skills and knowledge is heavy and will challenge contemporary conceptions and understanding of both state education systems and indigenous communities.

Language renewal

One way in which indigenous communities have started to recover education and culture is through language renewal and teaching in the mother tongue. Preserving the indigenous language is a means of preserving culture and strengthening identity.[45] In indigenous communities, where most children speak their mother tongue, many prefer school education to be taught in that language, preferably from kindergarten through grade 12. Few communities, however, have the resources to achieve this goal.[46] A major obstacle is the lack of bilingual teachers. The importance of capacity building thus cannot be overstated. The only way to provide adequate education for indigenous children in a bilingual environment is to prepare indigenous and non-indigenous teachers for the challenge of working in such an indigenous bilingual school environment.

National languages should not be ignored, but indigenous languages must be encouraged and preserved. Students should be given the opportunity of bilingual or multilingual capability and not made to choose one language over

---

[44] Glover, Anne (1994), 13, 16-17.
[45] See Assembly of First Nations (Canada) (2006); Larsen (2003), 29-33.
[46] Hays and Siegruhn (2005), 27-29; Hicks (2005), 9.

another.[47] Students with multiple language skills will be better adjusted, not having been subject to repression of their mother tongue. Furthermore, they enjoy significant cultural and intellectual advantages.

Progress in bilingual education in Bolivia

Important initiatives have been undertaken to ensure indigenous children's rights to education in Bolivia. In 1990, the Ministry of Education launched the Bilingual Intercultural Education Project for 114 rural primary schools with three majority indigenous languages: Quechua, Aymara and Guarani. The project developed into a national policy including more than ten ethno-linguistic groups.

Mother-tongue teaching starts with the first grade and continues throughout primary education, while Spanish is introduced gradually. The key strategies of the project were linguistic standardization to develop written forms of the indigenous languages involved, training of national human resources for the administration of the programs in the framework of the project, participation of parents, and coordination of efforts among the State, NGOs, and indigenous organizations. The latter remained actively involved throughout all stages of the project, from planning to evaluation.

The outcomes of the project included higher performance in reading and writing in the early years, better academic averages overall, greater self-esteem, better performance on the part of girls, and less disciplinary action in schools. The number of schools involved in the project increased because of demand from parents and communities.

Sources: UNICEF (2003) and d'Emilio (2001).

> increasingly, states and local authorities are recognizing that indigenous peoples want and should participate in running their schools, developing education policies and creating curricula

Self-determination in education

In addition to bilingual schools, indigenous communities and parents are increasingly demanding and taking greater control of their children's schooling.[48] One of the most important and most debated rights that indigenous peoples demand is the right to self-determination. Although self-determination is frequently associated with access to lands, territories and natural resources, it is also extremely relevant to indigenous peoples' education. Throughout the world, indigenous peoples have experienced education as an outside influence, something that has been imposed on them without consulting them or seeking their consent. From boarding schools to missionaries to state-run education

---

[47] Stavenhagen (2005a), 19-20.
[48] See May (1999); Pavel et al. (1997), 6; The Coolangatta Statement.

centres, indigenous peoples have had very little influence over the formal education system. Increasingly, states and local authorities are recognizing that indigenous peoples want to and should participate in running their schools, developing education policies and creating curricula. States must support the needs and desires of indigenous communities to assume greater management and responsibility for the education of their children.[49]

In different parts of the world, indigenous peoples are already managing their own schools. However, few community-based indigenous education projects have independent resources and most require outside financial help. Many community-based indigenous schools depend on foreign aid or private non-profit funds, and formal school systems have been less willing to adapt to the new education directions sought by indigenous communities. Dependency on external funding is a major weakness in many community-based and bilingual education programmes. States should develop strong ties to and provide support for the educational innovations sought by indigenous communities.[50]

An indigenous curriculum

Another demand that is often expressed by indigenous parents is that of having culturally-adapted and more practical and vocational-oriented school curricula that take the needs of the community into consideration.[51] Education should reproduce indigenous cultures for indigenous communities, and sustain indigenous identity rather than replace it.[52]

"What and when will I reap?"

In Kenya, a legal framework has been established to provide free and compulsory education for all children. However, there is no comprehensive strategy that ensures that the curriculum and the education system are relevant to the livelihood situation of pastoralists and hunter-gatherers. One of the issues of concern is therefore how the education system can benefit the pastoral community—or as one of the parents put it: "If I put my child in school, what and when will I reap"? Another comment was that school-educated children often detach themselves from their traditional lifestyle: "If, after finishing school, they remain unemployed, they end up belonging to nowhere".

Source: ILO/PRO169/IPEC (2006), 24.

Self-government, community-based initiatives and a strengthening of language, culture and values are all goals for indigenous education. Sophisticated presentations of indigenous history, culture and policy, as well as human and indigenous rights, will produce students and citizens who are knowledgeable and more capable of protecting culture and community interests.[53]

Indigenous students and communities need information and conceptual tools to defend and pursue their interests within the context of the state and international community. Inclusion of elders in the teaching and teacher-

---

[49] Hays and Siegruhn (2005), 32.
[50] Kaunga (2005), 41; Lasimbang (2005), 46.
[51] Vinding (ed.) (2006),16.
[52] Simon and Tuhiwai Smith (2001), 308-09; Abu-Saad (2006), 127.
[53] Krøijer (2005), 17-20; Larsen (2003), 33; Hays and Siegruhn (2005), 27; Fettes (1998), 250-271; Stairs (1994), 154-171; Vagner (2005) 24; The Coolangatta Statement.

training processes, including discussions of indigenous wisdom and spirituality, will help create well-informed indigenous students and teachers.[54]

Non-formal education systems

Schools need to work within the cultural and economic cycles of indigenous communities and adapt to specific situations. Adjusting school timetables and term schedules to the local work calendar is seen as one way of facilitating children's access to school education. But there are other ways, too. A number of countries in Latin America, for instance, have reacted to the low enrolment and high dropout rates of indigenous children by promoting flexible school projects in rural communities through education clusters or multigrade teaching (such as the *Nueva Escuela Unitaria* in Colombia, Guatemala and other Latin American countries), where children of different ages share a classroom. These projects, which have promoted bilingual learning, community and family involvement, and adequately trained teachers, are shown to have retained more students, improved achievement and increased parental satisfaction.[55]

Helping indigenous children who live in remote areas to receive an education is another challenge that indigenous communities have taken up, and several models have been applied, including the use of radio and mobile schools.

Providing education in remote areas

In the Nenets Autonomous Region of the Russian Federation, indigenous people maintain a nomadic lifestyle by following reindeer herds. They spend winters in the forests and summers on the coast of the Barents Sea. A nomadic school was founded in 1996 in the Bolshezemelskaya tundra region to provide education for Nenets children in their communities. Nenets-speaking teachers come to the town of Anderma and travel from there to herder communities, either by snowmobiles or with reindeer herds. Classes are held in tents, and the ages of students range from eight to 40 years.

In Thailand, mobile teachers travel to isolated communities by motorbike or on horseback. Namibia has adopted mobile "field schools" aimed at Himba children in the northwest remote areas of the country.

In Peru, teachers coordinate seven to 10 informal preschools, each of which is supervised by a young educated member of the community. Support is provided by daily radio broadcasts that review learning activities.

In Alaska, 155 new high schools, most of them in remote rural communities, have been built and staffed since 1974. These schools have made secondary education without leaving home a possibility. As a result, the percentage of 18- to 25-year-old Alaska Natives with high school diplomas rose from 48 per cent in 1980 to 73 per cent in 2000, and over the same period, the number of Natives who went to college tripled.

Sources: UNICEF (2003) and The Indigenous World 2005 (2005), 68.

---

[54] Vagner (2005), 24; Abu-Saad (2006), 142-44.
[55] Kline (2002).

Challenges

Although increased self-determination and local control is an indispensable element for improving indigenous peoples´ education, it is not enough. .This has been demonstrated in the United States and Canada where efforts toward local community control and multicultural education have not provided indigenous communities with the results desired in terms of performance or graduation rates.[56] Education cannot be separated from economic, social and political realities and in the absence of sustainable economic growth and improved social conditions, increased political autonomy can not bring about improved education results for indigenous peoples. This is especially true when continuing multi-generational poverty and trauma constrain educational participation and achievement. Severe poverty and exclusion also often contribute to multi-generational trauma, resulting in cycles of crime, high rates of suicide, alcoholism, domestic abuse and other social problems that inhibit school attendance and achievement and result in continuing limited economic opportunities.[57]

In other words, these issues are all interdependent. Poor education contributes to poverty and is also a direct result of poverty. Marginalization contributes to poor education and poverty. Poverty contributes to a poor study environment and less material support for education, and for many indigenous peoples, there is little return from education and thus little incentive for students to stay in school.

For many students, education will be valuable only if it provides skills and opportunities that assist the student and community to build a stronger local economy while preserving community, culture and autonomy. Local economic development may, in turn, encourage more indigenous students to return home.

Traditional education alone does not sufficiently prepare students for participation and competition within the national and global economy. Although indigenous students can benefit from the dominant education system, this does not mean that they should reject their communities and cultures for mainstream life, but rather that students need skills and knowledge to enable them to work in indigenous and non-indigenous economies and contexts. This is essential for individual indigenous students if they are to become active participants in their own communities and economies, and it is equally a collective right, essential for the sustainability of indigenous people's communities.[58]

Frequently, indigenous graduates are faced with the situation of having to choose between returning to their communities or pursuing their careers in the dominant society. There are too few opportunities to use their skills within their communities, either due to a lack of development there, or because their skills are inadequate for life in their community. An education system that meets the

> in the absence of sustainable economic growth and improved social conditions, increased political autonomy can not bring about improved education results for indigenous peoples

---

[56] Indian and Northern Affairs Canada (2003), 3-4.
[57] Danieli (1998), 307-402; Braveheart and Debrun (1998), 56-78.
[58] Hays and Siegruhn (2005), 27; Tshireletso (1997), 173-188; Le Roux (1999).

needs of indigenous peoples has to provide them with the opportunity to develop skills that are useful to them and allow them to pursue the life they choose.[59]

Educated but unemployed students and students who are trained to reject their indigenous economy and culture are of little value to indigenous communities.[60] It is essential that the knowledge gained from formal education can be translated into knowledge that is relevalnt to indigenous communities and that it promotes respect and understanding of indigenous culture, even if some indigenous students choose to live within broader economy.[61]

Concluding Remarks

Conditions of extreme poverty, exclusion and isolation are severe barriers to sustainable and multicultural indigenous education programmes. The recent move toward community-based education and local control has not, and probably will not close the gap with the non-indigenous population in terms of access to education and educational performance in the foreseeable future. There is, however, a growing awareness at international and national levels of the pressing need to support indigenous peoples' right to education—not only as a moral imperative and legal obligation, but also within the framework of inclusive and sustainable development that strengthens both individual students and whole societies, the latter benefiting from the presence of a strong, proud and well-educated indigenous population.

> students need skills and knowledge to enable them to work in indigenous and non-indigenous economies and contexts

Sustained economic development and greater political and cultural autonomy may enhance the chances for improving the education outcomes of indigenous students. However, community-based education and language programs need adequate funding and support from states. States can provide education resources and universities can assist in curriculum development, but indigenous education will require partnership between indigenous communities and state education structures and policymakers.

States need to support the cultural, economic and educational autonomy sought by indigenous peoples.[62] Education opportunities should affirm the history, culture and identities of indigenous peoples and provide opportunities for employment and work within both mainstream market economies and the mode of economy preferred by indigenous communities.

Indigenous students should be prepared and able to make choices to work in indigenous, non-indigenous or mixed economies. Such multi-culturally educated indigenous students will have the capability to participate in state institutions

---

[59] Hays and Siegruhn (2005), 32.
[60] Stavenhagen, (2005), 18; Kaunga (2005), 40-41.
[61] The Coolangatta Statement; Glover (1994), 13; Champagne (2006), 147-168.
[62] For a list of recommendations from the Special Rapporteur to states, indigenous communities and the international community for improving indigenous education, see Stavenhagen (2005a) and (2005b).

and civil society while not rejecting their identities and indigenous communities, nor rejecting the State and its mainstream culture(s). Indigenous education should provide a pathway to greater cultural, economic and political autonomy for indigenous peoples, but should also set the stage for participation and consensual commitment on the part of states and international institutions.

List of references

Abu-Saad, Ismael. 2003. "Bedouin Arabs in Israel. Between the Hammer and the Anvil: Education as a Foundation for Survival and Development" in The Future of Indigenous Peoples: Strategies for Survival and Development, ed. Duane Champagne and Ismael Abu-Saad. Los Angeles, CA: UCLA American Indian Studies Center.

Abu-Saad, Ismael. 2006. "Identity Formation among Indigenous Youth in Majority-Controlled Schools: Palestinian Arabs in Israel" in Indigenous Education and Empowerment: International Perspectives, ed. Ismael Abu-Saad and Duane Champagne. Lanham, MD: AltaMira Press.

The Age. 2005. "In a word, disgraceful" (Christopher Bantick). 28 November 2005. Available online at http://www.theage.com.au/news/education-news/in-a-word-disgraceful/2005/11/25/1132703378435.html

Assembly of First Nations, Canada (AFN). 2006. "Keeping Our Languages Alive". Presentation by Chiefs Committee on Languages to the UN Permanent Forum on Indigenous Issues, Fifth Session, New York, May 2006. Available online at http://www.un.org/esa/socdev/unpfii

Bando, Rosangela, G. López-Calva, Luis F., and Patrinos, Harry Thomas. 2005. "Child Labor, School Attendance, and Indigenous Households: Evidence from Mexico". World Bank Policy Research Working Paper 3487. Washington D.C.: World Bank.

Brave Heart, M. Y. H. and DeBruyn, L. M. 1998. "The American Indian Holocaust: Healing Historical Unresolved Grief". American Indian and Alaskan Native Mental Health Research, 8:2 (1998), 56-78.

Champagne, Duane. 2001. "A Holistic Emphasis: The UCLA American Indian Studies Center". Indigenous Nations Studies Journal 2, no.1: 21-28.

Champagne, Duane and Stauss, Joseph (Jay), eds. 2002. Native American Studies in Higher Education: Models for Collaboration Between Universities and Indigenous Nations. Walnut Creek, CA: AltaMira Press.

Coolangatta Statement. 1999. Coolangatta Statement on Indigenous Peoples' Rights in Education – adopted at the World Indigenous Peoples' Conference on Education, 6 August 1999 in Hilo, Hawai'i. Available online at http://www. tebtebba.org

Danieli, Yael, ed. 1998. International Handbook of Multigenerational Legacies of Trauma. New York: Springer Verlag.

d'Emilio, Lucia. 2001. Voices and Processes Toward Pluralism: Indigenous Education in Bolivia. Stockholm: Swedish International Development Cooperation Agency.

DeVoe, J.F., and Darling-Churchill, K.E. (2008). Status and Trends in the Education of American Indians and Alaska Natives: 2008 (NCES 2008-084). National Center for Education Statistics, Institute of Education Sciences, U.S. Department of Education. Washington, D.C.

ECLAC/CEPAL. 2006. Pueblos indígenas y afrodescendientes de América Latina y el Caribe: Información socio demográfica para políticos y programas. Chile: CEPAL.

Expert Mechanism on the Rights of Indigenous Peoples. 2009. Study on Lessons Learned and Challenges to Aciehve the Implementation of the Rights of Indigenous Peoples to Education: Report of the Expert Mechanism on the Rights of Indigenous Peoples to the Human Rights Council. UN Doc. A/HRC/EMRIP/2009/2

Fettes, Mark. 1998. "Indigenous Education and the Ecology of Community". Language, Culture and Curriculum 11:3(1998): 250-271.

Freeman, Catherine and Fox, Mary Ann. 2005. "Status and Trends in Education of American Indians and Alaska Natives". Washington, D.C.: National Center for Education Statistics.

Glover, Anne. 1994. "Moving into the System: Early Childhood Programs as a Bridge to School for Aboriginal Communities". The Aboriginal Child at School: A National Journal for Teachers of Aborigines and Torres Strait Islanders 22:1(Mar/April 1994).

Greene, Jay P. and Forster, Greg. 2003. Public High School Graduation and College Readiness in the United States. New York, N.Y.: Center for Civic Innovation at the Manhattan Institute.

Hall, Gilette and Harry Anthony Patrinos. 2006. Indigenous Peoples, Poverty and Human Development in Latin America 1994-2004. New York, NY: Palgrave McMillan.

Hays, Jennifer. 2004. "Indigenous Rights in Education: The San of Southern Africa in Local and Global Contexts". In Indigenous Peoples' Rights in Southern Africa, ed. Robert K. Hitchcock and Diana Vinding. Copenhagen: IWGIA.

Hays, Jennifer and Siegruhn, Amanda. 2005. "Education and the San of Southern Africa". Indigenous Affairs, Indigenous Peoples and Education, No. 01/2005: 26-34. Copenhagen: IWGIA.

Hicks, Jack. 2005. "Education in the Canadian Arctic: What Difference Has the Nunavut Government Made?" Indigenous Affairs, Indigenous Peoples and Education, 01/2005:8-15 Copenhagen: IWGIA.

ILO/PRO 169/IPEC. 2006. Handbook on Combating Child Labour among Indigenous and Tribal Peoples. Geneva: PRO 169/IPEC and the International Labour Organization.

Indian and Northern Affairs Canada. 2003. "Education Programs Report". Ottawa: INAC.

The Indigenous World 2005. 2005. Section on Alaska. Copenhagen: IWGIA. Available online at http://www.iwgia.org

International Labour Organization (ILO). 1989. ILO Convention concerning Indigenous and Tribal Peoples in Independent Countries (No. 169). http://www.ilo.org/ilolex/english/index.htm

Institute of Higher Education Policy. 1999. Tribal Colleges: An Introduction. Alexandria, VA: American Indian Higher Education Consortium.

Kaunga, Johnson Ole. 2005. "Indigenous Peoples' Experiences in the Formal Education System: The Case of the Kenyan Pastorialists". Indigenous Affairs, Indigenous Peoples and Education, 01/2005: 35-41. Copenhagen: IWGIA.

King, Linda and Schielmann, Sabine. 2004. The Challenge of Indigenous Education: Practice and Perspectives. Paris: UNESCO.

Kline, Rachel. 2002. "A Model for Improving Rural Schools: Escuela Nueva in Colombia and Guatemala". Current Issues in Comparative Education (CICE), 2002: 170-181. Teachers College, Columbia University, online journal available at http://www.tc.columbia.edu/CICE

Krøijer, Stine. 2005. "'We're Going Slowly Because We're Going Far': Building an Autonomous Education System in Chiapas". Indigenous Affairs, Indigenous Peoples and Education, 01/2005:16-20. Copenhagen: IWGIA.

Larsen, Peter Bille. 2003. Indigenous and Tribal Children: Assessing Child Labour and Education Challenges. Joint working paper from the International Programme on the Elimination of Child Labour (IPEC) and the INDISCO Programme. Geneva: International Labour Organization (ILO).

Lasimbang, Anne. 2005. "Giving the Best Possible Start: Preschool Programme for Rural Indigenous Children in Sabah, Malaysia". Indigenous Affairs, Indigenous Peoples and Education, 01/2005: 42-46 Copenhagen: IWGIA.

Le Roux, Willemien. 2000. Torn Apart: San Children as Change Agents in a Process of Acculturation. A report of the Educational Situation of San Children in Southern Africa. Windheok, Namibia: Working Group of Indigenous Minorities in Southern Africa (WIMSA).

May, Stephen. 1999. Indigenous Community-Based Education. Philadelpha, PA: Multilingual Matters.

Mellor, Suzanne and Matthew Corrigan. 2004. The Case for Change: A Review of Contemporary Research Non-Indigenous Education Outcomes. Camberwell, VIC.: Australian Council for Education Research.

Pavel, Michael D., Curtain, Thomas R., and Whitner, Summer D.. 1997. Characteristics of American Indian and Alaska Native Education: Results from the 1990-1991 and 1993-94 Schools and Staffing Survey. Washington, D.C.: US Department of Education.

Rural Development News, Spring/Summer 2006. University of Alaska, Department of Alaska Native and Rural Development.

Simon, Judith and Smith, Linda Tuhiwai. 2001. A Civilizing Mission? Perceptions and Representation of the New Zealand Native Schools System. Auckland, NZ: Auckland University Press.

St. Germaine, Richard D. 1995. "BIA Schools Complete First Step in Reform Effort". Journal of American Indian Education 35:1.

Stairs, Arlene. 1994. "The Cultural Negotiation of Indigenous Education: Microethnography and Model-Building". Peabody Journal of Education 69:2 (Winter 1994):154-171.

Stavenhagen, Rodolfo. 2005a. Indigenous Peoples and Education Systems: Human Rights Challenges. Fourth Annual Report to the Commission on Human Rights by the Special Rapporteur. UN Doc. E/CN.4/2005/88.

Stavenhagen, Rodolfo. 2005b. Conclusions and recommendations of the expert seminar on indigenous peoples and education. Addendum 4 to Fourth Annual Report to the Commission on Human Rights by the Special Rapporteur. UN Doc. E/CN.4/2005/88/Add.4.

Taylor, Jonathan B. and Kalt, Joseph P.. 2005. American Indians on Reservations: A Databook of Socioeconomic Change Between the 1990 and 2000 Census. Cambridge, MA: The Harvard Project on American Indian Development.

Tshireletso, Lucky. 1997. "'They are the Government's Children': School and Community Relations in a Remote Area Dweller (Basarwa) Settlement in Kweneng District Botswana". International Journal of Educational Development 17:2 (1997):173-188.

United Nations Committee on the Rights of the Child (CRC). 2000. "Concluding Observations of the Committee on the Rights of the Child: India. 23/02/2000". UN Doc. CRC/C/15/Add.115.

UNESCO 2008 Overcoming Inequality: Why Governance Matters. Education For All Golbal Monitoring Report. Paris: UNESCO.

UNICEF. 2003. "Ensuring the Rights of Indigenous Children". Innocenti Digest no. 11. Florence, Italy: UNICEF Innocenti Research Centre.

United Nations Organization. 2007. Declaration on the Rights of Indigenous Peoples. Resolution A/61/L.67 September 2007. Available online at UNPFII Web site http://www.un.org/esa/socdev/unpfii/en/declaration.html

United States Census Bureau. 2005. American Indian, Alaska Native Tables from the Statistical Abstract of the United States: 2004-2005. Available online at http://www.census.gov/statab/www/sa04aian.pdf

United States General Accounting Office. 1997. School Facilities: Reported Condition and Costs to Repair Schools Funded by Bureau of Indian Affairs. GAO/HEHS-98-47. Washington, D.C.: US General Accounting Office.

Vagner, Jytte. 2005. "Indigenous Wisdom in Bilingual Intercultural Education: A Field of Struggle". Indigenous Affairs, Indigenous Peoples and Education, 01/2005: 21-25. Copenhagen: IWGIA.

Villebrun, Dene National Chief Noeline. 2006. "Athabaskan Education: The Case of Denendeh Past, Present, and Future". In Indigenous Education and Empowerment: International Perspectives, ed. Ismael Abu-Saad and Duane Champagne. Lanham, MD: AltaMira Press, 2006.

Vinding, Diana, ed. 2006. Indigenous Peoples and the MDGs: Perspectives from indigenous communities in Bolivia, Cambodia, Cameroon and Guatemala. Geneva: PRO 169/ International Labour Organization.

CHAPTER V

HEALTH

By Myrna Cunningham[1]

The United Nations Declaration on the Rights of Indigenous Peoples states that "Indigenous individuals have an equal right to the enjoyment of the highest attainable standard of physical and mental health. States shall take the necessary steps with a view to achieving progressively the full realization of this right",[2] thus affirming the basic human right to life and health that is guaranteed under international human rights law. It also goes on to state, "Indigenous peoples have the right to promote, develop and maintain their institutional structures and their distinctive customs, spirituality, traditions, procedures, practices and, in the cases where they exist, juridical systems or customs, in accordance with international human rights standards".[3] This implies a greater obligation of states to uphold not only the indigenous individual's right to health but also the collective right of indigenous peoples to maintain and use their health systems and practices in pursuit of their right to health. The Declaration further specifies, "Indigenous Peoples have the right to their traditional medicines and to maintain their health practices, including the conservation of their vital medicinal plants, animals and minerals. Indigenous individuals also have the right to access, without any discrimination, to all social and health services".[4] The Declaration thus establishes a framework for addressing the health situation of indigenous peoples that includes the obligations of states both to provide accessible, quality health care to indigenous peoples and to respect and promote indigenous health systems, each of which must be fulfilled in order to ensure the health of indigenous peoples.

The commitment of United Nations Member States to the Millennium Development Goals (MDGs) is an important step forward in improving the health of millions of people who live in poverty around the world. However, by failing to ground the goals in an approach that upholds indigenous peoples' individual and collective rights, the MDGs fall short in addressing the health disparities that persist between indigenous peoples and other poor, marginalized groups. By advancing the dominant paradigms of health and development rather than an approach based on individual and collective human rights, the MDGs also promote projects that are potentially detrimental to indigenous peoples, and which violate their rights to their collective land, territories and natural resources. Moreover, because the cultures and worldviews of indigenous peoples are not taken into account in the formulation of the MDGs, the goals do not consider the indigenous concept of health, which extends beyond the physical and mental well-being of an individual to the spiritual balance and well-being of the community as a whole. To improve the health situation of indigenous peoples, there must thus be a fundamental shift in the concept of health so that it incorporates the cultures and world views of indigenous peoples as central to the design and management of state health systems.

The indigenous concept of health and health systems

National, regional and international health institutions have typically defined health as the biological, physical and mental well-being of an individual. The World Health Organization (WHO), for example, defines health as "a state of complete physical, mental and social well-being and not merely the absence of disease or infirmity".[5] However,

---

[1] Written in collaboration with the Center for Indigenous Peoples' Autonomy and Development (CADPI).
[2] United Nations Declaration on the Rights of Indigenous Peoples, Article 24.2.
[3] Ibid., Article 34.
[4] Ibid., Article 24.1.
[5] Constitution of the World Health Organization (1946), 1.

WHO has begun to debate this definition and to consider the possibility of incorporating a cultural aspect into its concept of health.[6] Many organizations that promote health are thus beginning to recognize that the conventional definition is insufficient to capture the full meaning of health in societies that are diverse in their cultures, religions and forms of social organization.

For indigenous peoples, health is equivalent to the "harmonious coexistence of human beings with nature, with themselves, and with others, aimed at integral well-being, in spiritual, individual, and social wholeness and tranquillity".[7] The indigenous concept of health articulates physical, mental, spiritual and emotional elements, from both individual and communal points of view, and involves political, economic, social and cultural aspects. It is shaped by indigenous peoples' historical experiences and worldviews, and is expressed in the rules and norms that are applied in the community and practised by its members. To promote health and prevent illness, an indigenous community seeks to recuperate and maintain its interior and exterior equilibrium, including the harmony between community members who are sick and the world around them.

> the indigenous concept of health articulates physical, mental, spiritual and emotional elements, from both individual and communal points of view

Traditional health systems in indigenous communities are complex and quite structured in their content and internal logic. They are characterized by a combination of practices and knowledge about the human body, and coexistence with other human beings, with nature and with spiritual beings. They involve all aspects of health promotion, prevention of illness and treatment and rehabilitation, but differ from most Western health systems in that they take an integral or holistic approach.[8] Many indigenous families address illness with a variety of approaches and practices, using either traditional or Western medicine, or a combination of the two. If treatment administered in the home proves insufficient, the choice is made—often by a woman, who is the primary decision-maker in this arena—as to whether to send the sick person to a practitioner of traditional or of Western medicine. In the absence of state health systems that incorporate the philosophies and practices of both traditional and Western medicine, the choice becomes polarized between the two systems, often to the detriment of the sick person.

---

[6] In its Session 101 in January 1998, the WHO Executive Board was requested to amend the WHO definition of health to include the concept of spirituality. WHO considers spirituality, religiousness and personal beliefs as three of the areas by which to analyze the quality of life of an individual. See WHO (1998).

[7] Health Workshop, Guaranda, Bolívar, Ecuador, 1995.

[8] It is important to present working definitions of the terms "Western" and "traditional" medicine. Western medicine, also called Occidental medicine, biomedicine, conventional, allopathic, or orthodox medicine, is a system of medical practices that use an approach of treating illness through remedies that produce effects that oppose the symptoms of the illness. The Pan-American Health Organization (PAHO) has defined traditional medicine and indigenous health systems to "include the entire body of ideas, concepts, beliefs, myths, procedures and rituals (whether explainable or not) connected with the maintenance of health or health restoration through the treatment of physical and mental illness or social imbalances in a particular individual, community, or people. This body of knowledge, grounded in the people's cosmic visions, explains the etiology, nosology and procedures for the diagnosis, prognosis, cure, disease prevention, and health promotion". See PAHO (1997).

Tuberculosis in indigenous and non-indigenous populations

Tuberculosis, a disease that primarily affects people living in poverty, affects at least 2 billion people in the world, according to 2008 statistics. As a result of poverty and associated issues, tuberculosis continues to disproportionately affect indigenous peoples around the globe. Indigenous peoples are at an increased risk of suffering from tuberculosis. Whilst programmes have been designed to combat tuberculosis, they often do not reach indigenous peoples because of issues related to poverty, poor housing, a lack of access to medical care and drugs, cultural barriers, language differences and geographic remoteness.

The statistics surrounding indigenous people in the context of tuberculosis indicate that

◈ in Canada, in 2006, the First Nations tuberculosis rate was 27.4 per 100,000, or 35 times higher than among the non-aboriginal population born in Canada. Tuberculosis is a particular threat to the Inuit in Canada, where the rates are 121 per 100,000, or just over 150 times higher than the non-aboriginal population;[9]

◈ in New Zealand, the ratio is 21.1 among Pacific Islanders and Maoris, making them at least 10 times more likely to contract tuberculosis than other people living in New Zealand;[10]

◈ in Kalaallit Nunaat (Greenland) the tuberculosis rate was 157 per 100,000, making them 45 times more likely to get active tuberculosis than the Danish population.[11]

Health and the collective rights of indigenous peoples

International human rights instruments such as the Universal Declaration of Human Rights, the International Covenant on Economic, Social and Cultural Rights, the Convention on the Elimination of All Forms of Discrimination against Women and the Convention on the Rights of the Child have traditionally provided the legal framework for the foundation of international human rights, including the right to health. These instruments include provisions for the right to life and for the "right of everyone to enjoy the highest attainable standard of physical and mental health",[12] with some specifically recognising the rights of individuals from marginalized populations, including indigenous peoples and ethnic minorities.

In the case of indigenous peoples, the right to health should not be conferred only on individuals, but should also be applied at the collective level. Until recently, however, few legal instruments had incorporated the concept of collective rights. In the same way that the establishment of individual rights has advanced over time, a set of collective rights is never beginning to be articulated at the international level, such as the approval of the Declaration on the Rights of Indigenous Peoples by the United Nations General Assembly.[13] This is perceived by indigenous peoples as a human rights instrument which, in time, will increase the political will of states to build new relationships with indigenous peoples, and to confront the exclusion to which they have been subjected.

---

[9] Public Health Agency of Canada (2006) and Statistics Canada (2006).
[10] Das, Baker & Calder (2006).
[11] Skifte (2004).
[12] International Covenant on Economic, Social, and Cultural Rights, Article 12.1.
[13] The Declaration was adopted by the newly established Human Rights Council in June 2006 and, on 13 September 2007, by the United Nations General Assembly.

In accordance with the international human rights instruments that provide for the right to health, most initiatives that seek to improve the health of poor and marginalized populations focus primarily on increasing access by individuals from those populations to state health systems. Indeed, full access to quality health care is a human right of all individuals, and it is therefore critical to ensure equal access to health care, including through efforts to eliminate the discrimination and marginalization faced by indigenous peoples. However, to address the root causes of indigenous peoples' health problems, there must also be full recognition and exercise of indigenous peoples' collective rights to communal assets and self-determination.

Gap in life expectancy between indigenous and non-indigenous people (in years)

Guatemala	Panama	Mexico	Nepal	Australia	Canada	New Zealand
13	10	6	20	20	7	11

Source: Hanemann (2006), 5 & Health Canada (2007).

Many of the most urgent health challenges faced by indigenous peoples, such as illnesses from pesticides and extractive industries, malnutrition, diabetes and HIV/AIDS, stem from the contamination and depletion of their land and natural resources, and from their forced displacement from their territories. The right to collective land, territories and natural resources is thus an essential component that lays the foundations for improving the health of indigenous peoples. In addition, the rights to preserve, practise and transmit traditional knowledge and to maintain cultural, spiritual and social beliefs and institutions are integral to ensuring the health of indigenous communities. Many mental health issues such as depression, substance abuse and suicide have been identified as connected to the historical colonization and dispossession of indigenous peoples, which has resulted in the fragmentation of indigenous social, cultural, economic and political institutions.

Similarly, the right to self-determination with respect to health implies creating conditions for the full and effective participation of indigenous communities in the design and management of health systems, in addition to adherence to the principle of free, prior and informed consent in the planning and implementation of health and development programmes and projects.[14] Furthermore, there must be a commitment to building the human resources necessary for the participation of indigenous peoples in health policy and management, as well as training non-indigenous health professionals in the cultures and languages of indigenous peoples. Finally, it is essential to recognize that the health situation of indigenous peoples is linked to the sustainable human development of

> to address the root causes of indigenous peoples' health problems, there must also be full recognition and exercise of indigenous peoples' collective rights to communal assets and self-determination

---

[14] For more on the concept of free, prior and informed consent, see UNPFII (2005).

indigenous communities in all aspects, which includes issues of education, political participation, environment and economic development; efforts to improve the health of indigenous peoples must therefore involve a multi-sectoral and multidisciplinary approach.[15]

Over the course of the last decade, some international and regional health initiatives have begun to pay greater attention to the specific needs of indigenous peoples, many of which were precipitated by the first International Decade of the World's Indigenous Peoples (1995-2004) proclaimed by the United Nations General Assembly. WHO, for example, has various initiatives administered by their Health and Human Rights Team that focus on improving the health of indigenous peoples, and the World Health Assembly (WHA) has passed a number of resolutions affirming its intention to tackle health disparities between indigenous and non-indigenous populations.[16] In addition, WHO has urged member States to "develop and implement, in close cooperation with indigenous people, national plans of action or programmes on indigenous people's health which focus on ensuring access of indigenous people to health care."[17] The Pan-American Health Organization (PAHO) has been one of the institutions most attuned to the demands of indigenous peoples. In 1993, within the framework of the United Nations International Year of Indigenous Peoples, PAHO held a meeting on the health of indigenous peoples.[18] The recommendations of that meeting were approved by the PAHO Directing Council as Resolution V, "Health of Indigenous Peoples", and secured a commitment from member Governments, at least at the policy level, to grant priority to improving the health of indigenous peoples while respecting their ancestral culture and knowledge.[19]

Core elements of PAHO Resolution V

◈ Promoting the participation of leaders and representatives of indigenous peoples and their communities in the formulation of health policies and strategies and the development of health and environmental activities directed at their people;

◈ Strengthening the technical, administrative and management capacity of national and local institutions responsible for the health of indigenous peoples, with particular attention to the need to overcome the lack of information;

◈ Ensuring greater access by indigenous peoples to quality health services;

◈ Facilitating inter-sectoral actions (government, non-governmental, universities, research centres and indigenous organizations);

◈ Promoting the transformation of health systems and supporting the development of alternative models of care, including research and certification of traditional medicine;

◈ Promoting programmes in disease prevention and health promotion to address the problems most relevant to each country; and

---

[15] This has been recognized by the Pan-American Health Organization. See PAHO (2003), 7.

[16] WHA (1994-2001). Resolutions 54.16, 53.10, 51.24, 50.31, 49.26, 48.24, and 47.27.

[17] WHA Resolution 51.24, International Decade of the World's Indigenous People, (1998), 1.

[18] The meeting was held in Winnipeg in April 1993, with the participation of indigenous peoples from the Americas and functionaries of WHO, Ministries of Health, and non-governmental organizations.

[19] PAHO Resolution V also includes the adoption of Document CD37/20, creating the PAHO Health of the Indigenous Peoples of the Americas Initiative.

> ❖ Forming reciprocal information and collaboration networks between organizations and institutions.
>
> *Source: PAHO/WHO Resolution V "The Health of Indigenous Peoples", adopted at the Fourth Plenary session, 28 September 1993.*

In addition, WHO, along with the specialized agencies of the United Nation system and international development institutions such as the World Bank, has begun to recognize that "when we marginalize indigenous peoples, we cut off a vast body of knowledge that is of great value to humanity."[20] This has spawned a number of efforts to support the preservation of indigenous knowledge with respect to traditional medicine and healing practices. Programmes such as UNESCO's Local and Indigenous Knowledge Systems Programme may not have an explicit health focus but, by focusing on sustainable development and resource management, they work on preserving and promoting the use of traditional knowledge, which is integral to indigenous health systems. In 1997, WHO established a programme on traditional medicine with the objective of interesting governments of member countries and other health institutions in supporting traditional health agents, and has since focused on supporting the development of national policies related to the practice of traditional medicine, advocating for the rational use of traditional medicine based on international standards, and developing technical standards and methodologies for research into traditional medicine therapies and products.[21]

Based on reports on the health of indigenous peoples and to follow up from the work initiated through Resolution V, PAHO approved Resolution VI, calling on member States to intensify their efforts to identify and eliminate the inequities in the health status of indigenous peoples. One of their strategic goals is to create an inventory of the region's best practices in incorporating indigenous perspectives and practices into health systems.[22] Various regional initiatives have followed, including the support of the United Nations Population Fund (UNPFA) for summits and associations of indigenous women that address health in Latin America and the Caribbean[23] and efforts by both UNIFEM and the United Nations Inter-Agency Support Group on Indigenous Peoples' Issues to convene indigenous women to discuss how to incorporate the demands of indigenous women into United Nations initiatives related to the MDGs.

The current health situation of indigenous peoples

Indigenous peoples suffer from poorer health, are more likely to experience disability and reduced quality of life and ultimately die younger than their non-indigenous counterparts. PAHO has stated that "the present epidemiological profile of the indigenous population is associated with high poverty indices, unemployment, illiteracy, migration, exclusion from the mainstream society, lack of land and territory, destruction of the ecosystem, alteration of the dynamic of life, and unmet basic needs".[24] Circumstances of extreme poverty are significantly more prevalent among indigenous peoples than non-indigenous groups, and are rooted in other factors, such as a lack of access to education and social services, destruction of indigenous economies and socio-political structures, forced displacement, armed conflict and the degradation of their customary lands and waters. These forces, which are inherited from colonization, are all determined and compounded

---

[20] WHO (1999), Statement by WHO Director-General, Gro Harlem Brundtland.
[21] WHO (2002), 5.
[22] See PAHO (2006).
[23] See UNFPA (2006) and Box on page 180, this chapter. UNFPA also makes efforts to consider gender mainstreaming and cultural sensitivity in all of its initiatives. See http://www.unfpa.org/culture/rights.htm and http://www.unfpa.org/gender/index.htm
[24] PAHO (2003).

by structural racism and discrimination, and make indigenous women and children particularly vulnerable to poor health.

The impact of these phenomena is that indigenous peoples experience disproportionately high levels of maternal and infant mortality, malnutrition, cardiovascular illnesses, HIV/AIDS and other infectious diseases such as malaria and tuberculosis. Indigenous women experience these health problems with particular severity, as they are disproportionately affected by natural disasters and armed conflicts, and are often denied access to education, land, property and other economic resources. Yet they play a primary role in overseeing the health and well-being of their families and communities. In addition, as the incidence of other public health issues such as drug abuse, alcoholism, depression and suicide increases, urgent and concerted efforts are needed to improve the health situation of indigenous peoples.[25]

> indigenous peoples suffer from poorer health, are more likely to experience disability and reduced quality of life and ultimately die younger than their non-indigenous counterparts

Health disparities from an epidemiological perspective

All around the world, there are health disparities between indigenous and non-indigenous populations in the incidence of virtually every health condition, from infectious diseases such as HIV/AIDS, malaria and tuberculosis to cardiovascular disease, diabetes, cancer and respiratory diseases. Moreover, many of the most widespread causes of mortality among indigenous children are preventable, such as malnutrition, diarrhoea, parasitic infections and tuberculosis. Box V.3 gives an example of the health disparities between indigenous and non-indigenous populations in Venezuela.

The health situation in Amazonas state, Venezuela

Although Venezuela is a middle-income country, health indicators in Amazonas state, which is home to twenty distinct indigenous peoples, are significantly lower than in the rest of the country. Living in areas short of infrastructure, indigenous peoples are disproportionately affected by malnutrition and infectious diseases. Consequently, the infant mortality rate in Amazonas state is 43.9 per 1,000 births, compared to the national average of 19 per 1,000 births, and between 76 and 250 per 1,000 births in the Yanomami population. In 2001, the rates of diarrhoea-related diseases, pneumonia and tuberculosis in Amazonas state were double the national rates. In 2004, the malaria incidence was 70 times higher than the national average, standing at 87.7 cases per 1,000, compared to 1.2 per 1,000, making malaria the main cause of morbidity and the seventh cause of infant mortality. The indigenous municipalities of Atabapo, Autana and Manapiare were the most affected, with the highest malaria rates in Venezuela.

Source: The Indigenous World 2004 (2004), 137-138.

---

[25] PAHO (2006), 3.

Poor nutrition is one of the health issues that most affects indigenous peoples around the world. In addition to circumstances of extreme poverty, indigenous peoples suffer from malnutrition because of environmental degradation and contamination of the ecosystems in which indigenous communities have traditionally lived, loss of land and territory, and a decline in abundance or accessibility of traditional food sources. These changes in traditional diet, combined with other changes in lifestyle, have resulted in widespread malnutrition among indigenous peoples. The World Bank has reported that "the rate of stunting [height/age] for Guatemala overall is 44 percent, but for indigenous children the rate is 58 percent, higher than either Yemen or Bangladesh, and almost twice the rate for non-indigenous children. In Ecuador, chronic malnutrition is more than twice as high in indigenous as compared to non-indigenous communities".[26] In El Salvador, an estimated 40 per cent of indigenous children under age five are malnourished, compared to the national average of 23 per cent, and in Honduras an estimated 95 per cent of indigenous children under age 14 suffer from malnutrition.[27]

However, this malnutrition manifests itself differently depending on the local circumstances. Whilst in some parts of the world malnutrition affects maternal and infant health and child development, in other regions it contributes to an increasing prevalence of non-communicable diseases such as obesity, diabetes and cardiovascular disease among indigenous peoples. In the State of Arizona in the United States, for example, the Pima Indian tribe has the highest rate of diabetes in the world, as "some 50 per cent of the Pima between the ages of 30 and 64 have diabetes."[28]

Indigenous people and diabetes

Indigenous people are particularly vulnerable to diabetes due to a combination of environmental, genetic and socio-economic factors. The contamination and destruction of natural habitats and the disappearance of wildlife plants and animals have resulted in the erosion of traditional food systems and decreased food security. This has led to increasing reliance upon imported processed foods that have little nutritional value but are often high in sodium and fat, causing obesity and diabetes.

The genetic selection processes that may have been advantageous when food was in short supply and had to be obtained through hard physical effort make indigenous people highly vulnerable to diabetes at the time of the rapid transition to a high-calorie diet and low levels of physical activity. The situation is aggravated by indigenous peoples' lack of access to health care. Most indigenous people are never diagnosed or treated for diabetes. Others are diagnosed too late to prevent the dramatic impact of the disease on the eyes, kidneys, nerves and circulation.

Because of economic constraints and lack of knowledge about healthy eating, many families choose affordability over nutritional value. In Tonga, for example, traditional low-fat sources of protein, such as fish, cost between 15 per cent and 50 per cent more than either lamb flaps or imported chicken parts. The local taro plant costs more than imported starches such as bread and rice. Thus, "not only are the health consequences of these imported foods detrimental, but the availability of these cheap imports is also constraining the development of domestic markets".

There is little research into diabetes prevalence in indigenous populations. However, available health statistics indicate that, in some indigenous communities, diabetes has reached epidemic proportions and

---

[26] Hall and Patrinos (2006), 14.
[27] PAHO (2002a), 181.
[28] PAHO (2002), 182.

places the very existence of indigenous groups at risk. In the Pacific, diabetes is present in 44 per cent of the Torres Strait Islanders of Australia, 28 per cent of the residents of the Kingdom of Tonga and 22 per cent of the residents of Nauru. In Australia, the estimated number of indigenous adults with type 2 diabetes is up to four times higher than that of Australians of European descent, and ten times higher than the national prevalence among 25- to 50-year-olds. In other areas of the world, diabetes prevalence is also high among Native North Americans, Inuit people of the Canadian Arctic and Greenland, and indigenous people in Asia. In Canada, diabetes prevalence among certain aboriginal peoples is three to five times higher than that of the general population in the same age group. Worldwide, over 50 per cent of indigenous adults over age 35 have type 2 diabetes, and these numbers are predicted to rise.

It is essential to recognize the severity of diabetes in indigenous people. A number of successful initiatives have been undertaken in order to protect traditional food systems in the Pacific region. Vanuatu declared 2001 as Yia Blong Aelan Kakae, or the Year of Island Food, to encourage the revival of traditional methods of food cultivation and consumption. Fiji banned the import of lamb flaps from New Zealand because of the proven links with obesity. Such initiatives need to be supported with research that will foster a better understanding of diabetes in indigenous communities. Furthermore, it is important to step up efforts to develop culturally appropriate methods of education, prevention and care within indigenous populations as part of broader efforts to improve the health of indigenous communities around the world.

Sources: International Diabetes Federation (2007); World Health Organization (2001); Nicolaisen (2006).

Infant, child and maternal mortality rates are good indicators of the general health status, as they are affected by a range of factors, most important of which are malnutrition and poor access to health care, which are preventable. Although the gap has narrowed in recent decades in most countries that collect disaggregated data, these rates continue to be significantly higher among indigenous peoples, compared to the non-indigenous populations. Child mortality (years 1-4) rates in 2005, for example, were twice as high for American Indian and Alaska Natives than for the total population in the United States,[29] while in Australia for the period 1999-2003, the indigenous infant mortality rates were almost three times that of non-indigenous infants, and child mortality twice as high.[30] Infant mortality rates in New Zealand are 1.5 times higher for the indigenous Maori than for non-Maori, whilst similar trends are visible in Canada.[31]

In Latin America, where disaggregated data is readily available, indigenous infant mortality rates are always higher than those of the total population, ranging from 1.11 times higher in Chile to 3.09 times higher than the general population in Panama.[32] "In Bolivia, Ecuador, Guatemala, México and Panama, which have collected information on ethnic group and mother's area of residence (i.e., urban vs. rural), infant mortality rates are consistently higher among rural indigenous populations than among their non-indigenous rural peers as well as among urban indigenous populations".[33]

Where disaggregated data is unavailable, it is sometimes helpful to look at regional differences, and the regions where indigenous peoples predominantly live tend to fare worse than other regions. In Ratankiri, the northeast

---

[29] DeVoe, J.F. and Darling-Churchill, K.E. (2008), 34.
[30] Trewin, D. & Madden, R. (2005), 88.
[31] Although these differences in these rich countries are striking, the gap has narrowed substantially in recent years.
[32] ECLAC (2007) 190.
[33] PAHO (2007) 32.

province of Cambodia, the infant mortality rate was reported estimated at 187 per 1,000 births, compared to the national rate in 1999 of 86.[34] Maternal mortality rates tend also to be higher than those of the general population. "In Viet Nam, access to maternal health care services ranges from 90 per cent in urban areas to as low as 20 per cent in remote areas of the Central Highland and Northern Uplands regions inhabited by indigenous peoples".[35] Similar trends have been recorded throughout Latin America[36] as well as in the richer developed countries.

The health gap in developed countries

The health of indigenous peoples in First World countries, measured by life expectancy, is significantly worse than that of the mainstream populations of those countries.

Broadly speaking, New Zealand, the United States and Canada saw major health improvements for indigenous populations up to around the 1980s, leading to an appreciable narrowing of the gap in life expectancy between indigenous and mainstream populations. However, between the 1980s and the end of the century, a slowing or stalling of indigenous health improvements measured by life expectancy meant that the gap failed to close significantly (Canada) or even widened (New Zealand and the United States).

Source: Griew, R. (2008), 41.

> because indigenous peoples are essentially invisible in the data collection of many international agencies and in most national censuses, the disparities in their health situation as compared to other groups continue to be obscured

A recent conference on diabetes among indigenous peoples noted that "poverty and the associated poor quality diet, physical inactivity, overcrowded living conditions, psychosocial stress, and high burden of infectious disease interact to increase the risk of these chronic conditions from early life".[37] At the same time, it has also been demonstrated in some parts of the world that "the heavy reliance on traditional, locally available foods seems to reduce the risk for certain health problems".

Lack of disaggregated data and of culturally relevant indicators

Although the above statistics provide a general picture of the health gap between indigenous and non-indigenous populations around the world, precise and comprehensive data are still extremely difficult to obtain. In fact, because indigenous peoples are essentially invisible in the data collection of many international agencies and in most national censuses, the disparities in their health situation as compared to other groups continue to be obscured. The lack of data means ongoing shortcomings in plans, programmes and policies that

---

[34] UNICEF (2003) 9.
[35] UNICEF (2003) 10.
[36] See for example PAHO (2004).
[37] International Diabetes Federation (2006), 2.

seek to improve global health, including efforts to achieve the MDGs, which are based on averages instead of disaggregated data. Similarly, even when indigenous peoples appear in health data, they are often conceived of as a percentage of a national population, which UNICEF has noted "can be misleading in as much as the distribution of certain indigenous peoples does not correspond to national boundaries. As an illustration, the Quechua in South America are found in significant numbers in six countries and the Fulani of West Africa extend across eight countries".[38] PAHO has thus continually stated that "the lack of vital statistics or breakdown by ethnic groups, gender, and age makes the generation of policies and managerial processes based on evidence more difficult, which, in turn, jeopardizes the formulation of priorities and appropriate monitoring and evaluation systems for indigenous populations".[39]

In order to design public policies aimed at improving the health situation and related conditions of poverty and discrimination faced by indigenous peoples, it is necessary to collect disaggregated data, to develop culturally relevant indicators of health and well-being rooted in the world views of indigenous peoples, and to advance methodologies for conducting research into indigenous peoples. Moreover, indigenous peoples must have full and effective participation and take leadership roles in the collection, processing, reporting and use of information that guides decision-making in health policies and programmes.

In the international arena, and especially in the United Nations system, there has been increased recognition of this need for improved data collection.

Aboriginal health indicators in Canada

The Assembly of First Nations (AFN) represents over 630 communities in Canada. Since its charter was adopted in 1985, it has lobbied for the rights of indigenous peoples, setting policy objectives, conducting research, and negotiating with the state on issues such as treaty rights, economic development, culture and language, education, health, housing, justice, and environment.

AFN's research and policy development on the health of indigenous peoples complements the First Nations Regional Longitudinal Health Survey (RHS), which was initiated in 1997 as the most extensive national health survey on indigenous peoples and the only national research initiative controlled by indigenous peoples. It was stewarded by the National Aboriginal Health Organization and governed by the First Nations Information Governance Committee, comprising First Nations regional health coordinators from ten regions across Canada. The RHS was based on the principles of Ownership, Control, Access and Possession (OCAP) to ensure self-determination over the data collection process. The survey used the framework of holistic health and gathered information on areas such as demographics, languages, culture and religion, education, employment, water quality, food and nutrition, community development, housing, physical activity, health conditions, HIV/AIDS, diabetes, drug and alcohol use, and suicide attempts.

In 2005, the National Chief of the AFN proposed that all governments in Canada work toward "Closing the Gap" between indigenous and non-indigenous populations in health and well-being. AFN thus devised a "Closing the Gap Reporting Framework" of indicators, and a First Nations Holistic Policy and Planning Model, which guides policy interventions and the development of performance indicators.

AFN's indicators of well-being are linked to each of the core issues in the holistic health model, which is based on the following principles:

---

[38] UNICEF (2003), Innocenti Digest, No.11, 8.
[39] PAHO (2006), 3.

◈ Holistic focus on determinants of well-being

◈ Individual placed in the context of the community

◈ Governance as its underpinning, including self-government, fiscal relationships and capacity building

◈ Premised on the components of the Medicine Wheel, with the four directions articulated as spiritual and social, cultural and physical, emotional and environmental, and economic and mental

◈ Inclusive of the four cycles of the lifespan (child, youth, adult, elder)

◈ Inclusive of the three components of social capital (bonding, bridging, linkage)

The indicators include the following categories: health care; education/lifelong learning; housing; community control over services/community relationships; economic development; environmental stewardship; social services; justice; lands and resources; language/heritage/culture; employment; gender; on/away from reserve and urban/rural.

Sources: Assembly of First Nations Canada (2004), (2005) and (2006), 6.

Even where the political will exists to generate disaggregated data, however, the mechanisms and methodologies for collecting data that both give greater visibility to indigenous peoples and incorporate their participation are still lacking. The Permanent Forum on Indigenous Issues has been promoting processes to define indicators of well-being. Organizations such as the International Indigenous Women's Forum/Foro Internacional de Mujeres Indígenas (FIMI)—a network of indigenous women who facilitate the participation and advocacy efforts of indigenous women in the international arena—has called for the development of analytical paradigms, research methodologies and training programmes that can strengthen the capacity for relevant and useful data to be collected from indigenous women.

Health outcomes influenced by structures inherited from colonialism

Many illnesses that have a disproportionate impact on indigenous peoples, especially problems of mental health, are related to the colonialist and racist structures that cause indigenous communities to be some of the poorest and most marginalized in the world. Not only have indigenous peoples experienced a collective history of genocide, dispossession and dislocation, manifestations of these violent forces persist today in the form of development aggression, forced displacement and economic exploitation. WHO has noted that "whatever the reasons—war, development, or lack of economic opportunity—the psychological consequences of dislocation are serious and often result in high rates of distress".[40] In addition, most armed conflicts around the world are being waged on indigenous peoples' territories, which contain most of the remaining sources of mineral wealth, water and biodiversity.

---

[40] Cohen (1999), 9.

Environmental contamination and degradation

Environmental contamination and degradation are often the direct result of violations of the collective rights of indigenous peoples and the continuation of colonial tendencies to exploit indigenous peoples' land and resources. The environmental contaminants from sources such as mining, oil and gas industries, as well as climate change and resource depletion have serious health consequences for local indigenous communities, and neither governments nor transnational corporations seeking profit in these industries share the values of conservation and sustainability practised by indigenous peoples for thousands of years. In some regions such as the Arctic, the contaminants do not even originate in the region; rather, "environmental contaminants such as mercury, other heavy metals, PCBs, DDT, dioxins and other organ chlorines mainly originate in the mid-latitude industrial and agricultural areas of the globe but have migrated to the Arctic via atmospheric, river and ocean transport. Their subsequent bio-magnification in the Arctic food-webs and appearance in subsistence foods such as fish, waterfowl, marine and land mammals, and in the indigenous people who rely on these foods, is of great concern to Arctic residents. Potential human health effects include damage to the developing brain, endocrine and immune systems".[41]

> contaminants from sources such as mining, oil and gas industries, as well as climate change and resource depletion have serious health consequences for local indigenous communities

Use of pesticides and the health of indigenous peoples

In 1997, the University of Arizona conducted a study into the health effects of industrial agricultural pesticides in the homeland of the Yaqui people in Sonora, México, who share a common territory between the United States and Mexico. Yaquis living or working near the fields are exposed to frequent aerial spraying of pesticides. For some, their only source of water is contaminated irrigation canals. They carry poisons home in pesticide-soaked clothing, spreading the contamination to their families. The study detected high levels of pesticides in the cord blood of newborns and in mothers' milk and found birth defects, learning and development disabilities, leukaemia and other severe problems in children, along with cancer and other illnesses among family members of all ages. Deaths from acute pesticide poisoning are increasing. U.S. tribal communities are also affected by contamination passed on through the food chain and the natural environment. Dangerous pesticide use in the United States has increased 33 times since 1945.

Source: Guillette, Elizabeth et al. (1998), 347-353.

---

[41] Statement by Alan J. Parkinson from the Arctic Investigations Programme (2006).

Mental and behavioural health issues

Another serious concern in indigenous communities is mental and behavioural health issues such as alcoholism, drug abuse, depression and suicide, particularly among indigenous youth. These have all been linked to past and current experiences of colonization as a clear "psychopathology" and are exacerbated by conditions of poverty and marginalization.[42] A WHO report stated the following:

> Mental health must be considered as being deeply enmeshed with economic and political concerns such as poverty, hunger and malnutrition, social change, and violence and dislocation... Furthermore, mental, social and behavioural health problems cannot be assessed in isolation from one another, because they "represent overlapping clusters of problems that... interact to intensify each other's effects on behaviour and well-being"... From this perspective, social pathologies (e.g., substance abuse and violence), health problems, (e.g., heart disease and depression) and social conditions (e.g., poverty) are interrelated to such an extent that it is impossible to differentiate one problem clearly from another.[43]

In addition to this interrelation, which complicates diagnosis of mental health issues, some Western methods of diagnosis are insufficient within the context of contemporary multicultural, multiethnic societies. Because social and cultural contexts determine the manifestations and symptoms of mental health illnesses such as depression, the methods of diagnosis are culturally constructed.[44]

Suicide

Youth suicide affects societies around the world. The issue has been a particularly painful and sensitive topic for a number of indigenous peoples, which have experienced disproportionately high rates of youth suicide.

Youth suicide in indigenous communities takes place in the context of contemporary discrimination and marginalization and historical trauma related to colonization, assimilation and loss of traditional livelihoods. During the 19th and 20th centuries, for example, some States implemented policies intended to destroy indigenous cultures, and which isolated children from their families and forcibly stripped them of their traditions, language and religion. Although the reasons for youth suicide are complex and difficult to define, such interference with, and destruction of, cultural structures has caused stress throughout subsequent generations that is generally considered to contribute to suicidal behaviour. Indigenous youth today face the challenge of striking a balance between their place within their indigenous community and within the mainstream society of the country and may feel marginalized from both, resulting in a sense of social isolation.[45] This isolation, compounded by contemporary manifestations of discrimination, such as disproportionately high levels of poverty and unemployment, may contribute to the high rates of suicide experienced by certain indigenous tribes or peoples.

In Australia, death from self-injury is higher amongst indigenous youth than among the overall Australian youth population. In 2005 the death rate from self injury for young people aged 15–24 years was 10.4 for the

---

[42] Cohen (1999), 12.
[43] Cohen (1999), 11 citing Desjarlais et al. (1995).
[44] Cohen (1999), 12.
[45] Center for Disease Control (2007)

total Australian population and 17.6 for the Indigenous Australian population.[46] In the United States, suicide rates for American Indian and Alaska Native youth are significantly higher than the national average for other population groups. For 5 to 14 year-olds, the suicide rate is 2.6 times higher than the national average. The disparity grows larger in the later teenage years and into young adulthood. The suicide rate for American Indian and Alaska Native youth aged 15 to 24 is 3.3 times higher than the national average.[47] In the state of Alaska, a study conducted by the Alaska Statewide Suicide Prevention Council found that, although Alaska Natives comprise 16 percent of the state population, they accounted for 39 per cent of suicides between 2003 and 2006. The disparity was even greater for Alaskan youth 19 years and younger where, since the early 1990s, Alaska Natives accounted for 19 per cent of the youth population and 60 percent of the suicide deaths in that age group.[48]

In Canada, while there is a great deal of variation among First Nations communities, overall suicide rates are 5 to 7 times the rate for Canadian youth overall: 126 per 100,000 for First Nations male youth aged 15-24, compared to 24 per 100,000 for Canadian male youth as a whole, and 35 per 100,000 for First Nations female youth, compared to 5 per 100,000 for Canadian female youth.

Suicide rates have also been disproportionately high among certain communities of Inuit peoples. One researcher has correlated suicide rates among Inuit peoples in Alaska, Nunavut and Greenland with the period when governments encouraged them to move from their traditional territories to villages and towns. The trend began in north Alaska in the 1960s, Greenland in the 1970s and Nunavut in the 1980s.[49] Today, suicide rates among Inuit are the highest in Canada, at eleven times the national average".[50] In Greenland, suicide rates by young men in East Greenland reached a rate of 1,500 per annum per 100,000 in the 1990s, before beginning to decline.[51] These figures contrast starkly with historical records, which indicate that Inuit suicide rates were traditionally low. The earliest existing data on suicide among Inuit comes from Greenland, and indicates a low annual suicide rate of 3.0 per year from 1900 to 1930.[52] Records for Nunavut suggest that there was only one suicide in the region during the entire 1960s.[53]

In Latin America, suicide rates have risen dramatically within some indigenous peoples that are facing severe disruptions to traditional ways of life, including "rapid sociocultural change, disturbances in traditional social life, progressive dismantling of extended family structure, and forced relocation to reservations."[54]

In Brazil, the Kaiowa, with some 30,000 people, have seen hundreds of young people take their lives in the last two decades as the tribe has fought to keep loggers and farmers off its land.[55] Data collected by the Brazilian Ministry of Health on suicide trends and characteristics in two Guaraní communities from 2000 to 2005 suggests that the suicide rate among Guaraní was 19 times higher during this time period than the national rate in Brazil and that suicides disproportionately affected Guaraní adolescents and young adults.[56]

---

[46] Australian Research Alliance for Children and Youth (2008), p.60.

[47] Carmona (2005)

[48] Alaska Injury Prevention Center, Critical Illness and Trauma Foundation, Inc. & American Association of Suicidology (2006), p. 12.

[49] Canadian Press (2008)

[50] Health Canada (2008)

[51] IWGIA (2007)

[52] IWGIA (2007)

[53] Health Canada (2008)

[54] Center for Disease Control (2007)

[55] New York Times (2004).

[56] Center for Disease Control (2007).

In Colombia, at least 15 youth from the Embera, Wounaan, Katio and Chami peoples committed suicide between 2003 and 2004. Given the tribes' population of some 3,000 individuals, "the yearlong spate of deaths adds up to a suicide rate of 500 per 100,000 people. The overall suicide rate in Colombia was 4.4 per 100,000 in 2003, according to government statistics."[57] The suicides took place at a time of extreme change, during which settlers depleted the jungles of animals that the indigenous peoples once hunted, forcing the once-nomadic Embera to form permanent communities and turn to farming. Their traditional lives have also been greatly impacted by guerrilla and paramilitary activity.[58]

The problems faced by adolescents are often further compounded by the lack of resources available to assist them. The Special Rapporteur on the right of everyone to the enjoyment of the highest attainable standard of physical and mental health has reported discrimination in access to and treatment in, health care and support services, stating that "[I]ndigenous populations are frequently ignored, with no specialist development of psychiatric and support services despite acute needs that are manifest in increasing suicide rates...".[59]

The erosion of traditional resources and authority frustrates the ability of traditional governments to make available the culturally appropriate services most needed by indigenous adolescents. This is extremely significant as suicide rates have been found to be negatively associated with integration of traditional culture in several Native American peoples and degree of self-government among Native Canadians.[60] Similarly, although a study of suicide risk among indigenous Sami in Arctic Norway found an increased risk of suicide for the Sami in comparison with the rural population of Arctic Norway as a whole, it found no increased risk of suicide among reindeer herding Sami males. This finding may be due to the significance of reindeer herding as a traditional, culturally significant occupation among the Sami in Norway. Today, Sami in Norway who are involved in reindeer herding occupy a unique cultural position and have a strong ethnic identity and high status within the Sami culture.[61] In this regard, improvements in the enjoyment of human rights by indigenous peoples, including the rights to self-governance, culture and land rights, and improved access to resources and reduction in poverty may be expected to decrease the disproportionately high youth suicide rates faced by some indigenous tribes or communities.

At the same time, some mental health problems may be perceived differently in indigenous communities that have a collective sense of loss of their cultures, territories, or social structures. One study on alcoholism and depression in an indigenous community in the United States noted that "depression... can be a positive expression of belonging.... To be sad is to be aware of human interdependence and the gravity of historical, tribal, familial and personal loss. To be depressed, and that includes tearfulness and sleep and appetite disturbances, is to demonstrate maturity and connectedness to the Indian world".[62]

---

[57] New York Times (2004).
[58] New York Times (2004).
[59] Hunt (2005), para 12.
[60] Silviken, Haldorsen & Kvernmo (2006)
[61] Silviken, Haldorsen & Kvernmo (2006)
[62] Cohen (1999), 14, quoting O'Nell (1993).

Applying culturally adapted strategies to prevent suicide

In 2002, suicide was the second leading cause of death among Maori youth aged 15 to 24. In that same year, young Maori males were almost 3 times as likely (43.7 vs. 18.0 per 100,000), and young Maori females twice as likely (18.8 vs. 9.1 per 100,000), to die by suicide than non-Maori youth. In addition, for every suicide, there are around eight times as many hospital admissions for attempted suicides and self-injury. Many factors are attributed to the disproportionate rate of suicide among Maori youth, including poverty and higher exposure to the welfare system, cultural alienation, drug and alcohol abuse, and high rates of family and community violence.

The New Zealand Ministry of Health has developed a comprehensive strategy in conjunction with the Ministry of Maori Development and the Ministry of Youth Affairs that departs from the cultures and world views of Maori communities. The plan includes the goals of strengthening collective identity, increasing the role of Maori youth in the development of their communities, supporting cultural development, increasing access to mainstream services, and conducting further research into the underlying causes of suicide among Maori youth. Within these goals, the plan recommends a variety of strategies, including promotion of the Maori concept of health and well-being, focusing on community support systems and collective practices, reviving cultural practices to reinforce the cultural identity of Maori youth, connecting youth to elders, and fostering greater dialogue around the forces that affect Maori communities, such as unemployment, racism, abuse and breakdown of traditional social and cultural institutions.

Sources: Canterbury Suicide Project (2007) and Lawson-Te Aho (1998).

Multi-sectoral plans such as the one developed by the New Zealand Ministry of Health involve a number of actors in diverse settings and therefore require a real commitment of resources and full recognition of the capacity of indigenous peoples to lead efforts to improve the health of their communities. For governments to undertake such efforts, there must be full willingness to identify and address the underlying causes of mental health issues in indigenous peoples, and to transform structures inherited from colonization that perpetuate violations of the collective rights of indigenous communities.

Violence against indigenous women

One health problem that indigenous women are disproportionately afected by is violence, ranging from domestic violence to rapes perpetrated because of militarization and armed conflict, to economic violence through policies of neoliberalism, to violence against women through their forced displacement from their ancestral lands.[63] It is inextricably linked to violations of the collective rights of indigenous peoples and colonization, because indigenous women play a central role as bearers of collective traditional knowledge and as stewards of the collective ancestral lands, waters and other natural resources. In this sense, "indigenous traditions and indigenous women themselves identify women with the Earth and therefore perceive degradation of the Earth as a form of violence against women. This conviction is more than a metaphorical allusion to Mother Earth. It is rooted in indigenous cultural and economic practices in which women both embody and protect the health and well-being of the ecosystems in which they live."[64]

---

[63] For an in-depth discussion of violence against indigenous women, see International Indigenous Women's Forum/Foro Internacional de Mujeres Indígenas (2006).

[64] International Indigenous Women's Forum/Foro Internacional de Mujeres Indígenas (2006),16.

Umoja: Combating violence against indigenous women in Kenya

Umoja, which means "unity" in Swahili, is an independent, women-run village for survivors of gender-based violence in Kenya. Founded by Rebecca Lolosoli, an indigenous Samburu woman, and 15 other women, Umoja serves as a place for women who have been forced to leave their communities after bringing "shame" on their families for having been raped by British soldiers stationed on their ancestral lands. After being granted a neglected field of dry grassland by the local District Council, the women collectively filed a lawsuit against the British military for the rapes of over 1,400 Samburu women during the 1980s and 1990s. The women of Umoja have since participated in human rights training sessions led by Rebecca Lolosoli, actively took part in local government, and organized to demand an anti-violence unit within the local police force.

As part of their anti-violence strategies, the women of Umoja have also developed systems of resource sharing and collective means for promoting women's economic independence, which they see as integral to women's ability to be independent from abusive men. Moreover, while they draw heavily on their traditions and cultures in their strategies to combat violence, they have also used economic independence to avoid the pressure to submit their daughters to female genital mutilation and marry them off at a young age. Instead, they ensure that their daughters attend school and draw on the parts of their culture that empower them rather than those that are used to limit their choices as women.

Source: International Indigenous Women's Forum/Foro Internacional de Mujeres Indígenas (2006), 45-46.

Barriers to accessing health services

Indigenous peoples' lack of access to adequate health care manifests itself in a variety of ways. There are practical obstacles such as geographical distance or seasonal isolation, and "although health care services are largely free to indigenous peoples, the real cost of care, including the out-of-pocket costs of transportation, food, accommodation, family care, medication, and loss of workdays, poses a threat to health care access".[65] When affordable health services do exist in indigenous communities, they are often of lower quality than the services that are available to the non-indigenous population.

Moreover, expressions of racism and other forms of discrimination are widespread, creating an even greater barrier to indigenous peoples' access to health services, even when full access to quality health care based on Western medicine is possible. This is because most state health systems are not culturally sensitive, and their services and management do not reflect the socio-cultural practices, beliefs or visions of the indigenous communities. The Pan-American Health Organization has noted

> *Cultural barriers present the most complicated challenge because there is little understanding of the social and cultural factors deriving from the knowledge, attitudes, and practices in health of the indigenous peoples. The bias towards Western medicine and intervention can be offensive or inappropriate for practitioners of traditional medicine. Finding health staff that speak and understand indigenous languages is difficult, and poor communication between providers and clients at all levels compromises access to quality care. Moreover, indigenous people are often*

[65] PAHO (2006), 3.

discriminated against in health centres by non-indigenous staff and both fear and distrust caused by the attitudes and behaviours of health care workers prevent indigenous people from seeking the health care they need.[66]

These factors are even more acute for indigenous women, many of whom face multiple layers of discrimination based on the fact that they are poor, women and indigenous.

Lack of recognition of, or support for, indigenous health systems

Another fundamental aspect in the status of indigenous peoples' health is that most national governments do not provide technical or financial support to indigenous health systems, nor do most state health systems recognize, respect or incorporate the abundance of knowledge and experience of traditional medicine. Thus, because state health systems neither incorporate the indigenous concept of health nor work in harmony with traditional health systems, indigenous communities are marginalized, and health disparities between indigenous and non-indigenous populations persist.

[most national governments do not provide technical or financial support to indigenous health systems]

Treating HIV/AIDS with traditional medicine in Senegal

Indigenous peoples are particularly susceptible to contracting HIV because of their situations of poverty, unemployment, and vulnerability to violence and displacement. Yet, there are few efforts that address HIV/AIDS among indigenous peoples. Traditional treatments for HIV are widespread in indigenous communities, however, and, if recognized and supported, they are promising practices for combating the illness among all populations.

French doctor and academic Yvette Parès trained for 15 years under African traditional healer Dadi Diallo, and in 1980 founded the Keur Massar Leprosy Treatment Center outside Dakar.[67] The center uses traditional therapies to treat a wide range of illnesses, including leprosy, tuberculosis, malaria and HIV/AIDS. The treatments are based on the indigenous concept of health, which sees the therapist as a spiritual mediator who stimulates the healing forces of the sick person rather than trying to cure the disease through a cocktail of synthetic drugs. Keur Massar's traditional healers have succeeded in developing treatments for HIV/AIDS that have the benefits of being non-toxic, of addressing secondary infections such as tuberculosis, and of being formulated with natural plant components that do not require the support of rich nations in order to be synthesized. Parès has noted, "In addition, traditional medicine does not attack a pathogen in only one way, but through a combination

---

[66] PAHO (2006), 4.
[67] For a detailed account of Parès's work in Senegal, see Parès (2004)

> of active substances… from several different plants or roots, sometimes as many as 50. Where modern medicine is analytic and attacks the problem with a single molecule, traditional medicine attacks it on several fronts. This prevents the development of resistance to the combined action of all these plants."[68]
>
> Indigenous knowledge and community-based medical practices have already played a significant role in treating AIDS patients, as traditional medicine, such as that practiced at Keur Massar, is more accessible, affordable, and culturally appropriate than most current Western treatments for HIV/AIDS. Further research should be conducted to determine its potential to treat or cure the illness, and both governments and international agencies should recognize the need to incorporate indigenous knowledge into efforts to fight the HIV/AIDS pandemic.

The advancement of indigenous peoples' individual and collective rights at the national and international levels opens up possibilities of reorganising health services so that they are more culturally relevant. This process of reorganization must, however, be carried out in a participatory fashion that is oriented toward the empowerment of indigenous communities within the framework of their own plans for self-government and integral community development.[69]

As part of its Health of Indigenous Peoples Initiative, PAHO uses a socio-cultural analysis approach to harmonize indigenous health systems with state health systems based on allopathic medicine. PAHO notes

> *This approach seeks to encourage recognition, respect and an understanding of the social and cultural differences between peoples, their knowledge and their resources to improve health strategies by incorporating their perspectives, medicines and therapies into the national health systems. This process requires the application of a legal framework that facilitates social participation, indigenous practices, and the protection and conservation of indigenous knowledge and resources. It similarly requires the generation of knowledge and paradigms that expand conceptual frameworks and facilitate an understanding of indigenous knowledge and its incorporation into the training and development of human resources.[70]*

Within indigenous contexts, however, illnesses are not just epidemiological and mental health sicknesses identified by Western medicine, but also those that have direct relationships with indigenous beliefs and world views. Some indigenous beliefs hold that illnesses may come from supernatural figures, from other humans who know how to manipulate supernatural forces, or from imbalances produced in nature by humans, any of which can be cured by spiritual mediators who maintain contact with the supernatural world.[71] Some communities believe that many illnesses have a spiritual character that can be understood only by the indigenous prophets, shamans, healers and other health agents who understand the spiritual past and present of the communities in which they live. Community ceremonies and rituals are believed to protect or restore harmony within and among individual members of the community, families, nature, and the ancestors and gods.[72] Western medicine does not recognize traditional healing techniques such as song and dance, or traditional training methods for medical practitioners, such as dreams, yet these practices are viewed as integral to the prevention, diagnosis and treatment of illnesses in indigenous health systems.

---

[68] French Ministry of Foreign Affairs (n.d.)
[69] Cunningham (2002), 38.
[70] PAHO (2002b), 9.
[71] Cox Molina (2003), 42.
[72] Cox Molina (2003), 44.

Grisi siknis in Nicaragua

For centuries, grisi siknis (also called pauka alkan) has been a syndrome that occurs occasionally in the Miskitu communities of the Caribbean Coast region of Nicaragua. The first case recorded by Europeans was in 1881, in which most of the victims were young women, with some rare cases in men. The symptoms observed included a loss of senses, believing they had had sexual relations with spirits, and people running from their houses. The syndrome has an epidemic pattern; it is highly contagious and can affect a large number of people within a specific community simultaneously. According to the indigenous Miskitu and Mayangna worldview, a lack of happiness and socio- environmental well-being is related to being "sick". Based on this life philosophy, the grisi siknis is considered a state of illness. In the Miskitu culture, there are spirits in the forms of elves, mermaids, spirits of the dead and the owners of the mountains, rivers and hills. They are part of the way of life of the communities with whom they coexist. There are several reasons that this co-existence is broken and causes the imbalance. When this happens, the spirits cause sickness. Only traditional healers can cure grisi siknis.

Source: Davis (2006)

Intercultural health systems

In most state health systems, the cultures and world views of indigenous peoples are ignored, dismissed or actively opposed. Instead, most states promote monocultural health systems based exclusively on Western medicine, which do not fully reflect the multiple cultures and ethnicities of that state. This monoculturalism marginalizes indigenous peoples, denying them access to basic health services and devaluing their traditional health systems. In order to evaluate the extent to which governments are meeting the health needs of indigenous peoples, the degree to which indigenous health systems are respected and integrated into the state health systems must thus also be examined. Most health systems can be classified as monocultural, multicultural or intercultural.[73]

Monocultural health systems are based on a concept of society being homogeneous, and privileging the dominant national culture over all other cultures. There may be nominal acknowledgement of ethnic, linguistic or cultural diversity but the design of policies and programmes, including the allocation of resources, does not adequately reflect this reality. For example, in monocultural systems, data collection is not attuned to ethnic or cultural differences and may not identify health issues that are determined by gender, socio-economic class or ethnicity. Furthermore, the education of health practitioners is based on a biotechnological approach and ignores the contributions of indigenous cultures. Few health personnel are qualified to work in multiethnic contexts and the development and distribution of human resources is not culturally relevant. In these monocultural health systems, decisions are centralized at the top, without the systematic participation or consultation of indigenous communities.

Multicultural (or pluricultural) health systems, in contrast to monocultural ones, welcome and promote the presence of different cultures in society, including their respective beliefs, customs, practices and ways of life. This degree of recognition of diversity is still insufficient if it fails to ensure equality among those cultures or to promote mutual learning.

---

[73] For a classification and description of monocultural, multicultural and intercultural systems, see Cunningham (2002).

Interculturalism goes beyond merely recognising the existence of different cultures to seeking exchange and reciprocity in a mutual relationship, as well as in solidarity, among the different ways of life. Interculturalism is thus a concept that refers to communication and action among people of different cultures, and involves "interaction… putting in contact elements of different cultures and peoples and overcoming barriers between peoples, promoting a dialogue focused on the pursuit of mutual acceptance and reciprocity".[74] Intercultural health systems not only improve the quality of the health services for marginalized populations, but also promote greater horizontality, respect and solidarity between cultural health knowledge and procedures within the context of national society. In practice, this implies that both Western and indigenous health systems should be practised with equal human, technological and financial resources, with spaces for exchange of knowledge, methodologies and practices that ensure the ongoing development of both systems.

Alternative approaches

The main approaches used in different countries to find intercultural health models have been as follows:

The promotion of the use of medicinal plants approach has been generalized. It has been implemented in response to WHO guidelines in terms of giving priority to the use of medicinal plants, assuring their scientific validation. Generally, this has served as a first step in the efforts to find an intercultural health model. This has been combined with the organization of traditional therapists and the delivery of both health systems in the same facilities. A review of the different experiences shows that emphasis has been placed on carrying out studies to "scientifically" validate the plants that are used in the communities, thereby concurring with the position of WHO. A growing tendency to legalize the use of medicinal plants can be noted, although very often, laws fail to recognize the property rights of indigenous peoples—those who carry their ancestral knowledge with them. They become reduced to marginal actors in implementation of the norms.

> intercultural health systems not only improve the quality of the health services for marginalized populations, but also promote greater horizontality, respect and solidarity between cultural health knowledge and procedures within the context of national society

One limitation to this approach is that it does not value the intangible knowledge that accompanies the use of medicinal plants in the practice of community health. The activities of cutting and using these medicinal plants in the communities are accompanied by ceremonial activities and norms linked to other elements of the surroundings, the stars, spirits and other things. In other cases, each plant has a spiritual owner from whom permission is solicited in order to use it, and so on. These aspects are obviated once the use of medicines based on medicinal plants is validated and generalized, as when, in some cases, medicines derived from medicinal plants are being offered in response to requests from health units.

Joint delivery of official and indigenous medicine in the same health facilities. Various countries have adopted another modality by which to organize their

---

[74] R. Moya, cited in Cunningham (2002), 9.

intercultural health systems, delivering Western and indigenous health services through the same assistance center. In the Ecuadorian case, the goals set out for this modality were to a) link indigenous and Western medicine by treating both the indigenous and non-indigenous population, b) deliver health services in harmony with the world vision of different peoples, and c) recover and re-validate indigenous medicine and the role of its representatives.

The Jambi Huasi clinic in Ecuador

In 1994, a local organization established the health clinic *Jambi Huasi* ("Health House" in Kichwa), designed to meet the health needs of the indigenous peoples living in the Andean city of Otavalo. Over 1,000 people come to the clinic seeking health care every month. *Jambi Huasi* offers care using both Western and indigenous traditional medicine, and while it focuses on family planning and reproductive health services, it also offers traditional healing with native plants, as well as general medicine and dentistry. In addition to direct health care services, the clinic also conducts outreach and educational programmes, and all of its services are rooted in an understanding of the culture, language, customs and values of the local indigenous communities. The staff includes indigenous doctors, other health practitioners trained in working with the local population, and a full-time specialist in communication and education.

While *Jambi Huasi* started out by concentrating on meeting the health needs of the local indigenous communities, it has since grown into a care facility for other populations as well. In addition, it has now branched out into developing programmes focused on gender, discrimination, and violence, and programmes focused on youth and adolescents. *Jambi Huasi* has been supported by the United Nations Population Fund (UNFPA), which recognizes it as having the potential to influence national health policy.

Source: UNFPA (2006).

People are offered the choice of using both health systems as they share the same health infrastructure. Referrals between both systems take place within the same health unit in accordance with the diagnosis. Western doctors are trained to diagnose cases whereby referral to indigenous medical practice is required. One of the most developed areas within this concept has been the institutionalization of traditional births, for which rural doctors have been trained and health units have been oriented.[75] In many cases, the presence of traditional midwives is accepted. This has contributed to reducing maternal mortality rates. Among the lessons learned is that these experiences facilitate the access of non-indigenous people to the indigenous health system and facilitate a "dialogue of wisdoms" between men and women practitioners in the health systems.

The complementarity approach between the indigenous and official health systems. Intercultural health experiences have led to mechanisms for coordination between indigenous and official health systems even where they do not share the same facilities. The coordination is based on referral and counter-referral agreements. The lessons learned are that promoting indigenous medicine enhances the self-esteem of its practitioners and strengthens indigenous identity. Moreover, it responds to social-cultural illnesses because it facilitates complementary therapy for patients. In addition, it increases community members' confidence in the official health system because they see that their beliefs are respected. It also facilitates relations of respect on the part of staff from the official health system because they get to know and understand indigenous health concepts and practices.

---

[75] This has been documented in experiences in México (e.g., the intercultural hospital in Cuetzalan, Puebla), Ecuador, Bolivia and Chile.

Promotion of intercultural health in laws, public policy and state programmes. Intercultural health aim to influence laws and public policy so that they can transform health systems, and there are some experiences where this has been the main emphasis. These experiences combine some of the above-mentioned approaches; they are also aimed at changing power relations within health ministries—whether through decentralization, promotion of national laws and programmes, gathering of data with information ethnically disaggregated, or establishing more inclusive forms of participation of indigenous communities and peoples.

Another method has been applied in countries such as Ecuador, Bolivia and Venezuela, where vice-ministries or National Commissions of Indigenous and Intercultural Health have been created. These entities have promoted indigenous health either as a cross-cutting axis or as a specific programme. In the case of Nicaragua, the 1987 approval of an autonomous regime for indigenous peoples and ethnic communities legally transferred the administration of health services to the autonomous regional authorities.[76] This approach enabled indigenous organizations and authorities to take the lead in a large number of political initiatives. The generally held stigma and perception of incapacity in relation to indigenous peoples changed. The channelling of public resources to indigenous programmes improved. Administrative and management experience was gained at different levels, and this reflected positively in other areas of work.

Addressing social health determinants. Another approach being promoted in the delivery of health services to indigenous peoples recognizes that to achieve structural changes, it is necessary to respond to the specific factors determining the health of indigenous peoples.[77] Social determinants of health can be grouped into the following categories: socio-economic circumstances, physical circumstances and environment, infant development, personal health practices, the individual capacities and skills of those in power, and investment in biological and genetic research and health services. These social determinants of health deal with the life and work circumstances of people and their lifestyles. They deal with how social and economic policies impact on the lives and health of individuals.

Some common measures applied in the identified approaches have been a) education of official health staff about cultural diversity and indigenous rights. b) coordination with traditional women and men therapists, especially midwives, c) discussion around indicators, especially regarding ethnic disaggregation, and the inclusion of social illnesses in health records, and d) efforts to improve forms of community participation, and decentralization of services.

Prerequisites for introducing intercultural health systems

All these experiences tell us that intercultural health systems must be based on building the autonomy and ensuring the empowerment of indigenous peoples, which derive from the full recognition and exercise of rights of indigenous peoples. The framework for an intercultural system therefore includes self-determination; sovereignty over land, territory and natural resources; full and effective participation in decision-making arenas (including processes based on the principle of free, prior and informed consent); the recognition of indigenous

---

[76] In 1987, a new Political Constitution was approved in Nicaragua. The collective rights of indigenous peoples and ethnic communities were recognised, and the region where they live and what amounts to 50 per cent of the national territory was divided in two Autonomous Regions. The same National Assembly approved an Autonomy Statute that defined health administration as a responsibility of the autonomous authorities. As a result, the Regional Autonomous Councils have defined an Intercultural Autonomous Health Model that has also been recognised in the General Health Law (2003), the General Health Plan (2005), and National Health policies.

[77] See WHO/CSDH report (2008). In its fifth meeting, in Nairobi in June 2006, the WHO Commission on Social Determinants of Health (CSDH) committed itself to making health for indigenous peoples a specific area of its work.

health definitions and norms; and the recognition and protection of collective traditional knowledge. Based on this framework, intercultural health systems can be more relevant to the socio-cultural realities of indigenous peoples, and better suited to their aspirations for development and autonomy.

Conceptually, there are four fundamental prerequisites that must be present in order for an intercultural health system to exist. First, there must be a fundamental respect for human rights as codified in international human rights instruments and international law. Second, there must be recognition of indigenous peoples, because if states do not acknowledge the existence of indigenous peoples, it is not possible to develop policies that respond to their health capacities and needs. Often indigenous peoples are included in broader categories such as "vulnerable groups" or "the poor", obscuring the particularities of their situation. Furthermore, this recognition entails the structural reforms necessary to exercise self-determination, which in the case of health, corresponds to supporting the development of indigenous health systems while also ensuring full and effective participation in the health services offered by the state. Third, there must be political will, since the mere existence of policies aimed at improving the health of indigenous peoples is insufficient if they are not successfully implemented. Finally, there must be a conscious decision on the part of the national society to engage in an exchange and sharing of knowledge, values and customs, which, if practised on a daily basis, would overcome monoculturalist structures. Each of these prerequisites can be described in terms of the fundamental elements of interculturalism.

For a health system to be truly intercultural, these principles must be reflected in national laws and policies that incorporate the reforms necessary for cultures to thrive together in a multiethnic society. These principles will thus establish the basis for multiethnic alliances, cooperation among actors, and shared responsibility among local communities, governments, international agencies, non-governmental organizations, the private sector and research and training institutions.

At the same time, there are approaches to health systems that may masquerade as attempts to incorporate the needs of indigenous peoples but do not fully meet the criteria for being intercultural. In these situations, an inequitable distribution of resources persists, while the state promotes an illusion of cultural sensitivity. Some of these policies are paternalistic or integrationist and are based on policies of assimilation or integration that seek to "resolve" the problem of indigenous peoples.[78] In integrationist models, the concept of health is defined from the top down, privileging a biomedical paradigm over indigenous health models, and indigenous cultures are treated as interesting folkloric elements without true value for health promotion. Similarly, culturalistic approaches recognize cultural pluralism as intrinsically valuable but prioritize the didactic, linguistic or folkloric aspects without delving into questions of participation or power. In this approach, there are minimal consultations conducted with indigenous peoples, and projects, programmes and policies are designed by actors external to indigenous communities who treat indigenous peoples as a "target population". There may be translation of educational materials into several languages, for example, but without a critical examination of the pedagogical or cultural implications. Finally, the harmonious living approach has been promoted in response to increases in

---

[78] The International Convention of Pátzcuaro, approved by the countries of the Americas in 1940, has served as a legal framework for the definition and application of public policies relative to indigenous peoples for the last 60 years. It is framed within the "indigenist" perspective, which was put forth to encourage the "integral development" of indigenous peoples. While it promoted the recognition of cultures and strategies to overcome the situation of colonization, it did so from an outside paternalistic perspective that posited the indigenous situation as a "problem" to be resolved by the countries. This was expressed as integrationist measures of acculturation (Del Val, 1996). Since the VIII Inter-American Indigenous Congress, celebrated in 1980 in Mérida, México, there has been a period of critical revision of "indigenism" with approaches that abandon this paternalism. There has been increased recognition of the management capacity of indigenous organizations, the right to participate in public management, the pluricultural and multilingual character of national societies, and the need to respect and support the human rights of indigenous peoples. It was recommended that they continue to evaluate "indigenism" more profoundly and propose modifications in cases where it is referred to in principles, actions or institutional frameworks.

internal and external migration that have generated increased contact among different cultures. This approach recognizes that knowledge of other cultures is indispensable to the success of a multicultural society, and that cultures must learn to understand and value each other beyond mere tolerance. It therefore promotes dialogue with the goal of reaching a harmonious coexistence. However, if this approach is taken without the full participation of indigenous peoples, there is a risk of merely advancing integration without more equitable decision-making or clearer power relations. Harmonious living approaches, for example, may encourage ethnographic studies that are conducted only with the objective of learning about other cultures so that the dominant group can feel that those who are different are indeed "normal" and, based on this, can create health programmes for them.

Challenges

There are a variety of challenges to building intercultural health systems. First, states continue to assert monoculturalism as a way of promoting national unity. Second, health care sector reform is leading to increased privatization, making it more difficult to hold health providers accountable even to international human rights standards, much less to any of the collective rights of indigenous peoples. In addition, as traditional medicine is explored by non-indigenous actors, there is an increased risk of piracy of the intellectual property of indigenous peoples, as well as a risk that indigenous practices will be popularized and performed in ways that do not adhere to the histories, values and visions of indigenous peoples. Finally, the ongoing challenges of a lack of human and financial resources, as well as a lack of adequate data and research methodologies, limit the capacity of governments to design policies that could serve to build an intercultural health system.

> the full and effective participation of indigenous communities in various decision-making institutions related to their health is imperative

Concluding Remarks

In summary, to improve the health situation of indigenous peoples around the world, it is critical to recognize that their health and well-being are inextricably linked to their collective rights, such as rights to land and natural resources and to conserve and practise traditional knowledge. Efforts that codify, protect and advance the individual and collective rights of indigenous peoples, particularly indigenous women, will therefore also have positive health impacts. Furthermore, there must be ongoing integration of the perspectives and needs of indigenous peoples into global health programmes, plans, projects and policies, including initiatives to achieve the Millennium Development Goals.

In addition, the full and effective participation of indigenous communities in various decision-making institutions related to their health is imperative. At the same time, states must recognize and respect indigenous health institutions and incorporate strategies that respond to the particular needs and visions of indigenous peoples in policies of health care, prevention, promotion and education. In order to design more effective health policies, there must also be concerted efforts to create improved systems of data collection and research methodology, including research into traditional medicine that incorporate the participation of indigenous communities and reflect cultural and social considerations relating to the health of those communities.

Furthermore, models of health care must take into account the indigenous concept of health, and preserve and strengthen indigenous health systems as a strategy to increase access and coverage of health care. This will demand the establishment of clear mechanisms of cooperation among relevant health care personnel, communities, traditional healers, policy makers and government officials in order to ensure that the human resources respond to the epidemiological profile and socio-cultural context of indigenous communities. In other words, state health systems must develop to become truly intercultural, and this will involve exchanges of experience and knowledge among various actors, with the goal of improving the health of indigenous peoples, as well as the health of other poor and marginalized groups.

List of references

Alaska Injury Prevention Center, Critical Illness and Trauma Foundation, Inc. & American Association of Suicidology. 2006. Alaska Suicide Follow-back Study Final Report. Available online at: http://www.hss.state.ak.us/suicideprevention/pdfs_sspc/sspcfollowback2-07.pdf

Assembly of First Nations, Canada (AFN). 2004. "First Nations Regional Longitudinal Health Survey Backgrounder." Ottawa, Canada: Assembly of First Nations.

Assembly of First Nations, Canada (AFN). 2005. 10-Year Challenge – AFN proposal for 2005 FMM on Aboriginal Issues. Available online at www.afn.ca/cmslib/general/TenYearChallengeDeck-ENG.pps

Assembly of First Nations, Canada (AFN). 2006. "First Nations' Holistic Approach to Indicators", submitted for the Meeting on Indigenous Peoples and Indicators of Well-being, hosted by the Secretariat of the UN Permanent Forum on Indigenous Issues in Ottawa, March 2006. Available online at http://www.un.org/esa/socdev/unpfii

Australian Research Alliance for Children and Youth (2008), p.60. Report Card on the Wellbeing of Young Australians. Available online at: http://www.aracy.org.au/AM/Common/pdf/report_card/report_card_A5_web.pdf

Canadian Press. 2008. "Research tracks Inuit Modernization with Suicide, offers hope for improvement", 6 January 2008. Available online at: http://aol.mediresource.com/channel_health_news_details.asp?news_id=14168&news_channel_id=10&channel_id=10&relation_id=10577&article_rating=1

Canterbury Suicide Project. 2007. Suicide and Suicidal Behaviour amongst Maori Youth. University of Otago, Christchurch. Available online at http://www.chmeds.ac.nz/research/suicide/maori%20and%20pacific%20youth.pdf

Carmona , Richard. 2005. Testimony before the Indian Affairs Committee of the United States Senate, 15 June 2005. Available online at: http://indian.senate.gov/2005hrgs/061505hrg/carmona.pdf

Center for Disease Control. 2007. "Suicide Trends and Characteristics Among Persons in the Guaraní Kaiowá and Nandeva Communities – Mato Grosso do Sul, Brazil, 2000-2005", Morbidity and Mortality Weekly Report, January 12, 2007. Available online at: http://www.cdc.gov/mmwr/preview/mmwrhtml/mm5601a3.htm

Cohen, Alex. 1999. "The Mental Health of Indigenous Peoples: An Overview". WHO Nations for Mental Health, WHO/MNG/NAM/99.1.

Coloma, C., Hoffman, J.S., Gawryszewski, V.P., Bennett, M.D., Crosby, A.E.. 2007. "Suicide trends and characteristics among persons in the Guarani Kaiowa and Nandeva Communities—Mato Grosso do Sul, Brazil, 2000-2005". Morbidity and Mortality Weekly Report, 12 January 2007. Available online at http://findarticles.com/p/articles/mi_m0906/is_1_56/ai_n27127442/pg_1?tag=artBody;col1

Cox Molina, Avelino. 2003. Sukias y Curanderos: Isingni en la Espiritualidad. Managua: URACCAN.

Cunningham, Myrna. 2002. "Etnia, cultura y salud: La experiencia de la salud intercultural como una herramienta para la equidad en las Regiones Autónomas de Nicaragua." Presentation for World Health Day in Managua.

Davis, S. 2006. Algo anda mal. Managua: URACCAN.

Das, Dilip, Baker, Michael and Calder, Lester. 2006. "Tuberculosis in New Zealand: 1995-2004". Journal of the New Zealand Medical Association, 13 October, 2006. Vol. 119, N0.1243. Available online at: http://www.nzma.org.nz/journal/119-1243/2249

Del Val, José. 1996. "Self-determined Development, Democracy and Participation". In Proceedings from the International Seminar on Indigenous Development: Poverty, Democracy and Sustainability (Santa Cruz de la Sierra, Bolivia, May 1995), ed. D. Iturralde and E. Krotz. Washington, D.C.: Inter-American Development Bank and the Indigenous Peoples Fund.

DeVoe, J.F. and Darling-Churchill, K.E. 2008. Status and Trends in the Education of American Indians and Alaska Natives: 2008. National Center for Education Statistics, Institute of Education Sciences, U.S. Department of Education. Washington D.C.

Desjarlais, R. et. al. 1995. World Mental Health: Problems and Priorities in Low-Income Countries. New York: Oxford University Press.

Economic Commission for Latin America and the Caribbean (ECLAC) 2007. Panorama Social de América Latina 2006. Santiago: United Nations.

French Ministry of Foreign Affairs. n.d. "Medicines of the World" at: http://www.diplomatie.gouv.fr/en/article-imprim.php3?id_article=5393

Guillette, Elizabeth, Meza, María Mercedes, Aquilar, María Guadalupe, Soto, Alma Delia, and García, Idalia Enedina. 1998. "An Anthropological Approach to the Evaluation of Preschool Children Exposed to Pesticides in Mexico". Environmental Health Perspectives, Vol. 106, no. 6 (June 1998): 347-353.

Griew, Robert, Tilton, Edward, Cox, Nick, and Thomas, David. 2008. "The link between primary health care and health outcomes for Aboriginal and Torres Strait Islander Australians". A Report for the Office for Aboriginal and Torres Strait Islander Health, Department of Health and Ageing. Waverly: Robert Griew, Ltd.

Hall, Gillette and Patrinos, Harry Anthony. 2005. Indigenous Peoples, Poverty and Human Development in Latin America 1994-2004. New York, NY: Palgrave McMillan.

Hanemann. Ulrike. 2006. "Literacy for special target groups: Indigenous peoples." Background paper prepared for the Education for All Global Monitoring Report 2006. Paris: UNESCO publication 2006/ED/EFA/MRT/PI/40.

Health Canada. 2007. "First Nations Comparable Health Indicators" Available online at: http://www.hc-sc.gc.ca/fniah-spnia/diseases-maladies/2005-01_health-sante_indicat-eng.php

Health Canada. 2008. First Nations, Inuit & Health Program Compendium, Available online at: http://www.hc-sc.gc.ca/fniah-spnia/pubs/aborig-autoch/2007_compendium/1_2_addict-toxico-eng.php#_1_2_8, visited 20 November 2008

Hunt, Paul. 2005. Report of the Special Rapporteur on the right of everyone to the enjoyment of the highest attainable standard of physical and mental health to the Commission on Human Rights. UN Document E/CN.4/2005/51

Hunter, E. 2001. Aboriginal and Torres Strait Islander Suicide, Accessed online at http://www.auseinet.com/suiprev/occpapers on 1 May 2007.

International Diabetes Federation. 2006. "Draft Position Statement: Diabetes in Indigenous Children and Adolescents", prepared for the International Diabetes Federation Conference in Australia, November 2006. Available online at http://www.meetingsfirst.com.au/meetings/Diabetes%202006/Images/DRAFT%20Child%204.8.06.pdf

International Diabetes Federation. 2007. "Globalization, diet, and health: an example from Tonga." Care for Everyone. World Diabetes Day leaflet of the International Diabetes Federation. Accessed online at http://www.worlddiabetesday.org on 4 May 2007.

International Indigenous Women's Forum/Foro Internacional de Mujeres Indígenas. 2006. "Mairin Iwanka Raya: Indigenous Women Stand Against Violence". A Companion Report to the Secretary-General's Study on Violence Against Women. Available online at http://www.madre.org/fimi/vaiwreport06.pdf

International Work Group for Indigenous Affairs (IWGIA) 2007. "The Social Determinants of Elevated Rates of Suicide Among Inuit Youth". Indigenous Affairs Journal, no. 4/07.

Lawson-Te Aho, Keri. 1998. "Kia Piki te Ora o te Taitamariki: Strengthening Youth Well being: New Zealand Youth Suicide Prevention Strategy". Wellington: Ministry of Youth Affairs/Ministry of Health/Ministry of Maori Development.

Moya, R. 1998. "Reformas educativas e interculturalidad en América Latina". Revista Iberoamericana de Educación, 17: 105-187.

New York Times. 2004. "In a Land Torn by Violence, Too Many Troubling Deaths", 23 November 2004. Available online at: http://www.nytimes.com/2004/11/23/health/psychology/23trib.html

Nicolaisen, Ida. 2006. "Overlooked and in Jeopardy: Indigenous People with Diabetes". Diabetes Voice, June 2006, Vol.51, 2.

O'Nell, TD. 1993. "Feeling Worthless: An Ethnographic Investigation of Depression and Problem Drinking at the Flathead Reservation". Culture, Medicine and Psychiatry, 16:447-469.

Pan-American Health Organization (PAHO)/World Health Organization (WHO). 1993. Resolution V. "The Health of Indigenous Peoples", adopted at the fourth plenary session, 28 September 1993. PAHO Doc. CD37.R5. Available online at http://www.paho.org/English/AD/THS/OS/Indig-home.htm

Pan-American Health Organization (PAHO). 1997. "Fortalecimiento y desarrollo de los sistemas de salud tradicionales: Organización y provisión de servicios de salud en poblaciones multiculturales." Indigenous Peoples Health Series. Washington, D.C: PAHO.

Pan-American Health Organization (PAHO). 2002a. "Health in the Americas", Scientific and Technical Publication No. 587, Vol. I. Available online at http://www.paho.org/English/AD/THS/OS/Indig-home.htm

Pan-American Health Organization (PAHO). 2002b. "Harmonization of Indigenous and Conventional Health System in the Americas: Strategies for Incorporating Indigenous Perspectives, Medicines, and Therapies into Primary Health Care". Washington, D.C.: PAHO.

Pan-American Health Organization (PAHO). 2003. "Strategic Directions and Plan of Action 2003-2007", Health of the Indigenous Peoples Initiative. Available online at http://www.paho.org/English/AD/THS/OS/Plan2003-2007-eng.doc

Pan-American Health Organization (PAHO). 2004. "Healing our Spirit Worldwide" Newsletter for Indigenous People, Edition No.2, May 2004.

Pan-American Health Organization (PAHO). 2006. "Health of the Indigenous Population in the Americas." 47th Session of the Directing Council, September 2006. PAHO Doc. CD47.R13. Available online at http://www.paho.org/English/AD/THS/OS/Indig-home.htm

Pan-American Health Organization (PAHO). 2007. Health in the Americas, 2007. Volume I – Regional Health. PAHO. Available online at http://www.paho.org/English/DD/PUB/csp27-stp622-e.pdf

Parès, Yvette. 2004. La Médecine africaine, une efficacité étonnante, témoignage d'une pionnière, [African medicine, an astonishing efficacy, the account of a pioneer.] Barret-sur-Méoug: Editions Yves Michel.

Parkinson, Alan J. 2006. Statement at a joint hearing of the Committee on Commerce and Committee on Foreign Relations of the US Senate by A.J. Parkinson from the Arctic Investigations Program, Centers for Disease Control and Prevention, United States Department of Health and Human Services, on the Arctic Human Health Initiative, 26 September, 2006. See: http://www.dhhs.gov/asl/testify/t060926.html

Public Health Agency of Canada. 2006. Tuberculosis in Canada 2006, Ottawa: Public Health Agency of Canada. Available online at http://www.phac-aspc.gc.ca/publicat/2007/tbcanpre06/pdf/tbpre2006_e.pdf

Silviksen, Anne, T. Haldorsen & KS Kvernmo. 2006. "Suicide among Indigenosu Sami in Arctic Norway, 1970-1988", European Journal of Epidemiology No.9 September 2006.

Skifte, Turid Bjarnason. 2004. "Tubeculosis in Greenland – Still a problem to bear in mind: development and strategy". International Journal of Circumpolar Health 2004; 63 Suppl 2: 225-9

Statistics Canada. 2006. Aboriginal Peoples Highlight Tables, 2006 Census.
Available online at
http://www12.statcan.ca/english/census06/data/highlights/Aboriginal/pages/Page.cfm?Lang=E&Geo=PR&Code=01&Table=2&Data=Count&Sex=1&Abor=5&StartRec=1&Sort=2&Display=Page

The Indigenous World 2004. 2004. Copenhagen: IWGIA. Available online at http://www.iwgia.org

The New York Times. 2004. "In a land torn by violence, too many troubling deaths". 23 November 2004.

Trewin, D. & Madden, R. 2005. The Health and Welfare of Australia´s Aboriginal and Torres Strait Islander Peoples. Canberra: Australian Bureau of Statistics and Australian Institute of Health and Welfare.

UNICEF. 2003. "Ensuring the Rights of Indigenous Children". Innocenti Digest no. 11. Florence, Italy: UNICEF Innocenti Research Centre.

United Nations Organization. 2007. Declaration on the Rights of Indigenous Peoples. UN Doc. A/61/L.67, September 2007. Available online at UNPFII Web site http://www.un.org/esa/socdev/unpfii

United Nations Populations Fund (UNFPA). 2006. "Working from within and from without: Jambi Huasi – a model for community empowerment". Available online at http://www.unfpa.org/news/news.cfm?ID=742

United Nations Permanent Forum on Indigenous Issues (UNPFII). 2005. Report of the Workshop on Methodologies Regarding Free, Prior and Informed Consent and Indigenous Peoples. UNPFII Fourth Session. UN Doc. E/C.19/2005/1. Available online at http://www.un.org/esa/socdev/unpfii

World Health Assembly (WHA). 1994-2001. WHA Resolutions 54.16, 51.24, 50.31, 49.26, 48.24, and 47.27 regarding WHO's contribution to achieving the objectives of the International Decade of the World's Indigenous People (1994-2003). Available online at http://www.who.int/gb/or

World Health Organization (WHO). 1946. "Constitution of the World Health Organization". Available online at http://www.who.int/gb/bd/PDF/bd46/e-bd46_p2.pdf

World Health Organization (WHO). 1998. Review of the Constitution of the World Health Organization: Report of the Executive Board special group. WHO Doc. EB101.R2, 22 January 1998. Available online at: http://apps.who.int/gb/archive/pdf_files/EB101/pdfangl/angr2.pdf

World Health Organization (WHO). 1999. Speech held by WHO Director-General Gro Harlem Brundtland at the opening of the International Consultation on the Health of Indigenous Peoples, Geneva, 23 November 1999. Available online at http://www.who.int/director-general/speeches/1999/english/19991123_indegenous_people.html

World Health Organization (WHO). 2001. "Globalization, diet, and health: An example from Tonga". Bulletin of the World Health Organization, vol.79 no.9. Geneva: WHO.

World Health Organization (WHO). 2002. "Traditional Medicine Strategy 2002-2005." WHO Doc. WHO/EDM/TRM/2002.1. Geneva: WHO.

World Health Organization (WHO) Commission on Social Determinants of Health (CSDH). 2008. Closing the gap in a generation: health equity through action on the social determinants of health. Final Report of the Commission on Social Determinants of Health. Geneva: WHO.

CHAPTER VI

HUMAN RIGHTS

By Dalee Sambo Dorough

Early conceptions of natural rights, and later human rights, in some ways share certain parallels or philosophical strains with the general practices, customs and values of indigenous societies: the social contract, the common good, the general will, equality and so forth. There are a number of notable distinctions or additional elements, however. For example, indigenous concepts are not confined to human beings but include all living things, underscoring an essential, unique element of the relationship of indigenous peoples to nature and their natural world that has permeated indigenous identity and is at the core of their world views and perspectives. The collective rather than individualistic nature of indigenous societies is another important attribute that has surfaced repeatedly in all international and regional human rights standard setting discussions. The narrow view of rights attaching only to individuals is regarded as wholly insufficient for the distinct cultural context of indigenous peoples. The collective dimension of indigenous societies cannot therefore be underestimated in the development and implementation of human rights standards concerning indigenous peoples.

Other notable distinctions include the values of honour, respect for one another, deference to Elders, family and kinship and related roles, sharing, cooperation, humour, knowledge of language, customs and traditions, compassion, humility, avoidance of conflict, spirituality,[1] peace and harmony. These and other values are common to many, if not all, indigenous communities.[2] The concept of *having responsibilities to the collective* rather than simply enjoying rights is a widely found component of indigenous cultures. The link between knowledge of language, customs and traditions and indigenous peoples' relationship to their natural world is directly related to inter-generational responsibilities and rights. The practice of consensus decision-making and consultation is also a common practice within indigenous communities.

The values, customs and practices of indigenous societies are in fact "norms" that have guided indigenous societies toward harmonious relations. Through expressions at various international fora, indigenous peoples have translated their worldviews into a human rights discourse, through the borrowing of terminology as well as the expansion of human rights ideals.

This expansion of human rights concepts has taken hold within the United Nations, the International Labour Organization, the Organization of American States and elsewhere. What has evolved is a set of standards that are more consistent with the values, practices and institutions of indigenous peoples. Indeed, Richard Falk notes that:

---

[1] Inupiaqatigiigniq, the Inupiat of the north and northwest coast of Alaska have interpreted a number of concepts crucial to collective relations within Inuit communities: Qiksiksrautiqagniq (respect) for Elders, others and nature; Ilagiigniq (family kinship and roles); Signatainniq (sharing); Inupiuraallaniq (knowledge of language); Paammaagiinniq (cooperation); Piqpakkutiqagniq (love and respect for one another); Quvianguniq (humor); Anuniagniq (hunting traditions); Naglikkutiqagniq (compassion); Qinuinniq (humility); Paaqtaktautainniq (avoidance of conflict); and Ukpiqqutiqagniq (spirituality).

[2] A table referencing Maori values similar to those of the Inupiat values discussed above was presented by Garth Harmsworth from Landcare Research (New Zealand) at the Seventh Joint Conference: "Preservation of Ancient Cultures and the Globalization Scenario", organised 22–24 November 2002 by Te Whare Wananga o Waikato, (School of Maori and Pacific Development, University of Waikato, Hamilton, New Zealand) & International Centre for Cultural Studies (ICCS), India. See Harmsworth (2002).

*This recent authentic expression of indigenous peoples'
conception of their rights contrasted with that of earlier
mainstream human rights instruments claiming universalism…
Such comparisons confirm the contention that participatory
rights are integral to a legitimate political order, as well as to
a reliable clarification of grievance, demand, and aspiration.
This alternative conception has been developed by indigenous
peoples in an elaborate process of normative reconstruction that
has involved sustained and often difficult dialogue among the
multitude of representatives of Indigenous traditional peoples.*[3]

Despite efforts over the last forty years to improve conditions and to increase recognition of indigenous rights through law and policy, litigation, national dialogue and enhanced leadership opportunities, full accommodation of indigenous rights remains elusive. Domestically, remnants of colonialism applied with nuance and subtlety have become difficult to specify or identify. But ever since Cayuga Chief Deskaheh and Maori religious leader W.T. Ratana[4] tried to gain the attention of the League of Nations in the early 1920s, indigenous peoples have increasingly felt compelled to speak out internationally about the abuses being perpetrated by one people against another and the need to check the limits of power and abuses of others. Largely due to indigenous peoples organising themselves nationally and internationally, we are seeing an important synergy develop between domestic arenas and international human rights standard setting. These actions may ultimately ensure indigenous peoples their rightful place within the international community and create new tools with which to reconstruct political and legal relationships with nation-states and others. In this regard, the adoption of the Declaration on the Rights of Indigenous Peoples by the United Nations General Assembly in 2007 was a very significant event and the Declaration will inevitably be instrumental in shaping indigenous peoples' relationships with both the international community as well as states.

> [full accommodation of indigenous rights remains elusive]

A human rights-based approach

Indigenous advocates believe the use of a human rights-based approach to advancing their rights, interests and concerns, and for resolving indigenous/ state conflicts, is critical to the future of indigenous peoples. As the Special

---

[3] Falk (2000), 151-152.

[4] See the Introduction to this volume. Although the Iroquois Confederacy engaged in international relations with Great Britain, France and other Indigenous nations, it was not until the creation of the League of Nations that they attempted to gain access to a formal international organization to resolve a conflict. See, generally, Akwesasne Mohawk Counselor Organization, Deskaheh: Iroquois Statesman and Patriot (1984); and also D. Sanders (1992), 485. Regarding W.T. Ratana see http://www.socialjustice.org.nz/?sid=32&id=99&print=artic les, wherein his efforts to have the Treaty of Waitangi upheld are discussed, and reference is made to his trip to Europe.

Rapporteur on the situation of human rights and fundamental freedoms of indigenous people, Rodolfo Stavenhagen, has noted, a human rights-based approach

> ...should take into account basic principles such as the indivisibility and universality of human rights; non-discrimination, especially in the case of vulnerable or marginalized groups; participation and empowerment; and accountability.[5]

Right to self-determination

> indigenous peoples have consistently regarded the right to self-determination as a prerequisite to the protection and promotion, as well as the exercise and enjoyment, of all other human rights

In the context of indigenous peoples, and consistent with the inter-related, interdependent and indivisible nature of human rights, a human rights based approach requires recognition of the fundamental right to self-determination. The fundamental nature of the right to self-determination is evidenced by the fact that it appears in the United Nations Charter,[6] the International Covenants,[7] the Declaration Concerning Friendly Relations and Cooperation among States in Accordance with the Charter of the United Nations,[8] and the United Nations Declaration on the Rights of Indigenous Peoples.[9] The right to self-determination has been acknowledged as essential to the exercise of all other human rights and referred to as the pre-condition for the exercise of all other rights:

> Human rights and fundamental freedoms can only exist truly and fully when self-determination also exists. Such is the fundamental importance of self-determination as a human right and a prerequisite for the enjoyment of all the other rights and freedoms.[10]

Likewise, indigenous peoples have consistently regarded the right to self-determination as a prerequisite to the protection and promotion, as well as the exercise and enjoyment, of all other human rights. Furthermore, they have consistently emphasized the principle of non-discrimination, despite repeated state efforts to qualify or limit the right of self-determination in relation to indigenous peoples. And they have articulated self-determination as an inherent right, not a right that is "given" or "created" by others but pre-existing.

Under international law, self-determination is considered to be jus cogens or a peremptory norm. Similarly, the prohibition of racial discrimination is a peremptory

---

[5] Stavenhagen (2007), para. 14.
[6] Charter of the United Nations, Article 1, para. 2.
[7] The International Covenant on Civil and Political Rights and the International Covenant on Economic, Social and Cultural Rights, common Article 1.
[8] Declaration on Principles of International Law concerning Friendly Relations and Coopera-tion among States in Accordance with the Charter of the United Nations. UN Doc. General Assembly Resolution 2625 (XXV), 1970.
[9] The UN Declaration on the Rights of Indigenous Peoples was adopted by the General As-sembly on 13 September 2007 (A/RES/61/295).
[10] Gros Espiell (1980), 10, para. 59.

norm of international law. It is therefore disconcerting that not only one but a range of state proposals were being made in relation to the language concerning self-determination of indigenous peoples in the United Nations Declaration on the Rights of Indigenous Peoples.[11]

Self-determination is also an integral part of democracy. The right to self-determination has been described as "the oldest aspect of the democratic entitlement". As international law Professor Thomas Franck explains:

> *Self-determination is the oldest aspect of the democratic entitlement... Self-determination postulates the right of a people in an established territory to determine its collective political destiny in a democratic fashion and is therefore at the core of the democratic entitlement.[12]*

Fortunately, indigenous peoples' views prevailed on this matter at the United Nations. The provisions of the UN Declaration, when read in context, ensure consistency with international law and the obligations of UN Member States to promote and protect human rights for all, including indigenous peoples.

The inter-related, interdependent and indivisible nature of human rights

The authors of the Universal Declaration of Human Rights clearly recognized the interrelatedness of human rights in this hallowed text by including reference to civil, political, economic, social and cultural rights. In addition, those drafters of the International Covenants who argued for a single covenant understood the importance of the interrelationship of the basic human rights and freedoms that form the International Covenant on Civil and Political Rights and the International Covenant on Economic, Social and Cultural Rights.

Similarly, indigenous peoples recognize the interrelatedness and interdependence of all human rights.[13] They do so in large part because of their worldview of the holistic nature of their relations and inter-relationships with all other beings and all living things. From their earliest interventions at the UN Working Group on Indigenous Populations (WGIP), indigenous peoples have seen the text of the UN Declaration on the Rights of Indigenous Peoples as a whole and have affirmed the view that human rights are interrelated, interdependent and indivisible.[14]

---

[11] The Declaration on the Rights of Indigenous Peoples was adopted by 143 votes in favor, 4 against and 11 abstentions (A/RES/61/295).

[12] Franck (1992), 52.

[13] There are a range of indigenous interventions, Joint Submissions, etc., on this point. Specifically, see Geneva Declaration on the Health and Survival of Indigenous Peoples, adopted at a 1999 World Health Organization health consultation; its preambular paragraph 11 states: "Reminding the international agencies and other bodies of the UN system of their responsibility, and the obligation of States, towards the promotion and protection of Indigenous Peoples' status and rights, and that a human rights approach to Indigenous health and survival is based on the said international responsibility and obligation to promote and protect the universality, indivisibility, interdependence and interrelation of the rights of all peoples". See WHO (1999).

[14] Numerous statements have been made by indigenous peoples about the provisions of the Declaration being dependent upon one another, and that the text must be read in context and as a whole. See, for example, the 1996 NGO Statement to the Commission on Human Rights Working Group on the Draft Declaration (WGDD) stating that, "the Preamble was fundamental to the overall draft because it lays the philosophical foundations and contextual clauses and it is responsive to the intent of the declaration". See WGDD (1997), para. 34. Also see the 1998 Statement of the Inuit Circumpolar Conference to WGDD stating that, "[the Declaration] was an integrated document to be read as a whole..." See WGDD (1998), 8. Finally, see the Joint Submission on the Urgent Need to Improve the UN Standard-Setting Process on Indigenous Peoples' Human Rights presented to the Permanent Forum on Indigenous Issues, Fourth Session, in New York UNPFII (2004), para. 10.

The World Conference on Human Rights, through the Vienna Declaration and Programme of Action,[15] affirmed that:

> *All human rights are universal, indivisible and interdependent and interrelated. The international community must treat human rights globally in a fair and equal manner, on the same footing, and with the same emphasis. While the significance of national and regional particularities and various historical, cultural and religious backgrounds must be borne in mind, it is the duty of States, regardless of their political, economic and cultural systems, to promote and protect all human rights and fundamental freedoms.*

There are a growing number of international instruments that make specific reference to this important aspect of human rights.[16] In addition, this interpretation of human rights has been embraced by numerous scholars[17] and advocates.

The point of such an understanding and associated pronouncements is the need to recognize the dynamic interplay between cultural diversity and universal norms, principles or ideals. Furthermore, such language helps to motivate respect for certain minimum standards and to promote the actual enjoyment of basic human rights, which may be taken for granted. There is no question that each state will (and must) take into consideration its "national and regional particularities and various historical, cultural and religious backgrounds."[18] However, they must do so in a fashion that is consistent with universally applicable minimum human rights standards.

These and other fundamental principles of the human rights framework cannot be overstated, especially from an indigenous perspective. It is quite elementary but important to reiterate that it is undesirable and inconsistent with the human rights framework to establish a "hierarchy" of rights[19] or to invite discussion over rights that may be derogable and those that may not. Consistent with the indivisibility of human rights and their interdependence, state governments have both specific and general duties to promote human rights and are not in a position to determine which rights they may or may not limit.[20]

The universality of human rights, and understanding the cultural context

The Charter of the United Nations can be considered the starting point for the internationalization of human rights. In particular, Article 1(3) establishes a central purpose of the United Nations as one of "promoting and encouraging respect for human rights and for fundamental freedoms for all without distinction as to race, sex, language, or religion." Although there was a tension between the West and primarily Asian countries as to the value systems embedded in the early human rights instruments,[21] the objective was to ensure that all peoples,

---

[15] Vienna Declaration and Programme of Action, as adopted by the World Conference on Human Rights on June 25, 1993. UN Doc. A/CONF.157/23, Part I, para. 5.

[16] For example, the Inter-American Democratic Charter adopted by acclamation by the Hemisphere's Foreign Ministers and signed by the 34 countries of the Americas at the 28th special session of the OAS General Assembly, Lima, Peru, 11 September 2001. Its Article 7 states: "Democracy is indispensable for the effective exercise of fundamental freedoms and human rights in their universality, indivisibility and interdependence, embodied in the respective constitutions of states and in inter-American and international human rights instruments." Also the United Nations Declaration on the Right to Development, Article 6.2 acknowledges that all human rights are indivisible and interdependent.

[17] Henkin (1999), 1214, where he discusses "cultural relativism" and "cultural imperialism" and states: "A holistic perspective on human rights is not merely faithful to the intellectual and political history of the human rights idea; it reflects the relationship in principle, in law and in fact, between national and international human rights in today's world."

[18] See Preamble to the Declaration on the Rights of Indigenous Peoples.

[19] See Meron (1986), which addresses the notion of a hierarchy of norms in international law.

[20] See Article 5 of the International Covenants, which addresses actions aimed at the destruction of any rights or freedoms recognized, and the purposes and principles of the United Nations.

[21] Henkin et al. (1999), 16: "The Western origin of rights was a source of some political resentment after the end of colonialism and became a political issue towards the end of the Twentieth Century, leading, for example, to the invocation of 'cultural relativism.' 'Asian values,' in particular, were invoked to challenge the universality of rights."

worldwide, enjoyed fundamental human rights. The purpose was not to replace national constitutions or internal laws[22] but rather to establish minimum standards at the international level to be guaranteed by every state to its peoples. Furthermore, there was no intention to create homogeneity.[23]

The concept of cultural context[24] is significant in order to reinforce the positive purposes of international human rights instruments. Dependent upon regional or cultural particularities and conditions, the manifestation of every right will require different weighting. This is also true in the context of the exercise of collective or group rights and those of an individual nature.

The United Nations Charter itself recognizes that regional organs and arrangements were anticipated by the United Nations[25] for the accommodation of regional differences. In fact, various regional arrangements have emerged and have been complementary to the international human rights framework. For example, the Organization of American States is a regional arrangement, with a corresponding Inter-American Court of Human Rights and institutions to "enforce" and monitor a variety of regional human rights instruments.[26]

Similar to these regional arrangements, the work of the United Nations in preparing the Declaration on the Rights of Indigenous Peoples reinforced the need for instruments and processes to accommodate cultural diversity. Indeed, this was the ultimate objective of the UN Declaration. Such an approach is a necessary element to ensure the effectiveness of universally recognized human rights. Furthermore, cultural diversity is preferable to cultural imperialism, which would be antithetical to the objective of respecting and promoting international human rights.[27]

> ultimately, the balancing of the universality of human rights and the accommodation of distinct cultural contexts are necessary to ensure and maintain the rich diversity of humankind

---

[22] See also Mabo v. Queensland (1992), per Brennan J: "[I]nternational law is a legitimate and important influence on the development of the common law, especially when international law declares the existence of universal human rights. A common law doctrine founded on unjust discrimination in the enjoyment of civil and political rights demands reconsideration."

[23] Falk (2000), 151-152: "[T]he interplay of different cultural and religious traditions suggests the importance of multi-civilizational dialogue involving the participation of various viewpoints, especially those with non-Western orientations. The world does not need a wholesale merging of different cultures and civilizations; rather, it simply needs to foster a new level of respect and reconciliation between and among its ever changing and ever diverse peoples and nations."

[24] Steiner and Alston (1996), 374, which cites the American Anthropological Association's "Statement on Human Rights" (1947): "Today the problem is complicated by the fact that the Declaration must be of worldwide applicability. It must embrace and recognize the validity of many different ways of life."

[25] Charter of the United Nations, Chapter VIII.

[26] Hannum (1990), chapters 5, 10 and 12.

[27] Henkin et al. (1999), 107, quoting Donnelly (1989): "Cultural relativity is an undeniable fact; moral rules and social institutions evidence an astonishing cultural and historical variability. The doctrine of cultural relativism holds that at least some such variations cannot be legitimately criticised by outsiders. But if human rights are literally the rights everyone has simply as a human being, they would seem to be universal by definition. How should the competing claims of cultural relativism and universal human rights be reconciled? I defend an approach that maintains the fundamental universality of human rights while accommodating the historical and cultural particularity of human rights."

Indigenous peoples recognize that there is no room for cultural imperialism in the context of human rights. Rather, indigenous peoples are demanding that human rights be interpreted fairly, holistically, and consistent with the peremptory norms of international law. Ultimately, the balancing of the universality of human rights and the accommodation of distinct cultural contexts are necessary to ensure and maintain the rich diversity of humankind.

Human rights, democracy, and the rule of law

Like the interdependence of human rights, there are important relationships between human rights, democracy and the rule of law.[28] Increasingly, the international community has recognized the importance of this relationship.[29] For any government institutions to have a measure of integrity, they must ensure access, participation and representation. In this way, democracy is not merely about one person, one vote. In order to exercise the human right to self-determination without any threat to the territorial integrity or political unity of sovereign and independent states, governments must guarantee effective representation of all.[30] Without such effective participation and accommodation, and without recognizing the rights of distinct peoples within their borders, states cannot possibly claim to respect social justice and democracy. Hence, democracy and the rule of law are necessarily interrelated.

In 1991, the Conference on Security and Co-operation in Europe noted:

> The participating States emphasize that issues relating to human rights, fundamental freedoms, democracy and the rule of law are of international concern, as respect for these rights and freedoms constitutes one of the foundations of the international order. They categorically and irrevocably declare that the commitments undertaken in the field of the human dimension of the CSCE are matters of direct and legitimate concern to all participating States and do not belong exclusively to the internal affairs of the State concerned. [31]

And, in 1992, United Nations Secretary-General B. Boutros-Ghali stated:

> Democracy within nations requires respect for human rights and fundamental freedoms, as set forth in the [United Nations] Charter... This is not only a political matter.[32]

More recently, the member States of the OAS adopted the Inter-American Democratic Charter in Lima, Peru, coincidentally on September 11, 2001, and affirmed, both in the preamble and operative paragraphs of the Charter,

---

[28] Steiner and Alston (1996), 387, citing Pannikar (1982): "Human rights are tied to democracy. Individuals need to be protected when the structure which is above them (Society, the State or the Dictator – by whatever name) is not qualitatively superior to them, i.e., when it does not belong to a higher order. Human rights are a legal device for the protection of smaller numbers of people (the minority or the individual) faced with the power of greater numbers."

[29] Steiner and Alston (ibid.), 1314, quoting Steiner (1999), 202: "...the rule of law, so vital to the growth of liberalism and democratic government, is invoked to urge greater predictability in the application of laws bearing on foreign investment and on business generally... In turn, it is argued, heightened business investment and activity under such a legal regime will ultimately strengthen the rule of law with respect to civil and political rights as well. Foreign investment and the development of the local economy in a broad Western model thus will contribute importantly toward, if not make inevitable, the realization of democratic and human rights culture... The causal flows are argued to be reciprocal, as global business activity both inspires and responds to the growth of democratic rule and its associated rule of law."

[30] See Declaration on Principles of International Law Concerning Friendly Relations and Cooperation Among States in Accordance with the Charter of the United Nations, (1970), General Assembly Resolution 2625 (XXV), 25 UN GAOR, Supp. (No. 28) 121, UN Doc A/8028 (1971), reprinted in 9 I.L.M. 1292 (1970).

[31] OSCE Document of the Moscow Meeting on the Human Dimension, Emphasising Respect for Human Rights, Pluralistic Democracy, the Rule of Law, and Procedures for Fact-Finding, 3 October 1991, in 30 I.L.M. 1670, at 1672.

[32] B. Boutros-Ghali (1992), 22, para. 81.

the fundamental connection between human rights, democracy and the rule of law.[33] In particular, Articles 7, 9, and 11 read:

> *Article 7*
> *Democracy is indispensable for the effective exercise of fundamental freedoms and human rights in their universality, indivisibility and interdependence, embodied in the respective constitutions of states and in inter-American and international human rights instruments.*

> *Article 9*
> *The elimination of all forms of discrimination, especially gender, ethnic and race discrimination, as well as diverse forms of intolerance, the promotion and protection of human rights of Indigenous peoples and migrants, and respect for ethnic, cultural and religious diversity in the Americas contribute to strengthening democracy and citizen participation.*

> *Article 11*
> *Democracy and social and economic development are interdependent and are mutually reinforcing.*

It is the underlying principles of democracy that are necessarily and intimately tied to the exercise of human rights by indigenous peoples as well as the equal application of the rule of law to indigenous individuals and groups.

All of the key aspects of a human rights-based approach adopted by indigenous peoples require consideration: self-determination; the inter-related, interdependent and indivisible nature of human rights; universality; and human rights, democracy and the rule of law. Too often, they have been overlooked and denied within the indigenous context. Without a comprehensive understanding of these human rights principles, the full and effective exercise of indigenous human rights will not be achieved.

> it is the underlying principles of democracy that are necessarily and intimately tied to the exercise of human rights by indigenous peoples as well as the equal application of the rule of law to indigenous individuals and groups

Relevant human rights instruments specifically concerning indigenous peoples

Though indigenous peoples are the beneficiaries or subjects of all existing international human rights instruments, it is important to focus upon those instruments that specifically address their distinct context.

The United Nations Declaration on the Rights of Indigenous Peoples

The General Assembly's adoption on September 13, 2007 of the United Nations Declaration on the Rights of Indigenous Peoples demonstrates the Organization's

---

[33] Inter-American Democratic Charter (2001).

capacity to accommodate the distinct status of indigenous peoples. The instrument now provides an important framework for the realization of indigenous peoples' human rights as well as a benchmark for state accountability in relation to their specific obligations.

In regard to its actual content, the United Nations Declaration is an extraordinary document, reflecting the important balance between individual and collective indigenous human rights as well as the legitimate interests and concerns of state governments. Though the entire Declaration is significant for indigenous peoples, there are a number of notable articles that deserve specific mention. Article 3 embraces the right to self-determination and, when read in context with all other relevant preambular and operative paragraphs, it strikes the necessary balance between the exercise of this right by indigenous peoples and the international obligations of state governments. The matter of free, prior and informed consent, contained most specifically in Article 19, is an important dimension of the right to self-determination and further ensures the "participatory" role of indigenous peoples in matters that affect them.

The articles addressing lands, territories and resources reinforce the distinct rights of indigenous peoples to their surrounding environment. These provisions have been consistently expressed in the context of the profound relationship that indigenous peoples have to their lands, territories and resources. Furthermore, the articles elaborate upon State obligations to recognize indigenous land rights and to take action to affirm and safeguard them. The linkage between lands, territories and resources and the ability to exercise human rights, including the human right to development, are embodied in Article 23, which addresses indigenous peoples' right to determine their own priorities for development.

Overall, the fact that the text is consistent with international law and its progressive development, and more importantly the purposes and principles of the UN Charter, ensures that it will play a dynamic and lasting role in the future of specific indigenous/state relations and international law generally.

> the United Nations Declaration is an extraordinary document, reflecting the important balance between individual and collective indigenous human rights as well as the legitimate interests and concerns of state governments

Australia endorses the UN Declaration on the Rights of Indigenous Peoples

On 3 April 2009, the Australian government officially endorsed the United Nations Declaration on the Rights of Indigenous Peoples, reversing the position of the previous government and fulfilling a key election promise. The Minister for Indigenous Affairs, Jenny Macklin delivered a statement in support of the document at Parliament House, saying that the move was a step forward in "re-setting" the relationship between Indigenous and non-Indigenous Australians. "The Declaration gives us new impetus to work together in trust and good faith to advance human rights and close the gap between Indigenous and non-Indigenous Australians," Ms Macklin said.

> Member of the UN Permanent Forum on Indigenous Issues and Australian of the Year, 2008 Professor Mick Dodson said the government should not be afraid of the contents of the Declaration, adding that Australians should embrace it as a framework for policy. Prof Dodson also said that supporting human rights was not a barrier to progress. "Human rights do not dispossess people. Human rights do not marginalize people. Human rights do not cause problems. Human rights do not cause poverty. Human rights do not cause life expectancy gaps," Prof Dodson said. "It is the denial of rights that is the largest contributor to these things".
>
> Source: Speeches made by both Ms Jenny Macklin and Mr Mick Dodson at Parliament House, Canberra, Australia 3 April 2009.

OAS Proposed American Declaration on the Rights of Indigenous Peoples

On a regional basis, the Organization of American States (OAS) has a history of dealing with indigenous peoples' issues dating back to the first Inter-American Indian Congress, held in Patzcuaro (Mexico) in 1940.[34] Since that time, the Inter-American Indian Institute has become one of the specialized agencies of the OAS and has played a primarily advisory role to the OAS on matters concerning indigenous peoples, including the work of the Inter-American Commission on Human Rights.[35] The OAS is currently considering a proposed American Declaration on the Rights of Indigenous Peoples.[36] This development emerged in early 1989 and was almost certainly prompted by both the revision of ILO Convention No. 107 and the elaboration of the Declaration by the United Nations.[37]

Since 1989, procedural issues and inadequate measures for indigenous peoples' participation have triggered the development of a wider discussion within the OAS around the use of a "civil society" accreditation system modelled on the UN's non-governmental organization procedures. As with the changes in indigenous participation within the United Nations, this has been a significant turning point in the history of the OAS.

Unfortunately, at this stage, the fundamental matters of self-determination, lands, territories and resource rights, plus a host of other articles, remain unresolved and contentious. Like the UN, the OAS does have the competence to deal with political rights. One of the most troubling issues to emerge is therefore the potential for language that attempts to "qualify" the term "peoples", similar to the misinterpreted debate within the context of ILO Convention 169 (see below).

Re-drafting of the text continues in earnest. With work ongoing, it is difficult to speculate upon the final outcome. Nonetheless, this is another strand that can be woven into the overall trend of the international community's willingness to visit, or re-visit, the human rights of indigenous peoples.

---

[34] Created under the 1940 Pátzcuaro International Convention, the basic objectives of the Inter-American Indian Institute are to assist in coordinating the Indian affairs policies of the member States and to promote research and training of individuals engaged in the development of indigenous communities. The Institute has its headquarters in Mexico City.

[35] The Inter-American Commission on Human Rights has a long history of dealing with indigenous matters under the American Declaration of the Rights and Duties of Man, adopted by the Ninth Conference of American States (Res. XXX, 1948). See OAS (1948). For a brief discussion of the work of the Commission in regard to the Yanomami and other indigenous peoples of the Oriente, see Shelton (2001), 240-242.

[36] See the Inter-American Commission on Human Rights Annual Report (1988-9), 245-52. As an ICC representative, the author of this chapter participated in a number of consultations leading up to the OAS decision to prepare this "juridical instrument." See also Hannum (1990) for a discussion on the overall Inter-American system and the "protection of Indigenous human rights" through the Inter-American Court of Human Rights, country reporting procedures and the proposed Declaration.

[37] Anaya (1996), 54. See also Suagee (1997), 365.

The ILO Conventions

Dating back to 1921, the International Labour Organization (ILO) is one of the few intergovernmental organizations to have concerned itself with indigenous and tribal peoples and the issues facing them. In June 1957, the ILO adopted Convention No. 107 concerning the Protection and Integration of Indigenous and Other Tribal and Semi-Tribal Populations in Independent Countries. This Convention[38] has been ratified by only 27 States and came into force in June 1959 (and remains in force for some). The 1957 instrument encourages the gradual assimilation of indigenous individuals into national societies and economies, thus legitimising the gradual extinction of indigenous peoples as such. Moreover, the Convention presupposes complete state control over the affairs of indigenous peoples. As one might guess, many indigenous peoples have strongly criticized the ILO and its early interest in the area of indigenous conditions for being "paternalistic" in its approach to "protecting these groups". The ILO itself has acknowledged this criticism.[39]

The Convention does not deal with political matters such as self-government or other political dimensions of self-determination. The ILO has made it clear that these matters fall outside the "competence of the ILO" and that, as an international organization, they cannot deal with political rights, in the context of the Convention or otherwise.

However, the revised ILO Convention No. 169 concerning Indigenous and Tribal Peoples in Independent Countries, 1989,[40] substantiates and reinforces indigenous rights. This updated instrument, which remains open for state ratification, provides standards and protections relating to the environment, development and direct participation of indigenous peoples in matters affecting their rights, lives and territories.

Conventions Nos. 107 and 169 are the only legally binding international treaties that deal specifically with indigenous rights and, furthermore, include a recourse mechanism: the Committee of Experts on the Application of Conventions and Review of Recommendations. If the Committee is actively used, it is an effective method for overseeing government behaviour and actions toward indigenous peoples in those countries where the Convention has been ratified.[41] This aspect of ILO Convention No. 169 cannot be underestimated. Because of the efforts of trade unions and support groups such as Survival International and Amnesty International, even application of the outdated Convention No. 107 has saved lives.

> setting aside the criticisms about Convention No. 169, it has proved useful to indigenous peoples in domestic policy development and litigation, as well as in formal human rights complaints to the Inter-American Commission on Human Rights

---

[38] 328 UNTS 247.

[39] Swepston (1978), 450, explained this as follows: "The problem with the Convention stems from the ethos of the period in which it was adopted, i.e., at the height of the paternalistic era of the United Nations system, the heyday of the "top down" development approach... the ILO did something perfectly acceptable at the time...but they omitted to ask the under-privileged themselves what they thought of the idea."

[40] ILO Convention No. 169 was adopted in Geneva on 26 June 1989 and came into force on 5 September 1991. Reprinted in 28 ILM 1382 (1989). See Barsh (1990), 209; Swepston (1990), 677 and (1998), 17.

[41] ILO Convention No. 169 has been ratified by 20 countries (source: ILOLEX 30.11.08)⊠Ed.

When read in context, there are many possibilities for interpreting the language in a positive fashion. Setting aside the criticisms about Convention No. 169,[42] it has proved useful to indigenous peoples in domestic policy development[43] and litigation,[44] as well as in formal human rights complaints to the Inter-American Commission on Human Rights.[45]

International Covenants

The Universal Declaration of Human Rights was utilized as a starting point for the codification of first and second generation rights, namely civil and political rights as contained in the International Covenant on Civil and Political Rights (ICCPR)[46] and economic, social and cultural rights as contained in the International Covenant on Economic, Social and Cultural Rights (ICESCR).[47] It is interesting to note that some of those engaged in the process grappled with the fact that civil and political rights and economic, social and cultural rights were interdependent.[48]

Common to both the ICCPR and the ICESCR is the fact that they are binding upon State parties to the Covenants— creating international legal obligations that relate to the very principles and purposes of the United Nations

---

[42] See S. Venne (1989).

[43] The following information was downloaded from the ILO website at http://www.ilo.org: "Prior to its submission to the Committee of Experts of the ILO, the Government of Norway sent its latest report on the implementation of Convention No. 169 to the Sami Parliament for its comments. These comments form an integral part of the report, under the terms of an agreement entered into between the Norwegian Government and the Sami Parliament. This co-operation is established as a permanent procedure to ensure the inclusion of the opinion of the Sami Parliament in the formal reporting procedure on Convention No. 169. The Sami Parliament has indicated its willingness to enter into an informal dialogue with the Committee of Experts, together with the Norwegian Government, to facilitate the implementation of the Convention. The Government has stated that it shares the wish to facilitate the implementation of the Convention in this way, believing that open co-operation between governments and representative indigenous bodies may contribute effectively to the international promotion of indigenous rights and cultures, and the Government therefore fully supports the suggestion of a supplementary dialogue."

[44] The following information was downloaded from the ILO website at http://www.ilo.org: "With regard to the environment, the Norwegian Ministry of Culture has instructed the regional board responsible for managing crown land in Finnmark to ask the opinion of the Sami Assembly before taking any decision concerning land-use projects. The reindeer herding districts are legally entitled to be consulted, have the right to be compensated, in the event of economic damage, and may bring lawsuits before the courts if they consider a project inadmissible." In this case, the provisions of ILO Convention No. 169 were invoked and utilised by the Sami peoples. Such use of the language of the Convention is only available to those whose respective state members have ratified the treaty.

[45] See the Petition lodged by Jaime Castillo Felipe, on his own Behalf and on Behalf of the Mayagna Indian Community of Awas Tingni Against Nicaragua, re-printed in 9 St. Thomas L. Rev. 164 (1996). This petition was prepared by S. James Anaya, Counsel of Record, and invokes various provisions of ILO Convention No. 169, as well as the United Nations draft Declaration on the Rights of Indigenous Peoples, the draft Inter-American Declaration on the Rights of Indigenous Peoples [discussed above], and the American Convention. See also the Petition by the Western Shoshone (1993); the Mayan Cultural Council of Belize (2000); and the complaint filed by S. J. Anaya and R. A. Williams, Jr., on behalf of the First Nation of Carrier Sekani of British Columbia, Canada (2000). See also Anaya (1998), 1.

[46] International Covenant on Civil and Political Rights was adopted by the United Nations General Assembly on 16 December 1966 and entered into force on 23 March 1976. General Assembly Resolution. 2200A (XXI), 21 UN GAOR Supp. (No. 16) at 52, UN Doc. A/6316 (1966), 999 UNTS. 171.

[47] International Covenant on Economic, Social and Cultural Rights (1966), adopted by the United Nations General Assembly on 16 December 1966 and entered into force 3 January 1976. General Assembly Resolution 2200A (XXI), 21 UN GAOR Supp. (No. 16) at 49, UN Doc. A/6316 (1966), 993 U.N.T.S. 3,

[48] Steiner and Alston (1996), 17. The authors re-print the "Annotations on the Text of the Draft International Covenants on Human Rights," UN Doc. A/2929 (1955), which include: "[Between 1949 and 1951 the Commission on Human Rights worked on a single draft covenant dealing with both of the categories of rights. But in 1951 the General Assembly, under pressure from the Western-dominated Commission, agreed to draft two separate covenants]…to contain 'as many similar provisions as possible' and to be approved and opened for signature simultaneously, in order to emphasise the unity of purpose….Those who were in favor of drafting a single covenant maintained that human rights could not be clearly divided into different categories, nor could they be so classified as to represent a hierarchy of values. All rights should be promoted and protected at the same time. Without economic, social and cultural rights, civil and political rights might be purely nominal in character; without civil and political rights, economic, social and cultural rights could not be long ensured…."

Charter. It is important to underscore also the common Article 1, which recognizes the right of peoples to self-determination. Article 1 is clearly a collective right of "peoples" to self-determination that contrasts with the overall individual rights orientation of the two Covenants. Both the ICCPR and the ICESCR also outline State party obligations for the fulfilment of these basic human rights. Finally, in regard to implementation and monitoring, the treaty-based bodies established by the Covenants are significant not only to the realization of such human rights by individuals and the monitoring of violations of human rights by state governments but also to an understanding of the content of such rights to both individuals and groups.

The rights enshrined in the Universal Declaration and the Covenants do attach to indigenous individuals and collectivities, who also strive for human dignity and enjoyment of their natural rights as human beings. Hence, the use by indigenous peoples of the treaty bodies responsible for overseeing state implementation of the rights embraced by the Covenants. Such actions have dramatically increased due to the efforts of indigenous peoples, the elaboration of an indigenous cultural context and reliance upon such expressions by treaty body members. Though indigenous peoples, nations and communities have remained distinct from existing state governments, such actions are even more critical because the creation of states is a historical, legal and political reality that indigenous peoples must deal with.

In regard to accommodating the human rights of indigenous peoples, we are seeing a noticeable difference in the more recent comments and concluding observations of the human rights treaty bodies. There is increasing awareness and use of the treaty-based human rights bodies by indigenous peoples, as well as greater sensitivity toward indigenous peoples' rights and issues being shown by their respective members.

> there is increasing awareness and use of the treaty-based human rights bodies by indigenous peoples, as well as greater sensitivity toward indigenous peoples' rights and issues being shown by their respective members

These treaty bodies are providing for an indigenous cultural context in the interpretation of the existing international instruments, such as the Human Rights Committee under the ICCPR and the Committee on the Elimination of Racial Discrimination[49] (CERD) under the International Convention on the Elimination of All Forms of Racial Discrimination.[50] Though each of the treaty bodies have had the opportunity to review cases emerging from indigenous individuals, on behalf of their communities, the more recent work of the treaty bodies is evidence of a much more expansive and inclusive interpretation of human rights and their attachment to the distinct circumstances of indigenous peoples. Now, with the adoption of the United Nations Declaration on the Rights of Indigenous Peoples, it is highly likely that the treaty bodies, Special Rapporteurs and others will rely

---

[49] For a description of the Committee's work in regard to indigenous peoples, see Anaya (1996), 100-101 and 162-166.

[50] The International Convention on the Elimination of All Forms of Racial Discrimination was adopted by UN General Assembly on 21 December 1965, opened for signature on 7 March 1966, and entered into force on 4 January 1969. General Assembly Resolution 2106A (XX) UNTS, Vol. 660 (1966), 195; reprinted in ILM.1966 (5), 350.

upon the Declaration for purposes of context and interpretation of indigenous human rights standards.

There has been a blossoming of United Nations initiatives, ranging from the establishment of the UN Permanent Forum on Indigenous Issues to the appointment of the Special Rapporteur on the situation of human rights and fundamental freedoms of indigenous people and of the Expert Mechanism on the Rights of Indigenous Peoples. This groundswell of positive progress has had a contagious effect upon other international and regional instruments as well as inter-governmental institutions, and bodies including the World Bank, the Asian Development Bank, the Inter-American Development Bank, the World Intellectual Property Organization, the Commission for Sustainable Development and numerous other fora.

Indigenous Peoples' human rights— on the ground

Despite all the positive international human rights standard-setting developments, indigenous peoples continue to face serious human rights abuses on a day-to-day basis. Issues of violence and brutality, continuing assimilation policies, marginalization, dispossession of land, forced removal or relocation, denial of land rights, impacts of large-scale development, abuses by military forces and armed conflict, and a host of other abuses, are a reality for indigenous communities around the world. Examples of violence and brutality have been heard from every corner of the indigenous world, most often perpetrated against indigenous persons who are defending their rights and their lands, territories and communities.

> despite all the positive international human rights standard-setting developments, indigenous peoples continue to face serious human rights abuses on a day-to-day basis

Violence against indigenous women

According to a United States Department of Justice study on violence against women, more than one in three American Indian and Alaska Native women will be raped during her lifetime. A comparable figure for the United States as a whole is less than one in five. Furthermore, half of Native American women reported suffering physical injuries in addition to the rape, while the comparable figure for women in the United States as a whole is 30 per cent.

Amnesty International reports that between 2000 and 2003, Alaska Native people in Anchorage were 9.7 times more likely to experience sexual assault than others living in the city, and a medical professional responsible for post-mortem examinations of victims of rape and murder told Amnesty International in 2005 that of the 41 confirmed cases in Alaska since 1991, 32 involved Alaska Native women.

> Following a history of discrimination against indigenous peoples by national judicial systems, indigenous peoples frequently distrust formal justice systems. "When an emergency call comes in, the sheriff will say 'but this is Indian land.' Tribal police will show up and say the reverse. Then, they just bicker and don't do the job. Many times, this is what occurs." Victims often do not report incidents of sexual violence to the police because they believe they will be met with indifference and inaction, or even blamed for the incident. As a result, this non-reporting creates a climate of impunity where sexual violence is seen as normal.
>
> *Source: Amnesty International (2007), 2-36.*

In 2005, Mapuche leaders in Chile were jailed, threatened and had their homes burned down solely because they were working in defence of their land rights.[51] The Special Rapporteur, in his analysis of 15 different countries ranging from Myanmar to the Russian Federation to Australia, identified this unfortunate dynamic in the context of indigenous human rights violations:

> *In many countries, indigenous people are persecuted because of their work in defence of their human rights and fundamental freedoms, and are the victims of extrajudicial executions, arbitrary detention, torture, forced evictions and many forms of discrimination.[52]*

there are a myriad of examples and testimony at the international level of the forced relocation of indigenous peoples and dispossession of their lands

There are a myriad of examples and testimony at the international level of the forced relocation of indigenous peoples and dispossession of their lands. For a number of years now, the San (formerly known as Bushmen) living in their traditional hunting grounds in the Central Kalahari of Botswana have been struggling with forced relocation from their homelands, without any substantive address of their fundamental human rights.[53] For over two decades, the conflicts between indigenous peoples and gold miners, cattle ranchers and other outsiders have been raging throughout Brazil with little international notice or attention. Though legislation to demarcate lands has been adopted, the reality on the ground is dramatically different from the laws of the nation-state. For example, the Special Rapporteur has received Urgent Appeals from the Guarani-Kaiowa in the State of Mato Grosso do Sul, Brazil concerning eviction notices received despite the fact that their lands were demarcated as indigenous lands in 2004.[54]

In regard to large-scale or major development projects, the Special Rapporteur has summarized some of their effects on the human rights of indigenous peoples by stating that:

---

[51] Stavenhagen (2006), para. 20.
[52] Stavenhagen (2006), para. 6.
[53] Stavenhagen (2006), para. 77.
[54] Stavenhagen (2006), 8.

The principal human rights effects of these projects for indigenous peoples related to loss of traditional territories and land, eviction, migration and eventual resettlement, depletion of resources necessary for physical and cultural survival, destruction and pollution of the traditional environment, social and community disorganization, long-term negative health and nutritional impacts as well as, in some cases, harassment and violence.[55]

In this particular discussion of large-scale development projects, there was also reference to the impact of large dam projects upon indigenous communities in Colombia. Unfortunately, in this case, the human rights violations became so grave as to include forcible removal from homes and lands, destruction of property as well as assassinations and disappearances carried out by paramilitary forces.

The Special Rapporteur has noted other similar dam projects and the resulting violations of indigenous peoples' human rights. Forced removal, clear-cutting of forests, military abuses, and deaths and disappearances are taking place in India, the Philippines, Panama, the United States, Canada, Malaysia, Costa Rica and Chile. This is not an exhaustive list—such cases are only the known violations based upon communications to the Special Rapporteur or the Office of the High Commissioner for Human Rights. It is highly likely that many other cases have not been reported or communicated to the UN or any other agencies.

Other development projects being imposed or forced upon indigenous communities include logging, mining, resort developments and highway construction, establishment of national parks and reserves as well as oil and gas exploration and exploitation. For example, in the Russian Far East, little or no consideration has been given to the indigenous peoples' demands to safeguard their hunting, fishing and gathering territories in the face of oil and gas development.[56] These cases arise as urgent measures primarily due to the fact that state governments have not even established the ways and means for indigenous peoples to bring claims to gain any recognition or affirmation of their distinct rights to own and control their lands, territories and resources.

More recently, leaders of the Ardoch Algonquin First Nation (Canada) have had legal action taken against them for their efforts to block uranium exploration and mining on lands that have been claimed by the Algonquins.[57] The lack of procedures to identify and affirm indigenous land rights is exacerbated by the imposition of major, adverse developments that favour others, such as multinational corporations, and "criminalize" indigenous peoples' protests. The rampant actions of large economic and corporate forces often appear to go unrestrained by governments, who are ultimately responsible for the prevention of violations and abuses of indigenous human rights by third parties.

Discrimination against indigenous peoples

Indigenous peoples frequently raise concerns about systemic discrimination and outright racism from the State and its authorities. This discrimination manifests itself in a number of ways such as frequent and unnecessary questioning by the police, condescending attitudes of teachers to students or rudeness from a receptionist in a government office. At their most extreme, these forms of discrimination lead to gross violations of human rights, such as murder, rape and other forms of violence or intimidation. These forms of discrimination are often either difficult to quantify and verify or are simply not documented by the authorities, or not disaggregated based on ethnicity.

---

[55] Stavenhagen (2003), 2.
[56] Stavenhagen (2003), para. 68.
[57] "Ontario Algonquins suspend uranium site occupation", Friday, October 19, 2007, CBCNews.ca.

There are however some indicators of discrimination, which are documented and disaggregated, such as disproportionately high incarceration rates. In 1991 indigenous peoples accounted for less than 2.0 per cent of the total population of Australia, yet 14 per cent of all adult prisoners were indigenous. By 2001, this number had risen to 19.9 per cent, while the indigenous population had risen to just 2.4 per cent of the total population. Indigenous Australians were thus 8 times more likely than non-indigenous Australians to be imprisoned in 1991. In 2001 the ratio was 9.6.[58] In Canada, indigenous offenders represented 16.6 per cent of the federal prison population, while comprising only 3.38 per cent of the Canadian general population, making indigenous Canadians 5 times more likely to be imprisoned, than their non-indigenous fellow Canadians.[59] In the United States, in the state of Alaska, Native Alaskans are incarcerated at a rate 3.2 times higher than that of white Alaskans, and Native Alaskan juveniles are 1.8 times as likely to be adjudicated delinquent as white juveniles.[60] In New Zealand, of 10,452 cases resulting in a custodial sentence in 2005, 5,293, or just over 50 per cent, were Maori. Sixty-one per cent of women sentenced to prison in New Zealand in 2005 were Maori.[61] Ten years earlier, Maori women were 49.3 per cent of sentenced inmates and Maori men were 45 per cent of sentenced inmates.[62] In 2006, the Maori were 14.6 per cent of the total population, making them 3.4 times more likely to be imprisoned, than non-indigenous New Zealanders.

The overrepresentation of indigenous peoples in correctional institutions can be linked to discrimination in earlier stages of the justice process. For example, indigenous peoples are disadvantaged when their rights are adjudicated in non-indigenous languages. The Special Rapporteur has reported that, for example, this "is often the case in some Asian countries, where legal texts and proceedings are written and carried out in English or a national language not understood by an indigenous community."[63] He has also found that interpreters and public defenders for indigenous people may not be available, and if they are, may not be adequately trained in indigenous culture. Moreover, court officials may be biased against indigenous people in their district." [64]

Little systematic data on incarceration rates of indigenous peoples is available for most countries. However there is information available on the detention and imprisonment of indigenous peoples, and although this information is not compiled by means of census data collection, a review of some reports submitted to the Special Rapporteur on the human rights and fundamental freedoms of indigenous peoples paints "a disturbing picture of the situation of indigenous people in detention, which in many cases violates international principles for the treatment of prisoners." [65]

Indigenous peoples are all too often held in overcrowded prisons, in substandard conditions and with inadequate access to basic health and other services, and far from their communities, which makes it difficult for them to maintain contact with their families. Restrictions on religious rights have also been reported.[66] In Canada, the Special Rapporteur has reported that, not only are indigenous women held in disproportionately high numbers in federal prisons, they are also singled out for segregation more often

---

[58] Wijeskere (2001), 6.
[59] Welsh (2008), 492.
[60] Stavenhagen (2004), para. 29.
[61] New Zealand Ministry of Justice (2006).
[62] New Zealand Ministry of Justice (1996)
[63] Stavenhagen (2004), para. 37.
[64] Stavenhagen (2004), para. 37.
[65] Stavenhagen (2006a), para. 22.
[66] Stavenhagen (2006a), para. 22.

than other inmates and suffer higher rates of inmate abuse.[67] In Mexico, reports indicate that indigenous women tend to be abused and harassed while in detention, and may become involved in drug and prostitution schemes operating in prisons.[68]

Indigenous peoples have frequently faced detention due to the criminalization of social protest activities. According to the Special Rapporteur, "[o]ne of the most serious shortcomings in human rights protection in recent years is the trend towards the use of legislation and the justice system to penalize and criminalize social protest activities and legitimate demands made by indigenous organizations and movements in defence of their rights."[69] The Special Rapporteur has reported, for example, receiving "many reports from countries such as India, Indonesia, the Lao People's Democratic Republic, Malaysia and Thailand, of arbitrary arrest or fake criminal charges made against members of indigenous and tribal peoples, as well as other forms of threats and intimidations, as a result of their mobilization to defend their rights against State authorities. In Mexico, the Special Rapporteur received complaints about indigenous community activities being prosecuted on "fabricated" charges for their participation in social mobilization over rights issues.[70]

Cases of ill-treatment and torture during detention, as well as extrajudicial killings have also been widely reported. In relation to his 2006 visit to Kenya, the Special Rapporteur received numerous reports of arbitrary detention, police harassment, and incidents of torture and rape suffered by local residents as a result of the punitive application of security measures. Reportedly, many police abuses took place in relation to social protests associated with land rights claims, with vocal community members being ill-treated and arrested.[71] The Special Rapporteur has voiced concerns regarding abuse of indigenous individuals in detention in a number of instances, including in cases reported from Bangladesh and Botswana.[72]

Sources: See Footnotes

Testimony of abuses by State-controlled military or paramilitary forces has also been repeatedly given. In Myanmar, according to information received by the Special Rapporteur on the human rights and fundamental freedoms of indigenous people, members of the village of Tagu Seik, near Einme, were tortured and their community ransacked on the basis of purported communications with another armed opposition group.[73] In the Philippines, a similar military attack upon indigenous peoples took place. This was again on the basis that the indigenous individuals were allegedly members of a "splinter group of communist terrorists".[74]

Needless to say, these and numerous other gross human rights violations and abuses are perpetrated against indigenous peoples—as collectivities or as individual men and women—on the basis of their identity and marginalization, and, in the case of indigenous women, on the basis of their sex. Unfortunately, such discriminatory actions have been constant, from the time of first contact with outsiders to the present. Little has changed, despite the groundswell of developments in the area of human rights standards specifically addressing indigenous peoples' human rights.

---

[67] Stavenhagen (2005), para. 56.
[68] Stavenhagen (2004), para. 26.
[69] Stavenhagen (2006a), para. 19.
[70] Stavenhagen (2004), para. 49.
[71] Stavenhagen (2007a), para. 60.
[72] See for example,Anaya (2008), para. 70 and Stavenhagen (2007a), para. 53
[73] Stavenhagen (2003), para. 60.
[74] Stavenhagen (2003), para. 66.

Concrete and urgent action must therefore be taken by the international community to curb such abuses and violations, and to actually move toward implementing the instruments discussed in this chapter. In so doing, indigenous peoples may then have some potential for genuinely exercising their human rights. In order to implement the UN Declaration on the Rights of Indigenous Peoples, for example, it may be useful for indigenous peoples to develop, either independently or in cooperation with states or others, benchmarks for the realization of human rights.

> ## Apologies for Past Wrongs
>
> In February 2008, the newly elected Government of Australia, at its first sitting of Parliament House apologized for the removal of Aboriginal and Torres Strait Islander children from their families, their communities and their country. In a statement, the Prime Minister, Kevin Rudd apologized "for the laws and policies of successive Parliaments and governments that have inflicted profound grief, suffering and loss on these our fellow Australians…For the pain, suffering and hurt of these Stolen Generations, their descendants and for their families left behind, we say sorry. To the mothers and the fathers, the brothers and the sisters, for the breaking up of families and communities, we say sorry. And for the indignity and degradation thus inflicted on a proud people and a proud culture, we say sorry. We the Parliament of Australia respectfully request that this apology be received in the spirit in which it is offered as part of the healing of the nation. For the future we take heart; resolving that this new page in the history of our great continent can now be written. We today take this first step by acknowledging the past and laying claim to a future that embraces all Australians. A future where this Parliament resolves that the injustices of the past must never, never happen again".
>
> On the 11 June 2008, Prime Minister Stephen Harper made the apology in Parliament House, Ottawa, to the indigenous peoples of Canada for forcing aboriginal children to attend state-funded Christian boarding schools aimed at assimilating them. Mr Harper said aboriginal Canadians had been waiting "a very long time" for an apology. "I stand before you today to offer an apology to former students of Indian residential schools. The treatment of children in Indian residential schools is a sad chapter in our history". He said the system had been based on the assumption that "aboriginal cultures and spiritual beliefs were inferior and unequal". He went on: "We now recognize that, far too often, these institutions gave rise to abuse or neglect and were inadequately controlled, and we apologize for failing to protect you. The government of Canada sincerely apologizes and asks the forgiveness of the aboriginal peoples of this country for failing them so profoundly. We are sorry".
>
> *Sources: Apology to Australia's Indigenous Peoples House of Representatives Parliament House, Canberra (13 February 2008); BBC News Canada apology for native schools (11 June 2008).*

little has changed, despite the groundswell of developments in the area of human rights standards specifically addressing indigenous peoples' human rights

Restoration of Ainu rights step nearer

A Diet resolution last week recognizing the Ainu as indigenous to Hokkaido and neighbouring parts of northern Japan has created hope that progress will be made in restoring the rights of the Ainu people.

In response to the resolution, which was approved unanimously in both chambers of the legislature Friday, the government drew up out a policy the same to give official recognition of the indigenous status of the Ainu for the first time.

A slew of problems still need to be addressed from this point on, including how to deal with such issues as the land and natural resources the Ainu were deprived of in the process of Japan's modernization.

Tadashi Kato, chairman of the Hokkaido Utari Association, was visibly overwhelmed with emotion at a press conference in the Diet Building following the adoption of the resolution.

The Hakkaido Utari Association – Utari signifies brethren in Ainu – was formerly known as the Ainu Association of Hokkaido. This body has working since the end of World War II to enhance the social status of the Ainu, many of whom live in Hokkaido.

"Mr. (Nobutaka) Machimura, the chief cabinet secretary, has made of clear that the government has recognized us as an indigenous people," Kato said.

"After a lapse of 140 years (since the Meiji Restoration), we can finally see some light. I can hardly find the words to fully express our gratitude."

by Mariko Sakai and Shozo Nakayama, Daily Yomiuri, June 11, 2008

Possible indicators of exercise and enjoyment of human rights

A number of key questions about equality, racism, non-discrimination, access to justice systems, political representation, participation in the political life of the state, exercise and enjoyment of the right of self-determination and so forth may be useful starting points for an analysis of the exercise of human rights by indigenous peoples. Of course, any such indicators would have to be discussed and adapted on a case-by-case basis and dependent upon the issues facing particular indigenous communities.

In regard to assessing the exercise or manifestation of the right of self-determination by indigenous peoples, communities and nations, some basic indicators might include analysis of state government positions and policies in relation to indigenous peoples' self-determination. For instance, to what extent have various states been requested to take action on the implementation of the right of self-determination of indigenous peoples as understood in international law? What state policies impede or help to accelerate the exercise of self-determination by indigenous peoples?

The inter-related, inter-dependent and universal aspects of human rights are crucial indicators of the exercise of the right of self-determination. The right of self-determination is recognized as a pre-requisite to the exercise and enjoyment of all human rights. Hence the language of Article 3 of the UN Declaration on the Rights of Indigenous Peoples:

> *Indigenous peoples have the right of self-determination. By virtue of that right they freely determine their political status and freely pursue their economic, social and cultural development.*

In this regard, do indigenous peoples exercise their human right to development, including social development, economic development, cultural development and spiritual development? Do indigenous peoples control all forms of development in their communities? In terms of universality, do some indigenous peoples' communities enjoy greater exercise of self-determination than others?

There is also an inter-relationship (meaning you cannot attain one without the other) between development, security and human rights. And, in this context, "security" is not confined solely to military security. Rather, in an indigenous context; do indigenous peoples enjoy environmental security? Do indigenous peoples enjoy security in relation to their hunting, fishing and other gathering rights? If self-determination had been effectively attained, it would embrace such indigenous priorities and such questions would not have to be asked.

The right to free, prior and informed consent is another crucial element of self-determination. Is it recognized and respected in relations, agreements, etc., with states? Or is it diminished through mere "consultations" or denied and violated through unilateral state actions?

There is a strong correlation between the health of individuals and communities and the exercise or denial of the right of self-determination, with a growing body of evidence to support this thesis. Self-determination is intended to strengthen communities, not weaken or devastate them. What are the health conditions of indigenous communities, psychological, physical, etc.? Are the members of indigenous communities healthy?

Similar to health, is there equity of options and opportunity for indigenous peoples and indigenous peoples' communities? Poverty or the overall health and viability of a community are other relevant indicators of the exercise or denial of self-determination.

Democracy, the rule of law and human rights are inter-related and important dimensions of self-determination. Democracy in this context does not mean majority rule. Rather, it suggests a review of democratic principles and whether they are in operation within indigenous communities and in their relations with others.

These are only preliminary suggestions for possible indicators with which to analyse the extent to which indigenous human rights are respected, recognized,

do indigenous peoples exercise their human right to development, including social development, economic development, cultural development and spiritual development?

exercised and enjoyed. Most indigenous communities already have a clear sense of the impact of human rights abuses. Yet such indicators may be useful in specifying and linking human rights violations to specific existing and emerging standards in international human rights law.[75]

Concluding Remarks

This short chapter has only hinted at the severity and range of issues that require greater attention. Given the reality and condition of indigenous human rights and this brief cataloguing of abuses, it may be necessary for the United Nations to bolster the role and mandate of the Special Rapporteur on the human rights and fundamental freedoms of indigenous people in order to specifically monitor state action or inaction. The newly established Expert Mechanism on the Rights of Indigenous Peoples by the Human Rights Council may also help the United Nations to substantively respond to the urgent human rights conditions being suffered by indigenous peoples worldwide. Let us hope that the existing treaty bodies enhance and influence indigenous/state dialogue and state actions through their interpretation of the Declaration and corresponding review and receipt of state reports as well as consideration of human rights complaints. For example, the CERD and its potential for more active use of their early warning and urgent action procedures in the context of indigenous peoples may be critical. Yet at the same time, state governments, as the pivotal source of aggression toward indigenous peoples, must be compelled to respect and recognize the human rights of indigenous peoples. All such actions and more are necessary intermediate steps to be taken before the political milieu can become favourable to transforming the UN Declaration into a legally-binding covenant with a corresponding treaty body.

In the meantime, indigenous peoples will continue to be proactive in the defence of their human rights. Further steps must be taken in the area of human rights education and learning. The success of self-determination largely depends on the extent to which human rights concepts are understood by indigenous peoples within their home communities. Dialogue and training are critical to strengthening political organizations as well as developing political, economic, social and legal strategies with which to promote and protect indigenous human rights.

[indigenous peoples will continue to be proactive in the defence of their human rights]

Are human rights concepts and the content of the collective and individual human rights known and understood by those who assert self-determination? Are human rights concepts integrated in the community? Through human rights education and learning, political leaders as well as community members can explore the real meaning or effect of exercising and enjoying human rights at the

---

[75] The United Nations Permanent Forum on Indigenous Issues has been promoting the development of indicators with the direct involvement of indigenous peoples themselves. After an intense period of regional and global meetings on the subject, a synthesis paper was presented at the Forum's Seventh Session. See UNPFII (2008).

grass roots level. In this context, it may be helpful for communities to translate the United Nations Declaration as well as other key international human rights instruments into their respective indigenous languages in order to prompt dialogue and community organising. It may also be useful for the United Nations to catalogue the various human rights training programmes, both public and private, and especially those operated or controlled by indigenous peoples.

> the urgent and dire condition of indigenous peoples' human rights worldwide requires serious political will and resources

Again, despite positive international developments, it is clear that the state of the world's indigenous peoples in relation to their human rights is very tenuous. Most indigenous communities are in extremely delicate situations; many have already been destroyed or weakened, their security and integrity compromised. The urgent and dire condition of indigenous peoples' human rights worldwide requires serious political will and resources. The Member States of the United Nations must therefore play a more substantive, proactive and central role in the campaign to respect and recognize indigenous peoples' human rights. They must take their obligations seriously, both at the international and domestic levels. The United Nations and others must call States to action. Inaction is not an option.

List of references

Akwesasne Mohawk Counselor Organization. 1984. Deskaheh: Iroquois Statesman and Patriot (1984) Rooseveltown, N.Y.: Akwesasne Notes, Mohawk Nation;

American Anthropological Association. 1947. Statement on Human Rights. 49 Amer. Anthropologist No. 4.

Amnesty International. 2007. Maze of Injustice: The failure to protect indigenous women from sexual violence in the USA. Amnesty International Publications

Anaya, S. James. 2008. Report of the Special Rapporteur on the situation of human rights and fundamental freedoms of indigenous people. Addendum: Summary of cases transmitted to Governments and replies received. UN Document A/HRC/9/9/Add.1, 15 August 2008.

Anaya, S. James. 1998. "Maya Aboriginal Land and Resource Rights and the Conflict Over Logging in Southern Belize," 1 Yale Hum. Rts. Dev. L.J. (1998)

Anaya, S. James. 1996. The Awas Tingni Petition to the Inter-American Commission on Human Rights: Indigenous Lands, Loggers, and Governmental Neglect in Nicaragua. 9 St. Thomas L. Rev. 157, 165 (1996).

Anaya, S. James. 1996. Indigenous Peoples in International Law. Oxford/New York: Oxford University Press.

Barsh, R.L. 1990. "An Advocate's Guide to the Convention on Indigenous and Tribal Peoples," 15 Oklahoma City University L. Rev (1990).

BBC News "Canada apology for native schools", 11 June 2008. Available online at: http://news.bbc.co.uk/2/hi/americas/7447811.stm

Boutros-Ghali, B. 1992. "An Agenda for Peace". Report of the Secretary General, UN Doc. A/47/277, June 17, 1992.

CBCNews. 2007. "Ontario Algonquins suspend uranium site occupation",Friday, October 19, 2007. Available online at CBCNEWS.ca

Dodson, Michael "Australian government announcement on the UN Declaration on the Rights of Indigenous Peoples" 3 April 2009. Available online at:
http://www.un.org/esa/socdev/unpfii/documents/Australia_endorsement_UNDRIP_Michael_Dodson_statement.pdf

Donnelly, J. 1989. Universal Human Rights in Theory and Practice. Ithaca, N.Y.: Cornell University Press.

Falk, R. 2000. Human Rights Horizons: The Pursuit of Justice in a Globalizing World. New York/London: Routledge.

Franck, T. 1992. "The Emerging Right to Democratic Governance". 86 Am. J. Int'l L. 46.

Gros Espiell, H. 1980. The Right to Self-Determination: Implementation of United Nations Resolutions. New York: United Nations.

Hannum, H. 1990. Autonomy, Sovereignty, and Self-Determination: The Accommodation of Conflicting Rights. Philadelphia: University of Pennsylvania Press.

Harmsworth, Garth. 2002. Indigenous concepts, values and knowledge for sustainable development: New Zealand case studies. Paper presented at 7th Joint Conference: "Preservation of Ancient Cultures and the Globalisation Scenario", 22–24 November 2002. Available online at http://www.landcareresearch.co.nz/research/sustainablesoc/social/documents/UOWconferencepap2002.doc

Henkin, L. 1999. "Rhetoric and Reality," in Human Rights, ed. L. Henkin, G. Neuman, D. Orentlicher, D. Leebron. New York: Foundation Press.

Henkin, L. et al., eds. 1999. Human Rights. New York: Foundation Press.

Inter-American Commission on Human Rights (CIDH). 1988-9. Annual Report.IACHR.

Inter-American Court of Human Rights. 2000. Case of the Mayagna (Sumo) Awas Tingni Community v. Nicaragua. Preliminary Objections. Judgment of February 1, 2000. Series C No. 66.

International Covenant on Civil and Political Rights (ICCPR). 1966. General Assembly Resolution 2200 (XXI). UN Doc. A/RES/2200 (XXI).

International Covenant on Economic, Social and Cultural Rights (ICESCR). 1966. General Assembly Resolution 2200A (XXI) UN Doc. A/RES/2200 A (XXI).

International Labour Organization (ILO). 1957. Convention No. 107 concerning the Protection and Integration of Indigenous and Other Tribal and Semi-Tribal Populations in Independent Countries. 328 U.N.T.S. 247. Available online at http://www.ilo.org/ilolex/english/convdisp1.htm

International Labour Organization (ILO). 1989. Convention No. 169 concerning Indigenous and Tribal Peoples in Independent Countries, ILO. Available online at http://www.ilo.org/ilolex/english/convdisp1.htm

Mabo and others v. Queensland. 1992. 175 CLR 1 FC 92/014 High Court of Australia. 107 A.L.R. 1.

Macklin, Jenny MP Minister for Families, Housing, Community Services and Indigenous Affairs, "Statement on the United Nations Declaration on the Rights of Indigenous Peoples" 3 April 2009. Available Online at: http://www.un.org/esa/socdev/unpfii/documents/Australia_official_statement_endorsement_UNDRIP.pdf

Meron, T. 1986. "On a Hierarchy of International Human Rights". 80 Am. J. Int'l L. 1 (1986).

New Zealand Ministry of Justice. 2006. Conviction and Sentencing of Offenders in New Zealand: 1997 to 2006. Available online at: http://www.justice.govt.nz/pubs/reports/2007/conviction-sentencing-1997-2006/report/chapter-4.html?search=true#46

New Zealand Ministry of Justice. 2006. Census of Prison Inmates 1995. Available online at: http://www.justice.govt.nz/pubs/reports/1996/census/chapter-3.html

Organization of American States (OAS). 1948. American Declaration of the Rights and Duties of Man, Pan American Union, Final Act of the Ninth Conference of American States, Res. XXX. Reprinted in OAS, Basic Documents Pertaining to Human Rights in the Inter-American System (1996). Available online at http://www.cidh.org/Basicos/English/Basic.TOC.htm

Organization for Security and Co-operation in Europe (OSCE). 1991. Document of the Moscow Meeting on the Human Dimension, Emphasizing Respect for Human Rights, Pluralistic Democracy, the Rule of Law, and

Procedures for Fact-Finding, adopted at the Conference on Security and Co-operation in Europe, Moscow, October 3, 1991. 30 I.L.M. 1670, at 1672.

Pannikar, R. 1982. "Is the Notion of Human Rights a Western Concept?"' Diogenes Volume 120, pp.75-102. Ed. An-Na'im, Abdullahi.

Rudd, Kevin "Apology to Australia's Indigenous Peoples" House of Representatives Parliament House, Canberra (13 February 2008) Available online at: http://www.pm.gov.au/media/Speech/2008/speech_0073.cfm

Sanders, D. 1992. "Remembering Deskaheh: Indigenous Peoples and International Law" in International Human Rights Law [:] Theory and Practice, ed. I. Cotler & F.P. Eliadis. Montreal: Canadian Human Rights Foundation, 1992.

Shelton, D. 2001. "Environmental Rights," in Peoples' Rights, ed. P. Alston. New York: Oxford University Press.

Stavenhagen, Rodolfo. 2003. Report of the Special Rapporteur on the situation of human rights and fundamental freedoms of indigenous people, to the Commission on Human Rights. UN Document E/CN.4/2003/90, 21 January 2003.

Stavenhagen, Rodolfo. 2005. Report of the Special Rapporteur on the situation of human rights and fundamental freedoms of indigenous people, to the Commission on Human Rights. Addendum: Mission to Canada. UN Document E/CN.4/2005/88/Add.3, 2 December 2004.

Stavenhagen, Rodolfo. 2004. Report of the Special Rapporteur on the situation of human rights and fundamental freedoms of indigenous people, to the, Commission on Human Rights. UN Document E/CN.4/2004/80, 26 January 2004.

Stavenhagen, Rodolfo. 2006. Report of the Special Rapporteur on the situation of human rights and fundamental freedoms of indigenous people to the Commission on Human Rights. Addendum: Analysis of country situations and other activities of the Special Rapporteur. UN Document E/CN.4/2006/78/Add.1, 18 January 2006.

Stavenhagen, Rodolfo. 2006a. Report of the Special Rapporteur on the situation of human rights and fundamental freedoms of indigenous people to the Commission on Human Rights, submitted pursuant to Commission resolution 2005/51. Addendum: Progress report on preparatory work for the study regarding best practices carried out to implement the recommendations contained in the annual reports of the Special Rapporteur. UN Document E/CN.4/2006/78/Add.4, 26 January 2006.

Stavenhagen, Rodolfo. 2007. Report of the Special Rapporteur on the situation of human rights and fundamental freedoms of indigenous people to the Human Rights Council. UN Doc. A/HRC/6/15, 15 November 2007.

Stavenhagen, Rodolfo. 2007a. Report of the Special Rapporteur on the situation of human rights and fundamental freedoms of indigenous people. Addendum: Summary of cases transmitted to Governments and replies received. UN Document A/HRC/6/15/Add.1, 20 November 2007

Stavenhagen, Rodolfo. 2007a. Report of the Special Rapporteur on the situation of human rights and fundamental freedoms of indigenous people, to the Commission on Human Rights. Addendum: Mission to Kenya. UN Document A/HRC/4/32/Add.3, 26 February 2007.

Steiner, H. 1999. "Do Human Rights Require a Particular Form of Democracy" in Democracy, the Rule of Law and Islam, ed. E. Cotran and A. O. Sherif. London: Kluwer Law International.

Steiner, H.J. and P. Alston. 1996. International Human Rights in Context: Law, Politics, Morals. New York: Oxford University Press.

Suagee, D. 1997. "Human Rights of Indigenous People: Will the United States Rise to the Occasion?" 21 Am. Indian L. Rev. (1997).

Swepston, L. 1978. "Latin American Approaches to the Indian Problem". International Labor Review, Vol. 117, No. 2, (March-April 1978).

Swepston, L. 1989. "A New Step in International Law on Indigenous and Tribal Peoples: ILO Convention No. 169 of 1989". 15 Okla. City U.L.R. (1989)

Swepston, L. 1998. "The Indigenous and Tribal Peoples Convention (No. 169): Eight Years After Adoption" in Human Rights of Indigenous Peoples, ed. C. Price Cohen. New York: Transnational Publishers.

The United Nations Permanent Forum (UNPFII). 2004. "Assessing the International Decade: urgent need to renew mandate and improve the United Nations standard-setting process on indigenous peoples' human rights" Joint Submission by indigenous and Non-governmental organization, included as Paras. 10-13 in Report of the Secretary-General "Information concerning indigenous issues requested by the Economic and Social Council" to the Permanent Forum on Indigenous Issues, Fourth Session. Available online at http://www.un.org/esa/socdev/unpfii.

The United Nations Permanent Forum (UNPFII). 2008. Indicators of well-being, poverty and sustainability relevant to indigenous peoples. Summary report submitted by Victoria Tauli-Corpuz at UNPFII Seventh Session on regional and thematic workshops on indicators relevant to indigenous peoples under the Convention on Biological Diversity and the Millennium Development Goals. UN Doc E/c.19/2008/9. Available online at http://www.un.org/esa/socdev/unpfii.

United Nations Organization. 1970. Declaration on Principles of International Law Concerning Friendly Relations and Cooperation Among States in Accordance with the Charter of the United Nations, adopted by the General Assembly Oct. 24, 1970. UN Doc. General Assembly Resolution 2625 (XXV): A/8028 (1971), reprinted in 9 I.L.M. 1292 (1970).

United Nations Organization. 1986. Declaration on the Right to Development. Resolution / adopted by the General Assembly, 4 December 1986. UN Doc. A/RES/41/128

United Nations Organization. 2007. Declaration on the Rights of Indigenous Peoples. adopted by the General Assembly, 13 September 2007. UN Doc. A/RES/61/295. Available online at http://www.un.org/esa/socdev/unpfii

Venne, S. 1989. "The New Language of Assimilation: A Brief Analysis of ILO Convention 169". Without Prejudice, The EAFORD International Review of Racial Discrimination, Vol. II, No. 2 (1989).

Vienna Declaration and Programme of Action. 1993. Adopted at the World Conference on Human Rights. UN. Doc. A/CONF.157/23.

Welsh, Andrew. 2008. "Progressive Reforms or Maintaining the Status Quo? An Empirical Evaluation of the Judicial Consideration of Aboriginal Status in Sentencing Decisions" Canadian Journal of Criminology & Criminal Justice. July 2008, Vol. 60 Issue 4. p. 492.

Wijeskere, Gaminirate. 2001. Incarceration of Indigenous and non-Indigenous adults: 1991 – 2001: trends and differentials. Paper prepared for presentation at the 11th Biennial Conference of the Australian Population Association, 2-4 October 2001 Sydney: University of New South Wales.

Working Group on the Draft Declaration (WGDD). 1997. NGO Statement to Commission on Human Rights Working Group on the Draft Declaration. UN Doc. E/CN.4/1996/84.

Working Group on the Draft Declaration (WGDD). 1998. Statement of the Inuit Circumpolar Conference to the Commission's Working Group. Press Release HR/CN/834 27 March 1998.

World Health Organization (WHO). 1999. Geneva Declaration on the Health and Survival of Indigenous Peoples. Annex 4 of the Report of the International Consultation on the Health of Indigenous Peoples. WHO Doc. WHO/HSD/00.1.

CHAPTER VII

EMERGING ISSUES

By Mililani Trask

The designation by the United Nations General Assembly of a First and Second International Decade of the World's Indigenous People and the adoption of the United Nations Declaration on the Rights of Indigenous Peoples are major demonstrations of the progress that has been achieved in terms of raising awareness in the global arena about indigenous peoples' issues, and promoting the rights of indigenous peoples. The creation of the Permanent Forum on Indigenous Issues (UNPFII) and the designation of a Special Rapporteur on the human rights and fundamental freedoms of indigenous people are also significant milestones in integrating indigenous issues and advocacy within the United Nations system. These accomplishments, however, have also revealed inadequacies within the United Nations system, which need to be addressed if the goal of mainstreaming indigenous issues within the system and its programmes is to be achieved in the future.

This chapter presents a brief overview of emerging indigenous issues that need to be dealt with in the near future. These issues relate to:

◈ Policies and disaggregated data in order to address indigenous peoples' issues and protect their rights;

◈ Resolution of conflicts involving indigenous peoples, States, the United Nations system and civil society;

◈ Displacement of indigenous peoples, including issues of violence and militarization, conservation refugees and globalization;

◈ Migration and urbanization of indigenous peoples;

◈ Indigenous peoples living in voluntary isolation.

The critical need for policies and disaggregated data

The mandate of the Permanent Forum and its programme of work require that the Forum provide advice and make recommendations to the United Nations Economic and Social Council (ECOSOC) on indigenous issues in the areas of economic and social development, culture, education, the environment, health and human rights. The Forum is also tasked with the gathering and dissemination of information on indigenous peoples, awareness raisingand the promotion of their integration and coordination within the United Nations system.

In order for the Forum to adequately assess the situation of indigenous peoples and pursue its mandate, it must have access reliable data on indigenous peoples. The gathering and disaggregation of data by the United Nations system and States is undertaken pursuant to the policies adopted by them relating to indigenous peoples. On the one hand, the failure of many United Nations agencies, funds and programmes and States to adopt policies and guidelines relating to indigenous peoples means that there is also insufficient reliable data available to the Forum in critical areas. On the other, the lack of data represents a considerable obstacle to the development and implementation of sound policies.

Because of this gap in terms of policies and disaggregated data, it has been difficult for the Forum to monitor and assess in detail the many issues within its mandate. This also negatively impacts on the ability of the Forum and ECOSOC to evaluate progress made towards integrating indigenous peoples into broader United Nations goals and programmes such as the Millennium Development Goals (MDGs). The annual reviews of MDG Country Reports produced by the Secretariat of the Permanent Forum on Indigenous Issues (SPFII) have found that, with few notable exceptions, indigenous peoples' issues are not being addressed in these reports. Only 20-30 per cent of the reports analysed over three years included references to indigenous peoples. Furthermore, the desk reviews have found that indigenous peoples are largely not participating in MDG processes at country level.[1] A similar review conducted by the Office of the High Commissioner for Human Rights' Independent Expert on minority issues in 2007 found that indigenous peoples were mentioned in only 10 of 50 reports assessed.[2] In the few instances where States have collected and disaggregated data on indigenous peoples, the statistics verify that indigenous peoples face a significantly wider gap than others in society in the eight areas identified as MDG priorities.

Understanding these ethnic and cultural inequities has facilitated the ability of some States to implement poverty reduction strategies that positively impact on these problems. Mexico and the Philippines are good examples of States using disaggregated data to address MDG priorities. In the Philippines, projects have been adopted to prioritize education in under-served indigenous communities (Goal 2) and literacy programmes for indigenous women and girls have been initiated (Goal 3). In Mexico, where disaggregated data indicated that indigenous women had the highest national rates of maternal mortality and that indigenous child mortality was 300 per cent higher than the national average (Goal 4), the government is undertaking specific actions to overcome the high incidence of preventable diseases (Goal 6) suffered by indigenous peoples in order to have an impact on infant and maternal mortality rates.[3]

> [the lack of data represents a considerable obstacle to the development and implementation of sound policies]

With regard to policies, the lack of United Nations system-wide standards, policies and guidelines regarding indigenous peoples has diminished the ability of the Forum to effectively coordinate activities relating to indigenous peoples between agencies and specialized bodies, since some agencies have policies and guidelines which require their "active engagement" with indigenous peoples and others do not.

At present five United Nations system and other intergovernmental agencies have policies on indigenous peoples. They are: the United Nations Development Programme (UNDP), the International Fund for Agricultural Development (IFAD) the World Bank, the Inter-American Development Bank and the Asian

---

[1] SPFII's annual MDG Desk Reviews are available at: http://www.un.org/esa/socdev/unpfii/
en/mdgs.html
[2] McDougall (2007).
[3] McDougall (2007), paras. 30-34.

Development Bank. Some are working towards adopting guidelines and some include indigenous issues in their medium-term plans. One example is the United Nations Development Group (UNDG), which comprises all the United Nations system entities dealing with development. In February 2008, it adopted the UNDG Guidelines on Indigenous Peoples' Issues,[4] a document that will operationalize the UN normative framework on indigenous peoples, particularly at the level of United Nations country offices. The adoption of these Guidelines is a significant step in the right direction, and a great deal will depend on their implementation.

The UNESCO example

It is interesting to examine the work of UNESCO and the General Assembly of States that are party to the UNESCO Conventions for the Safeguarding of Intangible Cultural Heritage (2003) and the Protection and Promotion of the Diversity of Cultural Expressions (2005). These Conventions were developed and came into force in the First International Decade of the World's Indigenous People and early in the Second Decade respectively. UNESCO did not include indigenous peoples in the drafting of the Conventions nor was any effort made to engage indigenous peoples in a meaningful or comprehensive process of consultations before the Conventions came into force. Neither Convention adequately acknowledges the fact that a large part of the "cultural heritage" and "cultural expressions" referred to in the Conventions are the heritage of indigenous peoples and cultures. Rather, the Conventions present these cultural properties as the "heritage of humanity" subject to the rules of international cooperation.

Indigenous peoples have criticized the UNESCO Conventions because they authorize and legitimize the expropriation of indigenous cultural property, which is part of their heritage. In her study on the Protection of the Heritage of Indigenous Peoples,[5] Erica Irene Daes, Special Rapporteur of the Sub-Commission on Prevention of Discrimination and Protection of Minorities, notes that "heritage is ordinarily a communal right and is associated with a family, clan, tribe or other kinship group". Daes also recognizes that "only the group as a whole can consent to the sharing of heritage" and that consent is always "temporary and revocable; heritage can never be alienated, surrendered or sold, except for conditional use". Daes further notes that the individual and collective rights of indigenous peoples to cultural property are protected under Article 27.2 of the Universal Declaration on Human Rights, Article 15.1 of the International Covenant on Economic, Social and Cultural Rights and Article 5(d) of the International Convention on the Elimination of All Forms of Racial Discrimination.

UNESCO should consider adopting a policy on indigenous peoples that provides for their meaningful participation in UNESCO's undertakings, in accordance with UNESCO's Declaration on the Principles of International Cultural Co-operation, which affirms that each culture has a dignity and value that must be protected and preserved and that "every people has the right and duty to develop its culture".[6]

Issues relating to the peaceful resolution of conflicts

Indigenous peoples often find themselves involved in conflict with the dominant society, mostly relating to the loss of their lands, territories and resources or to the deprivation of their civil, political, cultural, social and economic rights. The rapid pace of globalization has accelerated such conflicts and indigenous peoples, like all other peoples, need access to mechanisms for peaceful conflict resolution.

---

[4] UNDG (2008).
[5] Daes (1995).
[6] Article 1 of the UNESCO Declaration on the Principles of International Cultural Co-operation (1996).

The United Nations system does not provide specific juridical mechanisms for the resolution of conflicts to which indigenous peoples are a party or which result in the victimization of indigenous peoples.

The International Court of Justice (ICJ) does not provide legal standing to indigenous individuals or collectives to pursue litigation against States and others. The human rights treaty bodies and the regional international courts, such as the Inter-American Court, have been accessed by indigenous peoples to a limited extent, i.e., in cases where a State party has agreed to optional protocols, or where a State party has reporting obligations under a treaty. It should be noted, however, that the decisions of these human rights treaty bodies are not binding or enforceable and are often ignored by offending States. Thus, indigenous efforts in these fora have not had significant results in the resolution of conflicts.

The indigenous problématique and United Nations intervention in cases of conflict

In his "Study of treaties, agreements and other constructive arrangements between States and indigenous populations", Special Rapporteur Miguel Alfonso Martínez discussed inherent problems relating to domestic and international juridical fora as venues for the resolution of conflicts between States and indigenous peoples. He notes:

> In practically all cases, both in Latin America and in other regions mentioned above, the legal establishment can be seen serving as an effective tool in [the] process of domination. Jurists (with their conceptual elaborations), domestic laws (with their imperativeness both in the metropolis and in the colonies), the judiciary (subject to the 'rule of [non-indigenous] law'), one-side international law (its enforcement assured by military means) and international tribunals (on the basis of existing international law) were all present to "validate" juridically the organized plunder at the various stages of the colonial enterprise.[7]

Noting that the indigenous problématique "cannot be approached exclusively on the basis of juridical reasoning" because the problems confronted are essentially political in nature, he concludes that:

> Juridical discussions and argumentation simply take too long, require copious resources (which the indigenous side almost always lacks or has only in limited amounts), and in many cases are prejudiced by centuries of sedimented rationale. In addition, the urgency of the existing problems simply leaves no

indigenous peoples often find themselves involved in conflict with the dominant society, mostly relating to the loss of their lands, territories and resources or to the deprivation of their civil, political, cultural, social and economic rights

---

[7] Martínez (1999), para. 196.

> *room to engage, at the threshold of the twenty-first century,*
> *in the type of juridico-philosophical debates ... pursued in the*
> *sixteenth century.[8]*

International legal expert Augusto Willemsen Díaz also dismisses the idea that domestic legal fora would be an alternative. In his opinion,

> *Judicial adjudication in specific disputes or conflicts by a court*
> *of law forming part of the State or of an intergovernmental*
> *organization is more clearly questionable, since it would entail*
> *surrendering fully the deciding powers of the Community to*
> *those outside entities.[9]*

Díaz proposes that the United Nations itself might utilize processes including facilitation, moderation, conciliation, mediation and arbitration, provided that the indigenous communities themselves freely and formally request such United Nations intervention.

The Manila Declaration

In December 2000, the Tebtebba Foundation, an indigenous organization based in the Philippines, convened an International Conference on Conflict Resolution, Peacebuilding, Sustainable Development and Indigenous Peoples. The outcome document, referred to as the Manila Declaration, affirmed the right of indigenous peoples:

> *...to create new systems and institutions of peace-making*
> *that are sourced in indigenous values and that co-exist with*
> *existing bodies such as the International Court of Justice*
> *and similar regional bodies. Such institutions could include*
> *independent indigenous peoples' tribunals; commissions of*
> *inquiry that are recognized as legitimate organs in any process*
> *of conflict resolution. [10]*

The Conference agreed that an "independent International Commission of Indigenous Peoples for Mediation and Conflict Resolution be organized not later than the year 2002. The mission of this body will be to promote and defend the rights of indigenous peoples, and to expose and denounce aggression and abuses of the rights of indigenous peoples in different parts of the world."[11]

The Manila Declaration contains detailed recommendations for peacebuilding, technical assistance, training in mediation and other approaches to conflict

> as indigenous issues become more prominent in the United Nations system, the need for an international forum for conflict and dispute resolution for issues between indigenous peoples and States is also becoming more critical

---

[8] Martínez (1999),para. 254.
[9] Willemsen Díaz (2004), 543.
[10] Manila Declaration (2000), Preamble.
[11] Willemsen Díaz (2004), 547-552.

resolution. It also recognizes the critical role that women play in peacebuilding in their communities. To date, the recommendations of the Manila Conference have not been implemented and there continues to be a need for conflict resolution mechanisms in the United Nations and at the national level.

As indigenous issues become more prominent in the United Nations system, the need for an international forum for conflict and dispute resolution for issues between indigenous peoples and States is also becoming more critical.

Emerging issues relating to the displacement of indigenous peoples

In the years that have elapsed since the Permanent Forum's creation, the significant participation of indigenous representatives in the Forum's work has greatly enhanced the United Nations system's understanding of the pressing issues faced by indigenous communities. This has allowed the Forum experts to clarify and further assess the nature of the problems facing indigenous peoples globally.

While there is a great diversity of problems confronting indigenous peoples today, it is clear that one of the most significant threats faced by indigenous peoples arises from their displacement, eviction and separation from their lands, territories and resources. These issues are expanding and represent significant challenges to the security, health and survival of indigenous peoples and their cultures.

The issues that the Forum will monitor and further assess in future years as it addresses the specific themes identified on its mandate include violence and militarism, conservation refugees and globalization.

> one of the most significant threats faced by indigenous peoples arises from their displacement, eviction and separation from their lands, territories and resources

Violence and militarism

In nearly every region of the world, indigenous peoples are being displaced and severely impacted by violence and militarism. Militarism in indigenous territories presents a direct threat to the lifestyle and survival of indigenous peoples and has significant effects on indigenous communities. These adverse effects include: the pollution of ancestral and sacred lands, forests and waters as well as the destruction of wildlife in impacted areas; the dumping of toxic, including nuclear, waste, which renders indigenous lands unproductive, and the use of explosives and landmines, which contaminate the land and cause injuries, mutilations and death among the civilian indigenous population.[12]

---

[12] WGIP (2006), paras. 11, 12 and 13.

Militarism includes not only armed conflict but rape and sexual violence, which are often employed by armed forces as a strategy to target women. These acts of violence may result in the victim being ostracized because of cultural norms or stigmatized, particularly if pregnancy results. In some instances, armed forces have forced indigenous women to engage in prostitution or used them as sex slaves.[13]

Indigenous women and militarism

The general pattern that holds for indigenous women worldwide is their vulnerability to sexual violence. In areas of conflict, indigenous women often fall victims to abuse by members of the military and are subject to sexual enslavement, forced pregnancy, gang-rapes, sexual mutilation and killing. Historically, violence against women was used as a weapon in colonial conquests of indigenous lands, but as recently as the 1980s and 1990s, 1,400 indigenous Samburu women of Kenya were raped by British soldiers stationed on their lands. In the 1980s, indigenous women were targeted for rape as a weapon of war in Guatemala. In the 1990s, indigenous women in Chiapas, Mexico were subject to compulsory servitude in paramilitary camps.

In times of crises, indigenous women are often forced to leave their communities and search for shelters and jobs elsewhere, which results in cultural and spiritual isolation as well as their exposure to sexual trafficking and prostitution as well as exploitation as domestic workers.

Source: International Indigenous Women's Forum (2006), 48.

Another tactic employed by armed forces occupying indigenous territories is the destruction of the social fabric of the indigenous community by assassinating its traditional authorities. This deprives the community of leadership and leaves it vulnerable to manipulation. As conventional roles held by women and men are destroyed, indigenous communities are unable to maintain their traditional social structure. This often leads to the loss of gender-differentiated roles and authority and may impact on critical community pursuits such as planting and food security. In addition, the occupation of indigenous territories by armed forces often results in the military restricting movement of members of the community engaged in hunting, fishing or the gathering of plants for traditional medicines.[14]

Displacement is often the result of intensified military activities in indigenous territories. Displaced communities are left without food, shelter or protection and are often forced to migrate to cities or other areas.

One recurring issue raised by indigenous peoples in United Nations fora has been the use of militarism as a pretext to gain control over natural resources, including land, minerals and oil, without restitution or compensation.[15]

---

[13] Rights and Democracy (2007), Section 9.
[14] Rights and Democracy (2007), Section 9.
[15] WGIP (2006), para. 13.

Violence in Colombia

Colombia is home to eighty-four distinct indigenous peoples who live in all areas of the country. There is great demographic and cultural diversity among these peoples, some of whom are nomadic while others live in rural communities. In addition, there is a growing indigenous urban population.

Since the 1980s, the indigenous regions in Colombia have become host to a number of armed groups involved in drug cultivation and trafficking. State military activity is also rampant in these areas and indigenous peoples are often caught in the crossfire. Armed groups make no distinction between combatants and non-combatants and the indigenous civilian population is sometimes forced to work for one side or another thus exposing themselves to reprisals.

In 2003, more than 100 indigenous peoples and leaders were murdered and the indigenous community in Sierra Nevada de Santa Maria was forcibly displaced. In the last 15 years, as political violence has escalated, more than 2,660 cases of human rights violations have been reported. Reports confirm that indigenous peoples have been the victims of several massacres perpetrated by paramilitaries, the guerrillas and other armed groups. State-sponsored military activities have included aerial bombing of rural and indigenous communities. Thousands of indigenous peoples have been displaced, resulting in increasing populations of refugees in the neighbouring countries of Brazil, Ecuador, Panama, Peru and Venezuela. Refugees have also fled to urban areas within Colombia where malnutrition and deaths due to hunger have been reported. Throughout the country, forced disappearances of indigenous leaders and representatives have been documented, as have reports of mass arbitrary detentions carried out by the military.

Source: Stavenhagen (2004).

Conservation refugees

In recent years, big international non-governmental organizations (NGOs) have worked with States to create Protected Areas for conservation purposes. These organizations include Conservation International, the Nature Conservancy, the World Wide Fund for Nature and the Wildlife Conservation Society. Funded by the World Bank, the Global Environmental Fund (GEF), States and transnational corporations, these organizations work with States through financial incentives such as debt-for-nature swaps to obtain huge areas of land for conservation purposes. These protected areas are often the traditional lands of indigenous peoples, which remain rich in biodiversity.

The expansion of protected areas has grown phenomenally. In 1962 there were 1,000 official protected areas worldwide; in 2003, there were 102,102 protected areas in the world,[16] covering 12 per cent (or 18.8 million square kilometres) of the Earth's surface, an area larger than the continent of Africa and equal to half of the world's cultivated land.[17]

---

[16] According to UN list on Protected Areas (2003). See webpage of UNEP-World Conservation Monitoring Centre at http://www.unep-wcmc.org/protected_areas/UN_list/index.htm

[17] Dowie (2006); See also Huertas Castillo (2004), 164-165.

Protected areas in Kenya and their impact

Kenya is widely admired in the world for its national parks and game reserves, which have become a major tourist attraction and therefore important for the national economy. It is estimated that direct and indirect revenues from wildlife conservationist policies amount to 10 per cent of GDP. Protected Areas cover over 3.5 million hectares, or 6 per cent of Kenya's total land area. The conservation of wildlife and the preservation of natural parks are considered high priority for the country, and this has involved separating indigenous peoples from the wildlife and the forests. Many families were evicted by the creation of protected areas, most of which were originally inhabited by pastoralists and hunter-gatherers.

On the mistaken assumption, held since colonial times, that subsistence hunting by indigenous communities is decimating wildlife. The Wildlife conservation Act prohibits game hunting inside and outside the protected areas. Those who persist are often arrested and prosecuted as poachers and in some areas "eco-guards" have been armed and have actually killed poachers to prevent illegal hunting. Despite centuries of coexistence with wildlife, nomadic pastoralists are not allowed to herd their cattle in the reserves, even in game reserves which are managed by the local authorities on behalf of the local communities. In the context of rising human population and escalating poverty, the restrictions imposed on the utilization of national parks and game reserves by pastoralists have severely affected their livelihood and their chances for survival.

The growth of the tourist industry in connection with the establishment of protected natural areas has created additional problems for these communities. In the Maasai Mara area, the construction of a private tourist resort has involved fencing off an area traditionally belonging to the Sekenani village, leading to the loss of access to one of the only three sources of water for everyday human and cattle consumption. Local Endorois communities similarly claim that the privately owned Laikipia Natural Conservancy Trust severely curtails their livestock grazing, and access to water sources in the area is only allowed once a week.

Local indigenous communities do not participate in the management of the parks and reserves and do not benefit from the revenue, which either accrues to the Kenya Wildlife Service in the case of national parks, or to the local districts in the case of national reserves. An exception in this regard is the Maasai Mara Game Reserve, where 19 per cent of the revenue is said to be invested in favour of the local Maasai communities. However, local Villagers claim that they do not see the benefit, and 60 per cent of the district remains in poverty.

the growth of the tourist industry in connection with the establishment of protected natural areas has created additional problems for these communities

> The revision of the Kenyan Wildlife Policy in 2003 was halted under pressure from indigenous communities and its adoption is still pending. A better practice, from a human rights and ecological perspectives, would be to involve the pastoralist and forest communities in the management and benefits of a conservationist strategy. Thus, wildlife and parks would be preserved, tourist dollars would be obtained and the livelihood of the local populations would be protected and strengthened. Throughout Kenya's recent history, it would appear that wild animals are protected, while peoples are not.
>
> *Source: Stavenhagen (2007b).*

Globalization

There is mounting evidence that the phenomenon of globalization has been devastating to indigenous peoples and their communities, lands and resources. Globalization has become a primary cause of conflict between indigenous peoples and others, including transnational corporations (TNCs), the World Bank (WB), International Monetary Fund (IMF) and the Overseas Development Agencies (ODAs).

Current manifestations of globalization are based on the premise that the best way to achieve universal economic prosperity is through a single worldwide system of trade and financial rules that promotes corporate large scale export-oriented commercial production such as commercial mining and industrial monoculture agriculture.

Trade and financial rules are mandated by international treaties and also include the rules governing member States of the World Trade Organization (WTO) and the conditionalities and requirements for aid set by the IMF/WB system. These trade and financial rules regulate the global market. The integration of national economies into the global market is achieved by the imposition of structural adjustment programmes (SAPs), which favour foreign investment and shift economic control away from States to TNCs through privatization. The impact of SAPs on indigenous peoples, the environment and developing States has been tragic and, in some cases, irreversible.

the transfer of highly polluting energy-intensive industries from the North to the developing South has displaced indigenous peoples from their lands and resources and destroyed indigenous subsistence economies

Financial and investment liberalization policies often require that States abandon controls on currency speculation and amend mining and forestry laws to allow for foreign ownership of resources. TNCs are also permitted to increase their equity to 100 per cent and to export profits rather than reinvest in the local economy. This drives out local control and transfers control of entire sections of the national economy to foreign TNCs.

The transfer of highly polluting energy-intensive industries from the North to the developing South has displaced indigenous peoples from their lands and resources and destroyed indigenous subsistence economies, replacing them with monoculture cash crops for export.

SAPs require that States curtail expenditure on national health, education and social services in favour of higher and more rapid repayment of the national debt to the IMF/WB. The impact on indigenous peoples and the poor can be seen in less access to education and social services and higher rates of illiteracy.

Trade and import liberalization policies require that countries abrogate tariffs and other measures intended to protect locally-produced food and commodities needed for domestic consumption in favour of increased incentives for corporate agribusiness producing exports for the foreign market. This not only undermines food security but results in environmental degradation and the over-exploitation of forest and subsurface mineral resources.

The hallmark of globalization is the privatization of government services and assets, which are replaced by corporate monopolies in many sectors of the economy that are crucial to national security. These sectors include food production, water allocation and health care delivery. Under the globalized model of development, these critical services are transferred to TNCs and G7[18] countries, which have reaped a huge windfall while indigenous peoples have been displaced from their traditional territories and livelihoods.

For an example of how globalization impacts negatively on indigenous peoples, their environment, lands, territories and resources.

The impact of globalization in the Pacific

In 2001, the World Council of Churches (WCC) undertook an inquiry into the impact of globalization in the Pacific region and an assessment of alternatives to economic globalization. The outcome of this effort was published by the WCC in a document entitled: "Island of Hope: A Pacific Alternative to Economic Globalization" (2001). The Council of Churches, in assessing the impact of globalization in the Pacific, examined impacts in several areas including social, political, ecological and economic impacts. The following are a few of the findings made by the Council and the Pacific churches:

Social impacts: The Pacific churches found a marked increase in the number of families living below the poverty line, largely linked to the liberal policies adopted by national governments, as well as worsening wages and working conditions. As the study points out, "national economic policies aim for greater liberalization and competition in the economy, ignoring their social and economic ramifications." Economic globalization has exacerbated social problems in the Pacific, including substance and drug abuse and the spread of HIV/AIDS. The Pacific has also experienced an increased erosion of traditional lifestyles and values.

Ecological impacts: The report describes an "intensive exploitation, rather than sustainable management of the Pacific's natural resources", with calls for sustainable exploitation of resources from regional

[18] The G-7 Countries are the world's major financial nations: Britain, Canada, France, Germany, Italy, Japan and the United States.

environmental NGOs largely being ignored. Much of this exploitation is carried out by transnational corporations, with resource owners getting a very small share of the profits.

Climate change: The very existence of small Pacific islands is threatened by climate change. According to the report, "six countries in the Pacific are faced with the threat of seeing islands disappear as a result of rising sea levels as a direct consequence of global warming". Livelihoods are being directly affected by climate change. In Tarawa, Kiribati, for example, salt water intrusion into the water table is causing the death of breadfruit trees, affecting an essential component of the local diet.

Economic impacts: Governments in the Pacific have been pursuing economic policies that are out of tune with the characteristics and realities of the economies of these small-island developing States. Pacific economies are largely reliant on agriculture and fishing, with large proportions of the population living in rural areas. Despite this fact, governments have pursued free trade policies that favour foreign investment. These policies "encourage foreign control of island economies and create increased dependency on externally devised economic initiatives, rather than promoting and supporting local initiatives".

Political impacts: The Pacific region has been affected by a series of political crises, notably in Fiji and the Solomon Islands, fuelled by disparities, land issues and a lack of confidence in Governments. Many of these sources of social discontent can be traced to the mixed impact of liberal policies.

Source: WCC (2001).

Migration and urbanization

For the first time in human history, the majority of humanity lives in urban areas. Although available data indicates that the majority of the world's indigenous peoples still live in rural areas, there is increasing evidence that indigenous peoples are part of a global trend towards urbanization, that this trend is irreversible and occurring in both developed and undeveloped regions.[19] For example, in Latin America, a multi-ethnic and pluricultural region with 671 state-recognized indigenous peoples, the majority of indigenous peoples in some countries (Bolivia, Brazil and Chile) reside in urban areas.[20] Likewise, in New Zealand, the Maori are highly urbanized, with over 80 per cent now living in major urban centres.[21] In some instances, urban migration is voluntary. It may be spurred by the prospect of better economic opportunities and the need to ensure survival of the traditional way of life in their territories through urban-rural remittances or a desire to be in closer proximity to social services and facilities for education or health.[22] New circumstances associated with globalization have led to an increase in migratory flows and mobility.[23]

In other cases, urban migration is involuntary. It may be the result of environmental degradation that has destroyed traditional livelihoods, dispossession, displacement, military conflict or natural disaster.[24] Common factors that

---

[19] Message from Ann Tibaijuka, Executive Director of UN-Habitat to the Expert Group Meeting on Urban Indigenous Peoples and Migration, Santiago de Chile, 27-29 March 2007. UNPFII (2007), 32.

[20] Statement by José Luis Machinea, Executive Secretary of the United Nations Economic Commission for Latin America and the Caribbean to the Expert Group Meeting on Urban Indigenous Peoples and Migration, Santiago de Chile, 27-29 March 2007. UNPFII (2007), 26.

[21] Statistics New Zealand (2007) 3.

[22] UNPFII (2007), 11 and 13.

[23] Statement by José Luis Machinea. UNPFII (2007), 27.

[24] Message from Ann Tibaijuka. UNPFII (2007), 32.

lead to involuntary or forced migration include poverty, conflict and inadequate legal protection of lands and resources, as well as environmental toxicity.[25]

Regardless of the factors prompting the migration, indigenous peoples in urban areas encounter substantial difficulties, including lack of employment and income, racism, limited access to services and severe housing needs. Indigenous youth are particularly vulnerable. The common denominator in these cases is structural discrimination, which is reflected in marginalization, exclusion and poverty.[26]

UN-Habitat has found that indigenous peoples who move to urban areas are often disadvantaged when it comes to employment opportunities and face numerous obstacles in accessing credit to start business or income-generating activities. Indigenous migrants have frequently become the slum dwellers of the cities. As such, they are more prone to disease, more at risk of HIV/AIDS and suffer as much from hunger and malnutrition as rural indigenous people. In addition, they are more vulnerable to natural and human-made disasters such as fire, flood and land slides and, because of the "illegality" of slums, often cannot access critical resources including clean water, sanitation and energy. Taken together, these factors and the ongoing violation of basic rights and fundamental freedoms of indigenous peoples reveal the underlying causes of persistent poverty and social exclusion among urban indigenous communities.[27]

One key issue relating to indigenous urban migration is the paucity of data on the migration process for indigenous peoples, which has contributed to a lack of adequate government policies aimed at urbanized indigenous peoples. Because of this problem, experts attending an International Expert Group Meeting, held in Santiago de Chile in March 2007, recommended that research institutions, universities, States and NGOs collect qualitative and quantitative data on urban indigenous communities and that these data be disaggregated by sex and indigenous group and compared with data from non-indigenous populations. The experts also called for the application of appropriate indigenous research methodologies and for the effective participation of the indigenous peoples themselves in data collection and research.[28]

In addressing forward-looking strategies, it is important that indigenous peoples' rights be considered in a holistic way, without dividing urban and rural members of indigenous communities. Indigenous peoples migrating to urban centres do not leave their identities behind but maintain strong attachments to their traditional lands and culture.

> indigenous peoples in urban areas encounter substantial difficulties, including lack of employment and income, racism, limited access to services and severe housing needs

---

[25] UNPFII (2007), 13.
[26] Statement of José Luis Machinea. UNPFII (2007), 26.
[27] Message from Ann Tibaijuka. UNPFII (2007), 33.
[28] Message from Ann Tibaijuka. UNPFII (2007), 33.

Indigenous peoples living in voluntary isolation

The Programme of Action for the Second International Decade of the World's Indigenous People calls for the establishment of a global mechanism to monitor the situation of indigenous peoples in voluntary isolation and recommends that States adopt special measures to ensure their protection and rights.[29] The United Nations Permanent Forum on Indigenous Issues has also prioritized the needs of indigenous peoples in isolation because these peoples and their cultures are facing imminent danger and extinction, and require the implementation of urgent measures to guarantee their survival.[30]

Although the term "indigenous peoples in isolation" is currently under discussion, there is a general understanding that these indigenous peoples share common characteristics and face recurrent situations and threats regardless of their geographic location or cultural affiliation.

Characteristics and challenges of indigenous peoples in isolation

Indigenous peoples in isolation are population groups that limit their contact to members of their own peoples and, in some cases, to the indigenous communities in the vicinity of their territories, refusing to establish sustained relationships or interactions with indigenous or non-indigenous populations that could endanger their physical and cultural integrity. They may be indigenous peoples in their own right, with their own culture, values and practices, or they may be segments of other peoples that have developed sustained relationships with national society. Indigenous peoples in isolation practice hunting, fishing, gathering and small scale sowing, for which purpose they cover a wide territory. They live exclusively from the resources provided by the forests and rivers, which are essential to their subsistence.[a]

Most indigenous peoples in isolation are nomadic. They establish travelling camps in areas where they find the necessary means for survival for a period of time. This production system requires a large area of land and so the invasion of small portions of their land can mean changes in settlement patterns and in their supply of products.[b]

Small indigenous communities that shun all contact with modern society and prefer to live in isolation and devote themselves to their traditional

> many of these communities are now on the brink of what some describe as genocide, owing to oil exploration, timber extraction, the introduction of vast commercial plantations, infrastructure works, missionary activity, drug trafficking and international tourism

---

[29] See United Nations Organization (2005), paras. 45 and 51.
[30] OHCHR (2007) Report of the Regional Seminar on Indigenous Peoples in Isolation and Initial Contact in the Amazon and Gran Chaco Region. See also the reports of the Fourth, Fifth and Sixth Sessions of the UNPFII.

> subsistence economy are to be found in different parts of the equatorial forests that still exist in the world. Contrary to the image portrayed by some media, these groups are not the original settlers "who have never had contact with civilization", but population groups that for generations have been avoiding contacts that have been extremely violent and deadly for them, leading them to seek refuge in forests. Many of these communities are now on the brink of what some describe as genocide, owing to oil exploration, timber extraction, the introduction of vast commercial plantations, infrastructure works, missionary activity, drug trafficking and international tourism. The few contacts that may take place can turn violent and the diseases carried by the new settlers continue to wipe out a large number of these population groups.[c]
>
> Sources: [a] Huertas Castillo (2004), 176-177; [b] OHCHR (2007); [c] Stavenhagen (2007a), 15.

Of the many factors that contribute to the vulnerability of indigenous peoples in isolation, the pressure to which their lands and territories are being subjected is the most significant. Experts and indigenous leaders attending the Expert Seminar on Indigenous Peoples in Isolation and Initial Contact in the Amazon Region and the Gran Chaco, held in Bolivia in November 2006, agreed that in most cases this pressure is attributable to an influx of private individuals and corporations, who are driving a rapacious effort to access and extract the wealth of natural resources from indigenous territories, resulting in the exploitation, expulsion and, increasingly, extinction of indigenous peoples living in isolation. In many cases, States have authorized and legalized these incursions, facilitating extractive industries (logging, mining, and oil) and tourism, pastoral uses and oil palm production.[31]

The infrastructure development related to globalization that is proceeding in the South American Amazon has had tragic and irreversible consequences for the indigenous peoples living on the remote rainforest frontiers of Peru, Brazil and Ecuador, including indigenous peoples in isolation or in initial contact.

> In the oil-producing regions of Ecuador's northern Amazon, thirty years of Texaco oil operations have left a dangerous toxic legacy for indigenous communities. Oil and toxic waste spills and seepages, and toxic air pollution, have caused the deterioration of terrestrial and aquatic ecosystems. Indigenous people who live, fish, bathe and drink from the region's rivers report high incidents of cancer, skin rashes and sores, stomach ailments and respiratory problems.

> Recent investigations indicate that cancer rates among indigenous communities living in Ecuador's oil-producing areas of Sucumbíos and Orellana provinces are three times higher than the national average. For certain types of cancer, this figure rises dramatically: the risk of throat cancer is thirty times greater than the national average; kidney and skin cancer is fifteen times greater; and stomach cancer is five times greater.

> This story is repeated throughout oil-producing areas of the Amazon. In October 2000, a Pluspetrol oil spill on the Marañon River in the Peruvian Amazon contaminated Peru's largest protected area, the Pacaya Samiria Reserve. The area's twenty thousand inhabitants, many from the Cocamas-Coacamillas people, suffered diarrhoea and skin diseases and saw their food and water supply decimated by toxic pollution. Many medicines provided by Pluspetrol never reached the affected communities, and food provided by the company did not meet their basic needs.

---

[31] OHCHR (2007), paras. 19 and 20.

The health impacts of large projects such as dams can be equally serious. The vast expanse of stagnant water that forms Brazil's Tucurui Reservoir led to a plague of Mansonia mosquitoes and a dramatic increase in malaria among local peoples. Cases of water-borne diseases such as river blindness and schistosomiasis[32] also rose. Forced resettlement also had damaging consequences for human health. Formerly dispersed indigenous groups were forced to live in settlements where they were exposed to new diseases, such as intestinal infections and influenza, which thrive in dense populations. Poor levels of official health care and the irregular system of vaccinations, along with unsuitable government-provided medicines led to many needless deaths among the indigenous peoples of the Tucurui area.

Throughout the Amazon region, there are many accounts of un-contacted populations being decimated by curable illnesses such as malaria, pneumonia and smallpox. In the Camisea region of Peru, in the mid-1980s, Shell Oil conducted preliminary exploration for oil and gas reserves. The exploratory work led to an influx of loggers who used seismic trails as access. The contact from oil workers and loggers exposed the Nahua to whooping cough, smallpox and influenza. An estimated 50 per cent of the population died. Most of the rest of the group fled the area.[33]

Although the Programme of Action for the Second International Decade of the World's Indigenous People refers to a need to establish an international mechanism guaranteeing the protection of indigenous peoples in voluntary isolation and in danger of extinction, and recommends a "special protection framework" for their protection,[34] these measures have not been implemented by the United Nations system and States.

Special measures, including legislation, adopted by some States in response to the recommendations made by the Forum and the Second Decade Programme of Action have been piecemeal and, in some cases, counterproductive, as in the situation whereby indigenous land reserves *(Zonas Intangibles)* are also subject to resource authorizations; or where indigenous territories are bisected by the boundaries of States with different legal systems.[35]

Most countries have not established specific institutions to protect the rights of indigenous peoples in isolation and in initial contact. Some States have

> throughout the Amazon region, there are many accounts of un-contacted populations being decimated by curable illnesses such as malaria, pneumonia and smallpox

---

[32] Schistosomiasis is also known as bilharzia, bilharziosis or snail fever.
[33] Lloyd, Soltani and Koeny (2006), 89.
[34] United Nations Organization (2005), paras. 45 and 51.
[35] OHCHR (2007), para. 30.

insufficient economic resources and few specialized staff able to address the situation of these peoples. In addition, most States have not established specific programmes or adequate action strategies that, based on the principle that the characteristic lifestyles of indigenous peoples in isolation should be maintained, would ensure their right to physical, social and territorial integrity. In some cases, States have even violated this right or allowed it to be violated.

The lack of regulations and oversight institutions has facilitated the arrival of extraction, timber and mining companies; of religious entities that seek to make contact with and to convert groups in initial contact; and of other social actors onto the lands of indigenous peoples in isolation and initial contact, with consequences that threaten their existence, including epidemics and deaths. The difficulty of bringing such cases of human rights violations before the courts has led to a situation of impunity.[36]

These factors taken together have created a situation of extreme urgency and emergency which has led the Permanent Forum to "urge Governments, the United Nations system, civil society and indigenous peoples' organizations to cooperate in immediately ensuring effective prohibition against outside encroachment, aggression, forcible assimilation and acts and processes of genocide. Measures of protection should comprise the safeguarding of their natural environment and livelihood and minimally invasive, culturally sensitive mobile health-care services".[37]

As the Forum continues its focus in this area, it will seek to implement recommendations from the Expert seminar held in Bolivia in 2006 and to work cooperatively with States and indigenous peoples through a human rights-based approach, recognising that isolation is the result of indigenous peoples' right to self-determination and, in the majority of cases, a consequence of aggression suffered in the past.

Concluding Remarks

This chapter has highlighted five of the most important emerging issues for indigenous peoples throughout the world. The approval of the United Nations Declaration on the Rights of Indigenous Peoples has given indigenous peoples and the international community the impetus to deal with these issues. The Declaration also provides a framework for the partnerships that are required to adequately address these issues and ensure that the rights of indigenous peoples are respected and protected.

---

[36] Santa Cruz de la Sierra Appeal in OHCHR (2007), 2.
[37] UNPFII (2006), para 83

List of references

Daes, Erica-Irene Protection of the Heritage of Indigenous People, Final Report of the Special Rapporteur, Jun. 21, 1995, U.N. Doc. E/CN.4/Sub.2/1995/26

Dowie, Mark. 2006. "Conservation Refugees", in Paradigm Wars: Indigenous Peoples' Resistance to Globalization, ed. Jerry Mander and Victoria Tauli-Corpuz. A special Report of the International Forum on Globalization Committee on Indigenous Peoples. San Francisco, CA.: Sierra Club Book.

Huertas Castillo, Beatriz. 2004. Indigenous Peoples in Isolation in the Peruvian Amazon. IWGIA Document No. 100. Copenhagen: IWGIA.

International Indigenous Women's Forum/Foro Internacional de Mujeres Indígenas. 2006. "Mairin Iwanka Raya: Indigenous Women Stand Against Violence". A Companion Report to the Secretary-General's Study on Violence Against Women. Available online at: http://www.madre.org/fimi/vaiwreport06.pdf

Lloyd , Janet, Atossa Soltani and Kevin Koeny. 2006. "Infrastructure Development in South American Amazon" in Paradigm Wars: Indigenous Peoples' Resistance to Globalization, ed. Jerry Mander and Victoria Tauli-Corpuz. A special Report of the International Forum on Globalization Committee on Indigenous Peoples. San Francisco, CA.: Sierra Club Book.

McDougall, Gay. 2007. "Achieving the Millennium Development Goals for Minorities: A review of MDG Country Reports and Poverty Reduction Strategies". Report of the Independent Expert on minority issues, Addendum 1. UN Doc. A/HRC/4/9/Add.1.

Manila Declaration. 2000. Manila. Declaration of the International Conference on Conflict Resolution, Peace Building, Sustainable Development and Indigenous Peoples, Metro Manila, Philippines, December 6 - 8, 2000. Available online from Third World Network' Web site http://www.twnside.org.sg/title/manila.htm

Martínez, Miguel Alfonso. 1999. "Study on treaties, agreements and other constructive arrangements between States and indigenous populations" Final report by Miguel Alfonso Martínez, Special Rapporteur. UN Doc. E/CN.4/Sub.2/1999/20.

Rights and Democracy. 2006. "Indigenous Women and Militarization", in Information Kit: Portrait of Indigenous Women of Asia, ed. the Asian Indigenous Women's Network (AIWN) and the Indigenous Peoples' Alliance of the Archipelago (AMAN: Aliansi Masyarakat Adat Nusantara), in partnership with Rights & Democracy. Available online at http://www.dd-rd.ca/site/_PDF/publications/indigenous/InfoKitEnglish_indig_asia.pdf.

Secretariat of the United Nations Permanent Forum on Indigenous Issues (SPFII). Annual MDG Desk Reviews, available online at: http://www.un.org/esa/socdev/unpfii/en/mdgs.html.

Statistics New Zealand. 2007. Census 2006, revised 2007. Available online at http://www.stats.govt.nz/census/2006-census-data/quickstats-about-maori/2006-census-quickstats-about-maori-revised.htm

Stavenhagen, Rodolfo. 2004. Mission to Colombia. Addendum 2 to the Report of the Special Rapporteur on the human rights and fundamental freedoms of indigenous people. UN Doc. E/CN.4/2005/88/Add.2 November 2004.

Stavenhagen, Rodolfo. 2007a. Report of the Special Rapporteur on the Human Rights and Fundamental Freedoms of Indigenous Peoples. UN Doc. A/HRC/4/32 27 February 2007.

Stavenhagen, Rodolfo. 2007b. Mission to Kenya. Addendum 3 to the Report of the Special Rapporteur on the situation of human rights and fundamental freedoms of indigenous peoples. UN Doc. A/HRC/4/32/Add3. February 2007.

UNESCO. 1996. Declaration on the Principles of International Cultural Cooperation. Available online at http://portal.unesco.org/en/ev.php URL_ID=13147&URL_DO=DO_TOPIC&URL_SECTION=201.html

United Nations Development Group (UNDG). 2008. UNDG Guidelines on Indigenous Peoples' Issues. Available online at http://www.un.org/esa/socdev/unpfii/documents/UNDG_Guidelines_indigenous_FINAL.pdf

United Nations Organization (UNO). 2005. Second International Decade of the World's Indigenous People: Programme of Action. UN Doc A/60/270.

United Nations Office of the High Commissioner for Human Rights (OHCHR). 2007. Report of the Regional Seminar on Indigenous Peoples in Isolation and Initial Contact in the Amazon and Gran Chaco Region, UN Doc E/C.19/2007/CRP.1,15 Feb. 2007.

United Nations Permanent Forum on Indigenous Issues (UNPFII). 2005. Report on the Fifth Session (15-26 May 2006) UN Doc. E/2006/43.

United Nations Permanent Forum on Indigenous Issues (UNPFII). 2007. Report of the International Expert Group Meeting on Urban Indigenous Peoples and Migration, Santiago de Chile, 27-29 March 2007. UN Doc. E/C.19/2007/CRP.8.

Williamson Díaz, Augusto. 2004. "The Role of the United Nations in Conflict Resolution" in Reclaiming Balance Indigenous Peoples, Conflict Resolution, and Sustainable Development, ed. Victoria Tauli-Corpuz and Joji Carino. The Philippines: Tebtebba, Indigenous Peoples' International Centre for Policy Research and Education.

Working Group on Indigenous Populations (WGIP). 2006. Report of the Working Group on Indigenous Populations on its 24th Session, Geneva. UN Doc. A/HRC/Sub.1/58/22 14 August 2006.

World Council of Churches (WCC). 2001. Island of hope 2001: An Alternative to Economic Globalization. Dossier 7. Fiji: World Council of Churches/Pacific Council of Churches. Available online at http://www.oikoumene.org/fileadmin/files/wcc main/documents/p3/dossier-7.pdf